READING "ADAM SMITH"

D0862396

MODERNITY AND POLITICAL THOUGHT

Series Editor: Morton Schoolman
State University of New York at Albany

This unique collection of orginal studies of the great figures in the history of political and social thought critically examines their contributions to our understanding of modernity, its constitution, and the promise and problems latent within it. These works are written by some of the finest theorists of our time for scholars and students of the social sciences and humanities.

READING "ADAM SMITH":

DESIRE,
HISTORY
AND VALUE

MICHAEL J. SHAPIRO

Modernity and Political Thought
VOLUME 4

SAGE Publications
International Educational and Professional Publisher
Newbury Park London New Delhi

For information address:

SAGE Publications, Inc.
2455 Teller Road
Newbury Park, California 91320

SAGE Publications Ltd.
6 Bonhill Street
London EC2A 4PU
United Kingdom

SAGE Publications India Pvt. Ltd.
M-32 Market
Greater Kailash I
New Delhi 110 048 India

Printed in the United States of America

Library of Congress Cataloging-in-Publication Data

Shapiro, Michael J.
    Reading "Adam Smith" : desire, history and value / Michael J. Shapiro.
        p. cm. —(Modernity and political thought : vol. 4)
    Includes bibliographical references and index.
    ISBN 0-8039-4584-1.—ISBN 0-8039-4585-X (pbk.)
    1. Smith, Adam. 1723-1790. Inquiry into the nature and causes of the wealth of nations. 2. Smith, Adam, 1723-1790. Theory of moral sentiments. 3. Economics—History—18th century. 4. Philosophy—History—18th century. I. Title. II. Series.
HB161.S66913   1993
330.15′3—dc20   93-6483

93 94 95 96 97 10 9 8 7 6 5 4 3 2 1

Sage Production Editor: Astrid Virding

To the memory of my parents,
Adelaide Lopiansky Shapiro
Irving Shapiro

Contents

Series Editor's Introduction

Michael Shapiro's *Reading "Adam Smith": Desire, History and Value* is the fourth volume to appear in the Sage Series **Modernity and Political Thought**. Shapiro's work follows the recent publication of the initial three volumes in the series, William Connolly's *The Augustinian Imperative: A Reflection on the Politics of Morality,* Richard Flathman's *Thomas Hobbes: Skepticism, Individuality and Chastened Politics*, and Fred Dallmayr's *G.W.F. Hegel: Modernity and Politics.* The series will continue with books on selected past political thinkers by leading contemporary political theorists. These will include a study of Hannah Arendt by Seyla Benhabib, of Edmund Burke by Stephen White, Michel Foucault by Thomas Dumm, Sigmund Freud by Jean Elshtain, Friedrich Nietzsche by Benjamin Barber, Jean-Jacques Rousseau by Tracy Strong, Ralph Waldo Emerson by George Kateb, and Henry David Thoreau by Jane Bennett. As those who are familiar with the previous works of these authors will expect, these studies adopt a variety of approaches and pose importantly different questions. As contributors to **Modernity and Political Thought**, however, their efforts are also commonly devoted to effecting critical examinations of the contributions that major political theorists have made to our understanding of modernity—its constitution, problems, promises and dangers which are latent within it.

During the past decade Michael Shapiro has produced an exceptional collection of critical studies of a range of cultural, political, and philosophical genres. Best known among these are *Language and Political Understanding: The Politics of Discursive Practices, The Politics of Representation: Writing Practices in Biography, Photography, and Policy Analysis,* and *Reading the Postmodern Polity: Political Theory as Textual Practice.*[1] Taken as a whole this body of work demonstrates the diversity and depth of his concerns, the most fundamental of which are the complex and intimate relationships between language and power. In each of his investigations the objective is to illuminate places where power is at work though hidden from view, believed to be absent, presumed to be neutralized or benign. Power is unmasked where its appearance is disguised by discourses that create the structures of meaning according to which we interpret our world and everything within it. It is in these acts of discovering power in social, economic, and political relations thought to be innocent of power and its effects that the oppositional, political significance of Shapiro's criticism lies.

It is immediately apparent from a consideration of Shapiro's work that his analyses draw their inspiration from many contemporary critical approaches as well as from those of Nietzsche and Adorno. But just as evident is that the theorist whose work he has found most instructive is Michel Foucault. As does Foucault, Shapiro views language as an arsenal of discursive assets out of which are fabricated structures of intelligibility that shape our valuations and limit, but also constrain and often determine, what is comprehensible and what is obscure, what is familiar and what is strange. Shapiro's intention is to disrupt these structures of meaning. By so doing, he undermines their ability to constitute individual and collective identities, construct the social spaces in which those who bear the identities are confined, and invent the assumptions which justify the social order within which these social spaces are contained.

Through Foucauldian genealogical strategies Shapiro intervenes in established "discursive economies," or systems of interpretation and exchange through which discourses acquire a range of values and gradually become entrenched. The "linguistic impertinence," as Shapiro describes it, of such intervention destabilizes these discursive economies and renders contingent and problematic beliefs that we accept as true and uncontested. Genealogical practices consequently can weaken the power that existing structures of meaning have in enabling and disenabling our identities and can expand the relations a social order makes available to them.

Shapiro devotes considerable attention to the construction of the modern "self" and the relations of power immanent in its identity. Consistent with strict genealogical approaches, he has no interest in defending some conception of an authentic or essential self from which the modern self can be claimed to be estranged or against which it can be appraised. Rather, his concern lies with the different periods in which the various forms of the self emerge and with the history of the discursive economies contributing to their formation. Shapiro's design is to show how, over the long stretch of time, discourses exert power in producing particular conceptions of the self and in overcoming rival ones. By demonstrating how power functions through the circulation of discourses, and through identities produced in the forms of knowledge and interpretation that normalize human subjectivity in various historical periods, Shapiro contributes to the destruction of any privileged ground that the modern self may stand upon. There can be no universal moral or rational claim to the effect that the self must be one way only and not any other.

Genealogical critique thereby proves the modern self to be but one possible and arbitrary result of the interpretive agonistics which appear to be the singularly defining characteristic of modernity. Through the deployment of genealogical tactics the modern self loses the power, which it otherwise would enjoy, to command our beliefs about what is true, rational, moral, right, and good. Although this discursive power cannot be broken entirely, through critique it can be attenuated to the point where alternative possible selves and competing judgments can be entertained, perhaps embraced, and, most importantly, never be suppressed through the ascendancy of a hegemonic self. For Shapiro, genealogy struggles against any mode of interpretation that naturalizes prevailing human identities and operates within the pretense that all possibilities are exhausted. Like Foucault and Nietzsche, he, too, assumes that there is an "indeterminant range of possible selves and that every institutionalized version of the self represents a political victory."[2]

Among the genealogical analyses Shapiro has produced "Political Economy and Mimetic Desire in *Babette's Feast*" is one of our most creative theoretical examples of genealogical strategies at work.[3] In an argument that anticipates the approach adopted in *Reading "Adam Smith"*, Shapiro brings to light an "economy" that is inherent in cultural practices and texts though repressed and hidden from view, as are the systems of authority and power to which the economy is related. At the outset, an important dimension of his study is the struggle over the definition of an economy. Shapiro contests the traditional practice of constructing narrow boundaries around "economy" by restricting its conceptualization to the familiar systems of exchange involving money. Value can be produced, accumulated, and exchanged in other forms, which can function systemically to create, maintain, and perpetuate a social order. Recognition of these alternative forms of value production expose structures of power and authority that remain disguised by interpretive frameworks functioning to veil and mystify relations of domination.

Isak Dinesen's *Babette's Feast*, Shapiro contends, chronicles the disruption of a "spiritual economy" by casting light on the various mechanisms involved in the relationship of economy and desire. The story revolves around life in a small Scandinavian village which, at one level of interpretation, survives by means of a static, medieval fishing economy where transactions are neither complicated nor fetishistic. At a deeper, implicit level of understanding, however, the community survives by closing off its moral boundaries. All systems and dynamics involved in signification, monetary and *otherwise*, Shapiro points out, are severly restricted. This is especially true of desire. In the absence of an Other who could arouse desire by being positioned with respect to all that which can be represented linguistically (signified) as desirable, the incitement of a desiring Self is arrested. When models of desire do manage to invade the narrowly circumscribed systems of representation, the community wards off desire, repairs its boundaries, and mends its identity by invoking its restricted linguistic economy. Desire is the value whose exchange must be the most closely regulated, for instability in the economy of desire can render precarious and perhaps topple the moral order resting upon it. In Shapiro's estimation, "this is not only the most persistent theme of the story but the major dimension of the culture-economy interface with which one can analyze such stories or situations."[4]

Babette's "feast" is compelling evidence of the linguistic dynamics of the village's restricted normative economy. Shapiro explicates the position that food itself occupies as a system of representation that contributes to preserving the existing social structure through its management of desire. Dinesen's Scandinavian community articulates its moral commitments through a culinary "language" that is impoverished, as is dramatically illustrated by the "dull and insipid fish soup," as Shapiro describes it, that is the staple of the village's daily menu. The linguistic poverty of this diet is highlighted through dramatic contrast with the rich and exotic culinary language of the feast, a unique event in the community's history to which many of its devout members are treated by Babette, originally an outsider who, in her earlier years, had been celebrated as one of Paris's memorable culinary artists.

The feast is heavy with a proliferation of worldly signs that threaten to disrupt the moral economy of the village by stimulating a panoply of appetites and desires. The management techniques inherent in the community's repressive linguistic system are reasserted implicitly through the invited guests' vow to remain silent about the meal as they consume it, an act which underscores the moral significance of linguistic economies. Ultimately, however, as the feast is elaborately enjoyed the moral challenge articulated by the invading culinary system succeeds in upsetting the stability of the existing linguistic economy. Shapiro captures the import of this victory by saying that "the rich system of culinary signification succeeds in penetrating the closed and reduced signifying system of the Scandinavian community, opening it to more meaning and thus to more life."[5]

It can be seen from Shapiro's analysis of *Babette's Feast* how a genealogical critique of Adam Smith would depart from traditional approaches to this eighteenth century philosopher and political economist. Though he would endorse the importance of their contributions, studies focusing on such topics as Smith's role in the Scottish Enlightenment, the influence of his friend, David Hume, on the development of his thought, his part in founding the school of classical political economy that included Malthus, Ricardo, Mill and Marx, Smith's contribution to liberal political economy through his defense of free trade and corresponding attack on mercantilism and the mercantilist state, or the complexities of his individualistic account of society and his relation to the natural law tradition would fall largely outside of Shapiro's compass. To the extent to which they enter into his concerns they do so importantly as supporting or contextual themes.

Rather, as evidenced by his examination of Dinesen's story and in keeping with his work in poststructuralist and postmodernist theory, Shapiro's *Reading "Adam Smith"* inquires into Smith's relation to the architecture of modernity, especially with regard to the construction of "self and other" internal to his political and economic thought. It is in this context that desire, among other sentiments, is examined for its collusion in creating and managing subjectivity and its expressions. Shapiro also extends his critique to the architectonics of discursive systems that play a decisive role in forming modernity's normative infrastructure—what he refers to as the "Smith effect." Here the inquiry turns to the textual dynamics of literary genres, as exemplified by Smith's writings, which act as powerful forces to constitute personal and collective identities and the orders that they are made to fit and sustain. At both of these levels of interpretation Shapiro's aim is twofold. On the one hand he seeks to expose the nature and extent of Smith's formative implication in modernity and of the "effect" of his discursive practices. On the other hand, Shapiro invites us to consider the ways in which Smith's thought and its "effect" implicates "we moderns," as Nietzsche puts it, in modernity, while also suppressing insight into our Smithian entanglement.

Readers of Shapiro who normally consign Adam Smith to a bygone era of capitalism will be startled to rediscover this "economist" to be one of the preeminent architects of this late stage of modernity. Smith's hand is revealed to have been at work, directly and indirectly, forging our world right down to the norms and desires which have replaced the foundations of the earlier Western industrial orders for which Smith, too, was partially responsibile. It is somewhat ironic that Smith himself proves, in peculiar ways, to be that "invisible hand" which he had promised in his *Wealth of Nations* would create harmonious public order.

The radically new perspective on Adam Smith introduced by Shapiro's study is equaled by the initial three volumes of the series on Augustine,

Hobbes, and Hegel. And as does *Reading "Adam Smith,"* the contributions to **Modernity and Political Thought** by Connolly, Flathman, and
Dallmayr improve our understanding of what modernity is while also
challenging us to speculate about what different cultural and political
projects societies must pursue if the problems of modernity are to be
overcome and its potential unlocked.

This challenge is made forcefully by Fred Dallmayr in *G.W.F. Hegel:
Modernity and Politics* (Sage, 1993). In *Betweeen Freiburg and Frankfurt: Toward a Critical Ontology* (1991), and in other works prior to his
contribution to **Modernity and Political Thought**, Dallmayr sets the
tone for his series study of Hegel by recalling that the fundamental
experience initiating the entire labor of Hegel's philosophical system
is the experience of division or, put more technically, "diremption," and
that the task Hegel pursues is the reconciliation of all forms of divisive-
ness.[6] This argument foregrounds the approach to Hegel's thought that
he adopts in *G.W.F. Hegel*, which is readily apparent where diremption
and reconciliation become the twin poles around which many of the
most important arguments of this study are constructed.

First and foremost, Dallmayr stresses in this new work, it is as a
theorist of division that Hegel possesses a profound understanding of
modern culture and modern consciousness. His thought is intensely
sensitive to the essentially divisive character of human existence, to
those of its features which impel conflict and opposition, contradiction
and differentiation. Throughout history existence is replete with such
ineliminable turmoil, but it is modernity's emancipation of the individual from tradition and other forms of conventional authority which con-
verts diremption into a qualitatively new phenomenon and modernity's
distinguishing feature. Hegel's concept of modernity thus corresponds to
our own historical experience, for when we think of modernity societies
rent with economic, political, and cultural divisions come to mind.

At the same time, the emancipation of the individual from traditional
forms of authority, which Hegel believed to be the paramount achievement of modernity, brought in its wake only *apparently* irresolvable
conflicts between the individual and the possibility for community, the
private and public spheres, man and nature, and between opposing
forms of thought articulating these and related interests. The gain in
individual freedom at the expense of traditions which orient individuals

toward a common good need not threaten to tear modern society apart. For Hegel diremption is an instrument of progress, unavoidably painful, though a particularly promising one in its modern formations. Here Dallmayr directs our attention to Hegel's turn toward Greek thought, a turn made not out of nostalgia for antiquity, but for insight into whether there could be a form of life able to resolve the conflicts rooted in the possibly exclusive prerogatives of individual freedom and those of shared ethical beliefs and values. Insofar as it finally subordinated individual autonomy to the needs of the community, the Greek experience failed to be instructive as to how this singular achievement of modernity might be preserved. Yet, in its ideal of an individuality nurtured with regard to shared ethical norms, the *polis* offered Hegel a model for the task of political theorizing which, as Dallmayr's puts it in *G.W.F. Hegel*, "was precisely to seek the integration and transcendence of the respective merits of antiquity and modernity through the conceptual formulation of a *modern polis.*"

In Dallmayr's estimation it is this "integrative move" that distinguishes Hegel as an outstanding theorist of modernity. In light of it, we come to see Hegel as a thinker who is more for our time, that of late modernity, because our modern self-understanding of freedom recognizes, however darkly, that it necessarily entails conflicts the resolution of which may require an abandonment of private self-centeredness and the transformation and reconstitution of autonomy from the standpoint of a shared ethical life. Hegel's *modern polis* embodies a critique of our present form of existence, but not as a reminder that individual freedoms can be pursued only at the cost of common goods, that our alternatives can lie only at one of either extreme, that we must chose between the ancients and the moderns. Rather, Hegel's concept invites consideration of an ethical life where individual and community undergo reconciliation, a transfiguration that preserves the interest and realizes the potential of each only by incorporating the aspirations of the other.

With the *modern polis* Hegel takes a decisive step on the "high road of modernity," Dallmayr contends, a road that does not merely celebrate Hegel's ideals and aspirations as he refuses to collapse modernity into its divisions and to sustain its diremptions. Rather, the high road articulates Hegel's conception of the possibilities for ethical life *actually inherent* in modernity. Winding, often torturously, toward the reconciliation of the modern world's deepest and most disruptive divisions, the high road leads eventually far beyond the conflict-ridden horizon of the technologically developed world to the reconciliation of its differences with the nations of the industrially developing world, differences over the nature of freedom, the claims on that freedom of public needs and values, over the limits to growth and the socially responsible role of scientific and technological progress, in short, over what is moral, rational, and true. And the same critical movement toward reconciliation characterizing the evolution of the developed world can take root *in* the developing world, as well, healing its internal divisions, assimilating the values of modern cultures without compromising the integrity of its own, pressing it toward the resolution of its normative conflicts with differently developed worlds. The "high road" is the direction taken by reason as it questions its commitments, tempers if not retreats from its imperialist drive toward mastery.

Dallmayr captures Hegel's vision of modernity by means of a beautiful and moving image. "Minerva at dawn" conveys the assistance Hegel's thought renders in allowing us to view the full sweep of modernity, rather than retrospectively as a shape of life that has grown old, through a philosophy which only at the falling of dusk takes wing with the Owl of Minerva. Through Dallmayr's image of "Minerva at dawn" Hegel enables us to grasp the history of modernity from the horizon of our future and its possibilities, to do nothing less than glimpse "the owl's wings against our hazy morning sky."

While Hegel cannot be exonerated of the charge of being a metaphysical thinker, by siezing upon those features of his thought which return it to our grasp whenever it threatens to spin out of control Dallmayr's argument about Hegel's theory of modernity proves the indictment too well-worn and facile. This is one, but only one of the many great strengths of Dallmayr's study from its first to its last thought. In the construction of this argument Dallmayr underscores the centrality of Hegel's *Philosophy of Right* and related writings, forging an inquiry that draws Hegel out of transcendental regions of experience into a direct and intense engagement with modernity, an engagement which shows Hegel to be situated at the very center of the debate about modernity and its future. Along the way Dallmayr interweaves contemporary theoretical voices, not only as parties to whom Hegel speaks, but as co-conspirators who realize the intent of Hegel's political theory even as they attempt to improve upon it. At the same time, Hegel's work is appraised in light of and defended against a variety of charges leveled by contemporary schools of thought which are, themselves, at war with each other's interpretation of modernity. What Dallmayr strives for is nothing less than a Hegelianism "transformed for political life."

Adopting an intellectual strategy similar to Dallmayr's, in *Thomas Hobbes: Skepticism, Individuality and Chastened Politics* (Sage, 1993) Richard Flathman aims to force a confrontation between Hobbes's thinking and "ours," a confrontation between Hobbes and the architects, critics and reformers, and everyday participants of modern liberal democracies. Flathman's approach is inspired, in part, by the belief that the perspectivism central to Hobbes's work is too little present in our liberal theory and practice. By foregrounding Hobbes's perspectivism and related features of his thinking, Flathman uses his engagement with Hobbes to apply intellectual pressure on our communities, aiming to alter not only our leading ideas but the very framework within which our ideas are conceived and translated into action. Through the intensity of this engagement Flathman presses us to become, self-consciously and despite opposing tendencies in our public cultures, the Hobbesians he thinks we already are in part and at our best.

Flathman has long been engaged with the challenges presented by Hobbes's political theory. Perhaps more than any other single political thinker, it has been Hobbes who has provided him with the theoretical tools to reconstruct liberal theory and practice, a project that in one form or another has occupied Flathman's attentions for much of his intellectual life. Because Flathman's study of Hobbes is deeply rooted in his preoccupation with liberalism, our appreciation of it can be enhanced by consideration of his most recent work in liberal theory (which he himself describes as a "companion" to the Hobbes volume), *Willful Liberalism: Voluntarism and Individuality in Political Theory and Practice* (1992).[7]

Willful Liberalism develops and defends a theory that moves aggressively against tendencies in and around liberal theory and practice in late modernity. The sharply controversial character of the voluntarist liberalism Flathman there endorses prompts him to anticipate that some will regard his argument as illiberal and therefore antiliberal. Although in his estimation (and in mine) such a response would be mistaken,

Flathman recognizes that the aversion of most liberals to Hobbes's authoritarianism will dispose them against a view that owes so much to Hobbes.

Though liberal theorists may mistakenly attribute an antiliberal stance to *Willful Liberalism*, they will be correct in discerning a certain skepticism, much indebted to Hobbes, toward democracy. Although inverting Hobbes's view that monarchy is the best and democracy the worst possible form of government, Flathman finds persuasive Hobbes's argument that an active and embracing democratic politics tends to add to the dangerous power and authority of the state. Thus Flathman argues that we should maintain democratic institutions and procedures but adopt what he refers to as Hobbes's "chastened" conception of the state and politics. On this conception, we seek important but few benefits from the state, and we view our political participation more as a means of protection against state excesses than as a means of putting its authority and power to our own uses or as a form of activity that is good in itself. Accordingly, Flathman opposes liberals who argue for a fervently participatory democracy and who promote a deepened and politically intensive conception of justice, social cooperation, and community. Also accordingly, he applauds Hobbes's view that we have a right—albeit not a "natural" one—to dissent, disobedience and rebellion, and goes beyond Hobbes in urging that we maintain a vigilant, defensive stance toward government.

An important part of Flathman's mission is to disrupt those currently influential tendencies in liberal thinking that celebrate reason and encourage and perhaps yearn for social and political unity based on rationally grounded and widely shared beliefs and values. He does so by confronting such views with Hobbes's powerful emphasis on difference, separation and incompatibility, indeterminacy, opacity and incomprehensibility. For Flathman, these features of Hobbes's thinking reorient liberal theory away from stifling homogeneity and conformity, away from those aspects of politics and political involvement which diminish the individual, and move it toward a conception of political association that protects and promotes individuality, plurality and hence group interactions that are at once mutually productive and as little intrusive as may be.

While acknowledging that Hobbes's thinking contains objectionably authoritarian tendencies, Flathman exonerates the great English political

philosopher of the charge that he was a statist and incipient totalitarian
who wanted to impose absolute rule on virtually all of social and
political life. In Flathman's reading, Hobbes's *Leviathan* was meant
unequivocally to serve individuality and the plethora of "felicities" that
are individuality's yield and its exclusive good. Hobbes rejects both the
possibility and the desirability of a common good and seeks no more
legal and political order than is necessary to facilitate the activities of
human beings pursuing a great and constantly changing variety of
goods. What is decisive here is the very special meaning of Hobbes's
individuality. For Hobbes individuals are primarily creatures of their
own making, creatures of "artificings" which flow first and foremost
from their passions and their wills, and only secondarily and instrumen-
tally from their reason. Hobbes's political theory, Flathman contends,
is thus "deeply voluntarist."

Flathman's willful liberalism rests on such a voluntarism where
passion and will rather than reason are the predominant moving forces
of human conduct. Reason is but the "scout" for the passions, as Hobbes
famously said. Flathman's liberalism presupposes, as he puts it, individuals whose conduct is for the most part voluntary in the familiar
sense of not being determined, coerced or compelled by other agents or
agencies and which occurs because of passions and desires, interests
and values, deliberations and decisions which are in some sense the
individual's own. By comparison with Hobbes, for Flathman most
liberal thinkers have embraced no more than heavily qualified versions
of voluntarism, versions too "weak" to satisfactorily account for the
kinds of voluntary conduct that *all liberalism* (tacitly) *presupposes*.
Moreover, these weak versions of liberal voluntarism are antagonistic
to the yet more vigorous forms of individuality for which Flathman
finds support in Hobbes. It is evident, in light of Flathman's reading of
Hobbes, why a Hobbesian inspired willful liberalism would find anath-
ema a single, substantive and life encompassing ideal, whether defined
by the state, the deliberations that occur in a public sphere, or an
inspiration to politics and political participation. On his view, for their
purposes liberal states, public cultures, and politics must seek no more
order than is necessary to the activities of diverse human beings pursuing a diversity of goods.

Willful Liberalism attempts a reconstruction of liberal theory only in part through engagement with the thought of Hobbes. It draws equally upon the voluntarist elements of the work of such philosophers as Ockham and Scotus, Schopenhauer, William James, Oakeshott, Arendt, and especially Nietzsche. With *Thomas Hobbes* Flathman escalates the terms of his earlier debates about Hobbes and liberalism. The aspiration here is to show emphatically and comprehensively that Hobbes is a precursor of not just any liberalism, but of one that promotes plurality and above all individuality. These ideas and ideals, Flathman shows, are vibrant throughout Hobbes's thinking, from his metaphysics and epistemology through his philosophy of mind and language right up to his morals and especially his politics. It is Flathman's own ideal that without individuals who are capable of self-making and self-command, self-discipline and self-control, self-reliance and self-responsibility, liberalism is hopelessly utopian. With *Thomas Hobbes* Flathman looks to the thought of a philosopher often believed to be the enemy of liberalism to save it from the utopianism it seems historically on the verge of becoming.

As does Flathman's *Thomas Hobbes*, William Connolly's *The Augustinian Imperative: A Reflection on the Politics of Morality* (Sage, 1993) has a strong bearing on liberal theory and practice. And like Flathman's contribution, too, its concerns are also rooted in its author's earlier work on liberalism, *Identity\Difference: Democratic Negotiations of Political Paradox* (1991).[8] Among other concerns, *Identity\Difference* shows how liberalism forgets the role politics plays in the very construction of personal and collective identity and its conversion of difference into otherness. Connolly pinpoints how liberalism unconsciously devalues the differences created by the identities it nurtures, and how liberal individualism and liberal individuality obscure the politics of identity and difference and deflate efforts to infuse these relations with the spirit of "agonistic respect." A politics of agonistic respect appears when contending identities mutually sacrifice their demands for self-certainty, exercising forbearance on their ambiguous relations of interdependence and strife. Only such a politics of "critical pluralism," as Connolly calls it in this study, can avert the conversion of difference into otherness and the naturalization and normalization of fixed identities that this conversion helps to effect. Politics now be-comes the vehicle through which we locate threats to diversity and difference in the state, civil society, and in the interior of the individual. A politics of critical pluralism becomes the medium through which we come to terms with the contingency of our own identities and the violence to others we produce by the effort to conceal this contingency. This is a politics through which difference can begin to flourish, or at least not be converted into otherness and victimized. Through such a politics, liberalism would be reconstituted, drawing inspiration from an unlikely combination of liberal skepticism, Nietzschean agonisms, and Foucauldian care.

A question of fundamental importance becomes, then, why does it seem so difficult for liberalism to make this decisive move to an agonistic politics? Although not explicitly concerned with liberalism, *The Augustinian Imperative* casts light on this question as it challenges the ideal of "intrinsic moral order" still implicit in some versions of liberalism. *The Augustinian Imperative* is an archeological investigation into the intellectual foundation of liberal societies. Connolly excavates and deciphers a complex of discourses which, because of the extent to which they have become insinuated into our linguistic practices, pos-sesses an inertia, not simply toward the determination, but toward the overdetermination of our identities. Augustinian in theory and practice, these discourses contribute to the formation of identity, to the sort of powers by which it is formed and the sort of power it becomes.

If we were to place *The Augustinian Imperative* side by side with *Identity\Difference*, we would learn this: The "Augustinian Imperative" is the moral infrastructure exercising hegemony over our words and thoughts and deeds. It is the structure that pulls identity toward its self-validation and dogmatization. It is the particular structure that constitutes order as intrinsic and identity as integral to the true order of things. The Augustinian Imperative is the holy father of moral order. And this imperative that there be an "intrinsic moral order" is lodged in the subterranean levels of liberalism.

In its theoretical insights and rhetorical power, *The Augustinian Imperative* compares with Michel Foucault's *Discipline and Punish* and his earlier *Madness and Civilization*, although in its genealogical stance Connolly's study has more in common with the later text.[9] As does

Foucault with madness and punishment, Connolly locates the points in Augustine's work where knowledge and power intersect, where they are imposed upon the body to constitute an authoritative identity and moral order taken to be intrinsic. Through his examination of Augustine's discourses—on god's will and human will, faith, mystery, divination, confession, condemnation, conversion, healing, self-discipline, heresy—the moral imperative, the tactics for its definition, the cultural forms the imperative assumes and the mechanisms of its cultural reproduction, and the extent to which it can order and organize our lives unfold before us as a densely textured universe of concepts, arguments, proofs. Of words, within which each of us becomes entangled because, as Connolly puts it, "the Augustinian Imperative assumes a larger variety of forms in modern doctrines that relax the demand for eternal life but relocate the spirit of eternity in the cultural identities they endorse and the conceptions of intrinsic moral order they represent."

So compelling is Connolly's image of the imperative that we come to recognize where Augustine's framework has impressed itself on our own cultural practices, where it is at work in contemporary philosophical and theoretical positions. Along the way we recognize, too, that Connolly himself is implicated in the confessional complex and moral imperative he exposes, perhaps all the more as he contests, combats, attempts to lighten its influence, to extricate his own thinking from its identitarian web. That Connolly cannot escape being drawn into the Augustinian maelstrom offers ironic support for his thesis. It also illustrates the departure he represents in contemporary studies of Augustine. Whereas Charles Taylor, for example, argues in his *Sources of the Self: The Making of Modern Identity* that Augustine's design is to move our attention away from the sensible to the insensible order, Connolly reveals how focusing our attention on the insensible is instrumental to riveting our attention on the order of the sensible world.[10] If Connolly's expose of Augustine's hidden agenda spells its failure, then the paradox is that Augustine succeeds even where he fails.

It will be apparent to readers of Shapiro, Dallmayr, Flathman, and Connolly's books that there are areas of agreement and disagreement on the problems and prospects of modernity and liberalism. As future series volumes appear we will have occasion to revisit these debates in the broader thematic context developed by each new study, and to take an accounting of the view of modernity the contributions to **Modernity and Political Thought** afford.

Members of the Sage Publications editorial staff have been particularly helpful over the nearly four years of labor required to produce this series. I am grateful to Blaise Donnelly for his contribution as in-house series missionary, to C. Terry Hendrix for acting as overseer, to Carrie Mullen for the professional care she has devoted to nurturing the concept underlying **Modernity and Political Thought** and for moving series volumes into and through all stages of production, and to Mary Curtis and Astrid Virding for their invaluable contributions to the editorial and production process.

–Morton Schoolman
–*State University of New York at Albany*

Notes

1. Michael J. Shapiro, *Language and Political Understanding: The Politics of Discursive Practices* (New Haven: Yale University Press, 1981); *The Politics of Representation: Writing Practices in Biography, Photography, and Policy Analysis* (Madison: University of Wisconsin Press, 1988); *Reading the Postmodern Polity: Political Theory as Textual Practice* (Minneapolis: University of Minnesota Press, 1992).

2. *Reading the Postmodern Polity: Political Theory as Textual Practice*, p. 16.

3. "Political Economy and Mimetic Desire in *Babette's Feast*," in ibid, pp. 54-67.

4. Ibid., p. 63.

5. Ibid., p. 67.

6. Fred Dallmayr, *Between Freiburg and Frankfurt: Toward A Critical Ontology* (Amherst: University of Massachusetts Press, 1991). These issues are discussed in the third chapter, "Critical Theory and Reconciliation."

7. Richard E. Flathman, *Willful Liberalism: Voluntarism and Individuality in Political Theory and Practice* (Ithaca: Cornell University Press, 1992).

8. William E. Connolly, *Identity\Difference: Democratic Negotiations of Political Paradox* (Ithaca: Cornell University Press, 1991). My discussion of Connolly's book focuses on arguments in its third ("Liberalism and Difference") and sixth ("Democracy and Distance") chapters.

9. See Michel Foucault, *Madness and Civilization* (New York: Random House, 1965) and *Discipline and Punish* (New York: Vintage, 1979).

10. Charles Taylor, *Sources of the Self: The Making of Modern Identity* (Cambridge: Harvard University Press, 1989), pp. 127-142.

Preface

This is not a book about Adam Smith in the usual sense of the word *about*, for it is neither a comprehensive explication of his views nor a careful tracing of the sources of them. Certainly Smith provides testimonial and textual evidence that his writing contains debts to early Greeks, especially the Stoics, to Rousseau, and to Hume along with other writers associated with the "Scottish enlightenment." He read widely and discerningly in a variety of intellectual domains, and the effects are well documented in both the contentious and celebratory pieces of Smith scholarship, which range over several disciplines. However, although some of the scholarship is critical, Smith's texts have yet to experience the catastrophic confrontation they deserve. A *catastrophe* in its etymological sense is "a turning down." This book is an enactment of the contention that despite the contribution Smith has made to creating and legitimating the conceptual space for modern commercial, liberal, and democratic society, and even though his ideas remain influential, he must be turned down by those who want an effective, politicized understanding of modernity.

Therefore, although what follows is a reading of some of Smith's work, it is less an intellectual history than it is a confrontation. *Reading Adam Smith* is a book about modernity with the aim of conceptualizing issues of the self or subjectivity, of orders, and of politics in ways that make the present available to one interested in a critical political perspective.

What, then, are the objects of confrontation? Although the name, Adam Smith, will be the representative for many of the objects of analysis, it lends more coherence to those objects than is warranted. *Adam Smith*, like the Judeo-Christian god, is a media personality. He is a function of the texts that bear his name, and throughout the history of the compilation of those texts Smith has been constructed to be as coherent an intellectual personality as possible. It is no doubt the case that the normativities surrounding modern liberal capitalism—which include a celebration of individual proprieties, a support for inhibition of state-level dominance over individual economic initiative, and a faith in the natural tendencies of interpersonal accommodation when not aggressively managed by government—has guided the Adam Smith one now reads.

Thus, like the Judeo-Christian god the textual Adam Smith has been normativized. The textual god is a product of interpretive work, having been fashioned over the centuries to accommodate the imperatives stemming from a tradition of priestly authority.[1] A very different authority domain, one involved with political rather than religious commitments, has guided the normativizing of Adam Smith. Nevertheless, as some of the better Smith scholarship has shown, many of the seeming contradictions between Smith's treatment of social and moral exchanges and his treatment of political economy have been lessened as various editions of both areas of writing have been assembled.[2]

However, my focus is not on finding the authentic Adam Smith, whether consistent or contradictory. For example, no attempt is made here to treat the so-called Adam Smith Problem, which changes depending on how it is formulated but which, perhaps at a general level, has been succinctly stated by Robert Heilbroner as "the question of the relationship between the intensely moral focus of . . . the *Theory of Moral Sentiments* and the moral indifference of the *Wealth of Nations*."[3] How such issues can be treated depend on which particular

Smithian construction of the self is isolated[4] and what assembly of statements (i.e., which editions) of the Smith texts are consulted.[5]

Because I am *not* after isolating a unique and coherent author, *Adam Smith*, the focus is on aspects of Smith's writing that one could call the *Smith Effect*,[6] a set of ways for scripting the self, for imagining spaces such as *the state*, and for constructing the dynamics of such selves within various spaces, dynamics involving the exchange of sentiments, goods, and recognition. All of these dimensions of the Smith Effect bear on understandings that are integral to modern capitalist political economy and the construction of the "social," "political," and "moral" within which such a political economy operates. The Smith Effect is also discernible as a way of doing narrative, of writing history, one that is characteristic of the kind of naturalizing perspective that imposes continuities on discontinuities, linearity on disturbed and inconsistent temporalities, and harmony on disharmony. Moreover, in focusing on the Smith Effect rather than attempting to strip away false or inconsistent representations in order to isolate the "real" Adam Smith, I hope to exemplify a way of doing political theory, one that challenges some traditional ways of constructing and celebrating the "political theory canon." Adam Smith is important for traditionalists because he helped to shape the modern political condition (as if that "condition" were quiescent, consistent, and unambiguous).

In a more critical sense, Smith is important because his writings exemplify some of the contending forces that tend to escape contention. His ideas are now textualized and, to some extent, institutionalized, and in the context of the present they militate in a pacifying direction. Their contentiousness is masked because they seem descriptive rather than appearing as arbitrary victories monumentalized in persons such as "the individual" and collectivities and spaces such as "the nation." These monuments exist in his kind of discourse, which not only forms them as if they are simply objects of description but also embeds them within narratives that naturalize them as consistent evolutionary developments.

Ironically, the very Smith whose writings helped to liberate the flows of capital by challenging the mercantilist discourse on wealth, now stands arrayed as part of the effect of the normalized present against forces that would liberate other flows, flows of forces that would constitute alternative individual and collective human identities, and alternative imaginings of space; forces, in short, that are the counter-forces lurking behind the arrangements that have been reified in prevailing dogmas.

Why, if the aim is one of elucidating aspects of the present, should one turn to Smith, whose thought developed in the context of the 18th century? It is because the Smith Effect continues to stand in the way of a politicized apprehension of modernity. The claim is not that a confrontational reading of Smith is the sine qua non for understanding modernity in a way that overcomes that effect. Rather, the more modest contention is that it is a useful strategy. Smith expressed himself at a time when the modern alternatives to various political, economic, and social issues were on the agenda, and, in general, he pushed the case for modernity. His thought was aimed at opening up the possibilities now reflected in modern arrangements. He challenged systems of authority and aspects of stasis that inhibited the flows we now associate with modern economic and political processes, and his ideas still provide many with discursive legitimations for some of modernity's arrangements.

Beyond the attitudes toward change that Smith's ideas embodied, the combinatory thematics he developed are significant. In addition to linking politics and economy, he was in the vanguard of those linking politics and society. In developing what was for his time a robust version of the common life, of the social, Smith was one of those most responsible for shifting the emphasis of political thinking away from the civic bond, the relationship between the ruler and the ruled, and replacing it with an emphasis on a politics based on the creative shaping and maintenance of social well-being.

With Smith the various modes of reciprocity constructing the political domain became more horizontal than vertical. In his writing, the sovereignty relation, familiar in canonical treatises through the 17th century, changes its locus and orientation. It derives its animus from exchanges within the common life rather than from the primordial exchange that some thinkers have used to justify unitary systems of rule. And Smith's emphasis on the common life as the locus of moral judgments shifted the emphasis away from a transcendent space within which conduct is to be valorized or deplored and toward the everyday process of interpersonal observation.

Given these various contributions of Adam Smith, he is always at least implicitly present when one negotiates modernity's codes and arrangements. Because his texts have remained inscribed within the political discourses of modernity and their echoes persist in contemporary conversations, it is wholly appropriate to summon him now. But as has been indicated, he is not being called forth to receive belated honors. Despite the enormity of his contributions to modernity's *self*-concepts and notions of the order, the treatment here is confrontational. Smith is not being constructed within the "hermeneutic ideal,"[7] the interpretive approach within which the commentator identifies wholly with the writer's work. However, to say that the reading is to be an encounter is insufficiently precise until the spatiotemporal parameters of that encounter are better specified. There are inevitable ambiguities in the fixing of a terrain of encounter between a past thinker and the present. Here, I will be alternatively placing Smith within both his and my terrains, appreciating his critical abilities in his period and the lessons that they dispense into the present and, at the same time, inquiring not only into what his contributions disclose and make possible but also what they block and render silent or invisible.

For the most part, however, Smith will be assessed within the here and now, for I am primarily involved in a speculation about modernity. It is, nevertheless, a mediated speculation in that I am bringing the past into the interpretive agonistics within which the present is negotiated. The facticity of the present is always contentious, whether recognized or not. The temporary concords through which it becomes possible to identify objects and kinds of persons and to ascribe meaning and value to them within a public discourse involves a negotiation of systems of representation, where certain past forms of inscription play a more central role than others. Not surprisingly, when the present is negotiated there is an inclination to mediate conversations and contentions through canonical texts, those with the most persistent ability to remain present.

But beyond the critical function of renegotiating the past to negotiate the present, there is a structural issue immanent in all critical argumentation. Criticism of systems of intelligibility must confront what I have elsewhere called "the dilemma of intelligibility," which necessarily hounds those who would distance themselves from canonical modes of thought.[8] This dilemma arises especially in connection with the desire

to create a politicized mode of apprehension. For to politicize something is, at once, to generate a frame with sufficient mutual intelligibility to allow for praxis or political engagement with what are recognized
as problems in the predominant public discourse, and to distance oneself sufficiently from common views to allow for a frame that can
disclose unrecognized commitments and forms of subservience to aspects of power embedded within what has seemed to be mere intelligibility, a natural structure of meaning. In this latter mode, one is interested not simply in addressing problems but also in showing the extent
to which thinking tends to be confined within a set of problematizations.

Like all dilemmas, this one has no simple resolution. All critical
enterprises must operate partly within established conversations such
as the one that Adam Smith helped to create, and partly outside of them
by showing that what is talked about is a limited mode of problematiza-
tion. For example, to understand the limits of the discourse on political
economy that Smith helped to establish, it is useful to take seriously the
spatial metaphor within which the notion of *limit* functions. Modern
reflection on issues of meaning and value has for some time overflowed
the space to which such issues were consigned by Adam Smith, just as
"with Adam Smith, reflection on wealth," the conception within which
mercantilists had interrogated issues of value, "overflowed the space
assigned to it [in what Foucault calls] the Classical age." [9]

Adam Smith should therefore be given his due as a quintessentially
critical theorist. In the case of his establishment of a discourse on
political economy, he attacked a conversation on value that had been
confined within a notion of the differential losses and gains of wealth
involved in trading policy and wage and price setting, a notion that
located the problem of wealth at the level of national regulations
involved in a struggle for wealth among nations. By focusing instead
on the production of goods and services that emerged from the structures of the division of labor, and by adding a system of calculation
based on labor power, Smith accomplished the two most significant
dimensions of any critical theory. First, he took a thing, in this case
wealth, and disarticulated it into the processes through which that thing
is produced. In the same way as the contemporary critical orientations
influenced by Freudian, Nietzschean, and Marxist discourses, Smith
helped to defetishize what was being treated as a natural object by

disclosing the practices involved in establishing the object. He took *wealth*, which was a thing to be hoarded within the mercantilist system, and turned it from a static thing into a *process*, something resulting from productivity. Since wealth for Smith was the sum of goods and services divided by the population, he had to turn his attention to its engendering rather than the more static and reified notion of it as a thing to be protected. Second, his perspective was critical (and politicizing) in that it overcame a silence surrounding working conditions. He shifted the focus from national rivalries to the conditions of work, thereby helping to enfranchise a neglected constituency, the working poor, and to draw them into a new conversation on problems of inequity, a conversation that could not be held within the old, mercantilist conversation on value.

Every conversation is established at the expense of other possible conversations. Just as a new critical perspective provides access to that which was formerly inaccessible, it administers silences and blocks access to something else. Smith's model of political economy was politicizing and critical in the context of the established mercantilist discourse but, given its pattern of volubilities and silences, was depoliticizing at the same time. And much of what remain as the "unthought contours and assumptions in the present"[10] are similar to those that were constituted as the unthought within Smith's theoretical system.

But whatever we may find its insufficiencies to be, Smith produced a comprehensive systematizing of the issues of *meaning* and *value*, situating them in a way that poses a range of important questions for social and political theory. His way of constituting the issues and posing questions both illuminates and obscures aspects of *his* age, and provides pregnant silences when we contemplate ours. To show its limitations both within its time and subsequently, my emphasis is on its temporal and spatial predicates, both of which are expressed within Smith's writing; they are evident in his textual practices.

The combination of critical and uncritical perspectives found in *The Wealth of Nations* is also evident in Smith's earlier *The Theory of Moral Sentiments*. There, the theatrical model of interpersonal judgments animating the text was a dual departure from the enchanted, preindustrial world that Smith's system of thought helped to make obsolete. For both the domains of epistemology and morals, Smith located much of the locus of control within the relationship between the individual and society. The knowledge from which moral sentiments was to issue derived in large part from the individual's personal and social experience, and the moral sentiment itself involved the exercise of an imagination that sprang from interpersonal observations wholly within the social domain. Although his language remained largely transcendental—he figured God as the great "Author" of the universe—Smith's deity had retreated from human, day-to-day existence, leaving behind mechanisms that Smith, in his virtually unbounded optimism, believed to be a structural guarantee that the self and the order would remain always attuned.

Among what Smith's "Author" had left behind as "nature" was the regulative mechanism of a socially felicitous tendency in individual human desiring, which, along with some inevitable tendencies in collective arrangements, would eventuate in an order that progressed toward general prosperity and broadly distributed human contentment. However, this optimistic dimension of Smith's thought, although dominant, had to contend with his less sanguine view, which he seemed to achieve when he was able to abandon his mythic narrative and scrutinize the effects of inequality and poverty.

If Smith's discourse on moral sentiments, like his subsequent treatment of political economy, functioned as an accommodative narrative that welcomed the new industrial society, what was so revolutionary? It was his emphasis on *society*, which moved the locus of morals from a transcendent, spiritual realm to the common life. To appreciate the impact of this move it is necessary to recall that politico-moral space in the 17th and 18th centuries, the period immediately prior to Smith's writing, was organized around an estate-dominated society in which the social domain was understood as a set of formal prerogatives authorized by God. Imagination, reasoning, discussion, and any other social process were irrelevant as founding bases of morals. Society was not a dynamic of human interaction but a structure regulated by a preexisting, formal system of authority.[11]

In locating morals in the domain of the sentiment, which involves the exercise of imagination and the exchange of sympathy within the common life, Smith was turning what had been a static, formal phenomenon into a dynamic, social one. This was therefore a critical contribution similar in structure to the one he was to make subsequently in his

Wealth of Nations, where, as noted above, he disarticulated the old mercantilist idea of wealth into the processes through which it is engendered, thereby substituting a dynamic of practices for a static object. This kind of substitution is one of the essential marks of revolutionary theoretical thinking.

Smith's constructions of morals and political economy are mobilizing; they evoke recognition of the human activities behind the normative codes regulating a society's proprieties and the human productive activity behind its exchanges and accumulations. But his perspectives are as notable for what they treat uncritically, formalize, and render static as they are for their critical recognition of dynamics and their displacing of static objects with human actions. Of prime significance in this regard is Smith's treatment of desire as a formal *a priori* of the social arrangement. Because he limited desire to an initiating condition and stable motivation, his position left no space for the articulation of desire with the dynamics of social perception, which are involved in a person's imposition of value on both objects and other subjects.

There is a possibility for such an articulation in Smith's position. Although he never incorporates his view of the immanent sociality of the self within his theory of the production and exchange of goods, his treatment of the exchange of sympathy contains the beginnings of a complex (even contemporary) view of desire. Some social objects (other subjects), insofar as they are discerned by a self involved in symbolic communication with an imagined other, are valued not directly but through a normative, social mediation. However, this inner dynamic does not, for Smith, disturb the initial impetus of a desire that constitutes the social domain. Desire is not fundamentally at odds with the normativities of the social. Subjects are influenced in their desiring by the desiring of others, but Smith does not suggest that subjectivity itself is either formed through the dynamics of desire or brought into situations of ambivalence and contestation. Desire's initial impetus and its continued effects move primarily in the same, socially pacifying direction.

Given this ambivalence in the Smithian texts, how are we to read him? As I have noted, the reading will be confrontational rather than pious, and it will involve an attempt to understand Smith not only within his time and space but also within the present. What must be added to this are some reflections that emerge when it is noted that I am reading Adam Smith *for us. We* must be situated in some of the problematic of modernity, for we exist not simply as a form of consciousness but as a set of tendentious practices. I do not propose to canvass many of them but to select those that help to reveal what I regard as the more interesting political aspects of those practices. Specifically, I explore (1) the dynamic tension between the impulses and practices of sovereignty and those of exchange, (2) the problematics of the self-order relationship in the context of the dynamics of desire, and (3) the problem of value, particularly as it is represented in historical narratives. Because much of contemporary social theory is addressed to these three issues, the confrontation between Smith and modernity will be mediated through those domains of social theory that I regard as most adequate to it.

The beginning of the Smith-modernity confrontation is an exploration of conflicting pressures that were keenly felt at the time Smith was writing. They emanated from a rapidly growing commercial society in Britain that was pressing to relax prevailing notions of sovereignty and territoriality. As a result of increasing levels of differentiation within the economy (which Smith welcomed and explicated in his *Wealth of Nations*), pressure arose to change the territorial and symbolic boundaries that create the context for political and legal stability. The conflict was essentially between the demands for an expanded level of exchange, which requires a relaxation of traditional sovereignty structures, and the countervailing attempts to hold on to traditional systems of authority based on a policing of forms of space or territoriality and subjectivity (e.g., the notions of citizen eligibility and property rights).

Inevitably, there is a conflict when elements within a society are searching for an external clientele that they cannot access adequately through traditional means, for instance, traveling monks in the case of proselytizing religions and traveling merchants in the case of commercial interests.[12] Niklas Luhmann describes the pressures that occur "when the structure of such subsystems become increasingly dependent on processes of exchange with what politically had been treated as their environment. Then, pressures increase . . . to extend the boundaries of society and to relax their political definition."[13] Inasmuch as Smith was an exchange-oriented thinker, he was prone to a position that welcomed this relaxation of sovereign prerogatives or, at least, to urge a model of sovereignty within which economic expansion would be encouraged. He thought, as do many still, that ultimately this relaxation of national boundaries would be redeemed in the form of a stronger national sovereignty.

However, before turning specifically to Smith's relevant writings, it is necessary to see how the conflicting impulses are being played out within a contemporary, increasingly globalizing modernity in which national boundaries are under increasing pressure. Doing a fast-forward from Smith's time to the present, chapter 1 begins with an analysis of a contention surrounding the attempts in 1990 by the British prime minister, Margaret Thatcher, to inhibit the movement toward European economic integration.

Notes

1. For an analysis of the textual work that supplanted the ancient, more poetically constructed Yahweh with the normativized and more consistent Judeo-Christian god, see Harold Bloom's treatment in *The Book of J*, trans. David Rosenberg (New York: Grove Weidenfeld, 1990).

2. See the excellent treatment of the Adam Smith Problem by Laurence Dickey, "Historicizing the 'Adam Smith Problem': Conceptual, Historiographical, and Textual Issues," *Journal of Modern History*, *58* (Sept. 1986), 579-609.

3. Robert Heilbroner, "The Socialization of the Individual in Adam Smith," *History of Political Economy*, *14* (1982), 427.

4. See, for example, Jean-Pierre Dupuy, "Deconstruction and the Liberal Order," *SubStance*, *62/63* (1990), 110-124, in which it is argued that the discovered inconsistency has been a function of a failure to understand the reflexive, Smithian self of the *Theory of Moral Sentiments*.

5. See Dickey, "Historicizing the 'Adam Smith Problem'," for this aspect.

6. This concept of *effect* is used similarly in Graham Burchell, Colin Gordon, & Peter Miller, eds. *The Foucault Effect* (Chicago: University of Chicago Press, 1991), and in Mieke Bal, *Reading Rembrandt: Beyond the Word Image Opposition* (Cambridge, UK: Cambridge University Press, 1991). (This latter book was entitled *The Rembrandt Effect* in its Dutch edition.)

7. This expression is taken from Charles Altieri, "An Idea and Ideal of a Literary Canon, " *Critical Inquiry*, *10* (Sept. 1983), 37-60.

8. Michael J. Shapiro, "Weighing Anchor: Postmodern Journeys from the Life World," in Stephen K. White, ed., *Politics and the Life-World* (Notre Dame, IN: University of Notre Dame Press, 1989).

9. Michel Foucault, *The Order of Things* (New York: Pantheon, 1971), 225.

10. This expression is from William Connolly, *Political Theory and Modernity* (New York: Basil Blackwell, 1988), viii.

11. The spatial configuration of the estate-based society is discussed in Donald Lowe, *History of Bourgeois Perception* (Chicago: University of Chicago Press, 1982).

12. This example and point is developed in Niklas Luhmann, *The Differentiation of Society*, trans. Stephen Holmes & Charles Larmore (New York: Columbia University Press, 1982), 246.

13. Luhmann, *Differentiation*, 246.

1

Sovereignty and Exchange in the Orders of Modernity

Introduction: Thatcher and the EMU

The story begins with the fall of a British prime minister, Margaret Thatcher. According to one of her staunch defenders, "Margaret Thatcher has taught us that you have to own your money before you can spend it."[1] Here, in one sentence, is contained the Thatcherian proposition that the interests of sovereignty must take priority over those related to exchange. It is supplemented by the corollary claim, emphasized in so many of her statements, that the dynamics of exchange threaten the achievements of sovereignty.

The tenacity of this commitment was at least partly responsible for Thatcher's fall from office, for it informed her resistance to a process of European economic integration endorsed by influential members of her party. At issue when her support crumbled was the mode of British entry into the EMU (European Monetary Union). As Sir Geoffrey Howe stated in summarizing his reasons for resigning as Thatcher's deputy prime minister, "The Prime Minister has appeared to rule out from the start any compromise at any stage on any of the basic components which all the 11 other countries believe to be part of EMU—a single currency or permanently fixed exchange rates, a central bank or common monetary policy."[2]

Like many national leaders in Europe, Howe did not see a strict trade-off between sovereignty and exchange as perceived by Thatcher. While she declared that "she would never witness the end of British sovereignty, nor countenance the demise of sterling,"[3] Howe argued against seeing the issue "as some kind of zero sum game." According to Howe, the forthcoming merger of economies is not to be understood as a loss of sovereignty but as a way to strengthen it, and, in support of this view, he quoted Winston Churchill's claim that such economic union is a step in "the gradual assumption by all nations concerned of that larger sovereignty, which can alone protect their diverse and distinctive customs and characteristics, and their national traditions."[4]

This exemplary contention between the impulses of sovereignty and exchange has been repeated in other European nations, even those with reputations for zealously guarding their sovereignty. For example, Sweden's qualms about relinquishing neutrality have turned out to be far less significant than the fear of damage to industrial development if Sweden remains outside of the European Union. Like Howe, such nations see preserving sovereignty and joining the European Union as compatible; what is feared "is a future outside the EC which sees industrial investment drain away and strips isolated national governments of any true influence over their economic fortunes."[5]

In sum, what is at issue in the disparate positions taken by Thatcher and Howe is the degree of compatibility possible between maintaining sovereignty and facilitating an expanded level of exchange. The fundamental tension between them has especially crucial implications for claims to political identity. To put it abstractly and comprehensively: The *sovereignty impulse* tends toward drawing firm boundaries around the self in order unambiguously to specify individual and collective identities, to privilege and rationalize aspects of a homogeneous subjectivity that is eligible for memberships and recognition and to constitute forms of nonidentical and ineligible otherness, and to specify and bound both the spaces in which subjects achieve eligibility and the space in which the collective as a whole has dominion.

In contrast, the *exchange impulse* encourages flows and thus (often) the relaxation of specifications of eligible subjectivities and territorial boundaries. The opposition between flows of exchange and the inhibitions of sovereignty is oriented around issues of selfhood and location, and consequently involves an emphasis either on ownership and the maintenance of authority and control or on reciprocity, substitutability, and the relaxation of control in order to produce expanded domains in which things can circulate.

However, the relationship between sovereignty and exchange exceeds in complexity this simple opposition. In various cultural configurations, in different epochs in the histories of states and economies, and with respect to different aspects of association, sovereignty and exchange can be either opposing, mutually facilitating, or relatively independent. The implications of this complexity will be examined later in a variety of different domains of human endeavor—linguistic exchange, the authorship of texts, the evolution of musical technology, the history of the art museum, and so on. However, because the issue of sovereignty and exchange involves elaborate connections between forms of subjectivity and forms of order, it is important to examine the frames within which the available possibilities have been theorized and circumscribed in canonical political treatises written in two earlier periods of British history.

Hobbes and Smith on the Self and the Order

Thomas Hobbes's *Leviathan*, written just after a fractious civil war, is an exemplar of a sovereignty-oriented treatise, for it is preoccupied with justifying a unifying, unambiguous, and absolutely dominant national proprietor. Hobbes's sovereign embodies the will and desire for protection of all subjects, who give up their individually sponsored coercive acts in order to achieve the paramount founding civic value, civil peace. *Leviathan* combines this valorizing and privileging of civil

peace with the ideas Hobbes generated from his fascination with math-
ematics and Galilean physics to produce a logical, rigorous, and virtually inescapable justification for an absolute model of sovereignty.

Hobbes's sovereignty orientation is notable not only for an absolutist
(preferably monarchical) view of sovereign displacement but also for
his conceptual building blocks, his proto-sovereign positions. A position on *proto-sovereignty*, as I am using the term, is a set of specifications of the attributes of citizen subjects that provided the pieces that
would fit into the model of a sovereign whole or collectivity. Hobbes's
views on the civically relevant dimensions of human subjectivity—his
proto-sovereign positions—are thus created with a legitimating end-in-
view. More specifically, like so many thinkers in the history of the
political theory canon, Hobbes offered a mythic narrative in which
drives toward consensuality, which are immanent in (or natural to)
subjectivity, become a basis for the existing system of sovereign authority. Hobbes's individual subjects are constructed as being, in their
initial condition, wholly "sovereign," that is, as the sole authors of their
actions or proprietors of their deeds, except in cases in which they are
duly constituted as representatives, authorized to act in behalf of another owner of the deeds to be carried out.

Hobbes's persons are therefore sovereign either as authors or actors.
As an author, the person is a natural person: A "natural person" is "he
whose words or actions are considered either his own, or as representing
the words or actions of another man."[6] As an actor, the person is an
artificial person: There are "Persons Artificiall" in that they "have their
words and actions *Owned* by those whom they represent."[7] In this latter
case, the representative is the "Actor," and the "owner" is the "Author."
In short, persons, insofar as they are persons, hold a copyright to their
words and deeds, and interactions among persons, which affect proprietorship, are matters of freely entered into covenants. Indeed, Hobbes's
rhetorical orientation toward the civic bond prefigured much of the
subsequent legal discourse constructing property rights.

Just as persons hire actors by covenants that stipulate substitutions
of actors for authors, they also hire an absolute sovereign. This choice,
which is the covenant of the civic whole, tends to persist, for although
persons exhibit a restless desire for power over others, they also have
an innate aversion to death and a desire for "commodious living." To

avoid the one and achieve the other, persons calculate that it is best to enter into the primary covenant by which they trade obedience for protection and accept the absolute power of the sovereign. This is the mythic tale that links proto-sovereignty with sovereignty, subjectivity with the sovereign order.

At an individual level, the entry of the Hobbesian self into the relationship with the sovereign is contractual. It amounts to a rational/consensual willingness to give up an aspect of proprietorship, of control over one's own protection. At an aggregate level, the sovereign state is constructed out of a series of covenants that, when viewed individually, are aimed at protection for each, and, when summed up, produce civil peace for the whole. The state as an entity thus amounts to a vast set of yielded proprietorships.[8]

Despite this version of a set of orderly submissions to authority, Hobbes recognized that there are rebellious aspects of human subjectivity. But rather than envisioning a less rigorous or normalizing form of civic order that would allow them space for legitimate articulation, he relegates them to the domain of the irrational. For example, he evokes the idea of madness, which manifests itself either as emotional extravagance (too much rage or laughter),[9] or as discursive aberration, an "abuse of words."[10] Concerned with maintaining a willed or consensual legitimation for absolute sovereignty, Hobbes marginalized all aspects of subjectivity that affront the order or appear to dilute consensuality.

It should be evident that this model of sovereignty has an immanent form of exchange. It is an exchange in the form of an implicit narrative that is very close to the one structuring Marx's discussion of the extended and general value form in volume 1 of *Capital*. When speaking of how value forms are extended, Marx states, "The value of any commodity, such as linen, is expressed in terms of numberless other elements of the world of commodities."[11] This extended form of value is analogous to the difference Hobbes noted between authors and actors, where another person—one of the "Persons Artificiall"—is substituted. Such extensions or substitutions are, for Marx, merely an intermediate stage in the movement of the capitalist system toward what he has called the general form of value represented by gold or money. The general form provides a means not only for substituting for various individual commodities but also, owing to its general representative character, for unifying exchange value. Hobbes's notion of the sovereign or monarch, whose will substitutes for those of all subjects, is thus analogous to Marx's notion of the sovereignty of gold, which monopolizes value just as the sovereign monopolizes normativity as a general representative. Gold, as a form of commodity, becomes sovereign inasmuch as, like a monarch, it achieves an "objective fixity and general social validity."[12]

The Hobbesian sovereign state therefore contains an implicit though atrophied economy. It is an economy that is inaugurated with a primordial exchange and is followed by an inhibition of substitutions. Once the substitutions are willingly made (if only mythically), the process is to cease, for although he allowed for a right of rebellion against abusive sovereigns, Hobbes wanted to give to the sovereign (the monarch or sovereign assembly) total control over selecting a successor.[13]

Another conceptual dimension must be added to determine what is at stake in Hobbes's repression of the economies within his version of sovereignty. It is necessary to raise the question of value, for value is always at least implicitly implicated in the sovereignty-exchange nexus. Jacques Lacan has raised it in a directly relevant way by noting the necessary complementarity between sovereignty and exchange in the process of discourse. Stating that "the signifier requires another locus—the locus of the Other,"[14] he is suggesting that value emerges precisely in the trade-off involved. To participate in intelligible exchanges, the subject must subordinate its identity to a hegemonic model of otherness. It is not a separate sovereign entity in its relationship to signification, for in its entry into discourse it must concede this form of subjugation to an otherness that is immanent in the social system of meaning or signification, and the value that emerges is a compensation. In exchange for the loss of control over meaning, subjects acquire the ability to enter into the social order within which the signification process is embedded and to which it refers.[15] In short, to speak is not to *ex*press one's individuality but to *sup*press it in order to participate within an institutionalized frame of intersubjectivity. A loss of individuality is compensated, then, by a gain in sociability.

This compromise of the sovereignty of the subject inherent in participation in linguistic exchange, this domination of the socio-symbolic domain over the will-to-mean of the subject, which is compensated by allowing participation, can be applied to an interrogation of Hobbesian thought at two levels. At the level of civic sovereignty, Hobbes institutes a strict form of inhibition that stifles the exchange dimension of sovereignty with an obsessive concern with peace and safety. Because of this, the value emerging from the collective sovereign relationship is compromised in that it is not re-experienced through continuous, participatory reactivation. Hobbesian sovereignty subverts exchange by being based on a single, mythic exchange that constitutes an end to all exchange. On the level of individual subjectivity, Hobbes represses the dimension of exchange by repressing the otherness of the social, which is always already there in the subject's ability to engage in self-recognition, for it is within a socio-symbolic discourse that the subject is able to objectify itself. Precisely because of his emphasis on the original sovereignty of the subject, its ownership or authorship of its acts (as though conduct has meaning without a prior system of social inscription), Hobbes neglects that aspect of otherness—the symbolic exchanges between self and other through which selves are constituted—that produces a socially available form of subjectivity.

This stifling of participatory exchange within the individual-level sovereignty relation is also reflected at the macro level. Hobbes's preference for a robust model of sovereignty, a strong centralized model of sovereign control, with power concentrated at the top of a steep hierarchy, suppresses the possibility for political forms that are open to increasing flows of all kinds.

A telling contrast with the Hobbesian privileging of both an absolutist, unifying sovereignty and a wholly self-contained model of proto-sovereign subjectivity is in the writings of Adam Smith who, like Hobbes, was writing in response to a sovereignty crisis. In Smith's case, the crisis was related not to the issue of maintaining civil peace but to the issue of fitting a model of home rule to the need for access to markets. Hobbes was certainly writing at a time when a bourgeois market society had already begun to emerge, but his gaze on this aspect of the order was inconsistent: "Now he saw it, now he didn't," as C. B. Macpherson puts it.[16] In sharp contrast, Adam Smith's gaze was well and consistently focused on this aspect of the order. Writing a century later, he was responding in part to the turmoil produced in connection with the Scottish-English Union, which had been effected in 1707 after a tumultuous national debate in Scotland. The debate had been primarily

concerned with the degree of compensation to be gained through an
increased trading advantage to be had by giving up a large measure of
Scottish sovereignty.[17] Ultimately, the Treaty of Union required Scotland to give up some venerable institutions in order to gain some
economic advantages.

There are some important continuities between Hobbes and Smith.
At a minimum, Hobbes anticipated one aspect of Smithian individualism in his emphasis on the interpersonal comparisons through which
persons determine their worth and his view that life is a race with
everyone attempting to achieve distinction through material success.
This view was expressed by Smith in his repeated emphasis on persons
striving to "better their condition."[18] Despite his emphasis on the
individual and his preference for a robust and broad economy and an
anæmic degree of centralized control, Smith was not without an elaborate view of sovereignty. He addressed himself assiduously (albeit with
highly selective historical evidence) to the proprieties of legislation as
well as to issues surrounding judicial and executive powers. Treating
these issues in his *Lectures on Jurisprudence*, he does much of his
reasoning on the basis of long historical fables, which are primarily
linear narratives of the changes from early hunter-gatherer economies
to commercial ones. He connects these narratives to forms of governance, imagining, for example, that hunting and shepherding societies
had little use for robust legislative functions. He also resorts occasionally to the writings of the ancients on the Greek city state and, putting
these together with his historical fables and anthropological fantasies,
comes up with a model of the *natural* progression of the art of government, which is a more-or-less materialist version of the evolution of
governmental forms. He sees a consistent match wherein the mode of
government appropriate to the mode of production and exchange always seems to emerge.

It follows, therefore, that Smith wanted to locate primary sovereignty
in a legislative body, for it fulfills his narrative in which he sees his
contemporary society as being at the appropriate evolutionary stage for
legislative sovereignty because of its emphasis on manufacture and
trade. In his view a society based on manufacture and trade is well
beyond the management capabilities of a chieftain, and he claims to
demonstrate that only parliamentary sovereignty can provide the man-

agement necessary for Britain's mode of economy (although, as is well known, Smith wanted a minimalist form of management that would allow the natural social mechanisms, especially those related to the division of labor and market impulses, to provide the necessary regulation).[19]

However non-absolutist Smith's version of sovereignty may be, what distinguishes him from Hobbes is not only his preference for a sovereignty shared between a legislature and social mechanisms rather than located in a monarch but also his well-elaborated version of society. Whereas in Hobbes the sovereignty relationship emphasizes owner/author subjects and representing rulers to whom the subjects defer to obtain social peace, in Smith it is a social body made up of social beings involved in economic exchange and the exchange of sentiments that provides the basis of the sovereign relationship. The political relation for Smith is oriented toward this robust version of the social, for politics is conceived in the classical liberal sense of subordinating the political relation to the natural mechanisms operating at the level of social relations.

What is especially notable also by way of the Hobbes-Smith contrast is the attenuated sovereignty implicit in Smith's proto-sovereign notions. The Smithian individual is not the sovereign, self-contained owner or author of actions but, rather, a dynamic, reflective, immanently social system of symbolic exchanges. This Hobbes-Smith difference is consonant with the different rhetorics within which they construct the subject-object and intersubjective relationships. Hobbes figured the person -thing relationship within a scientific rhetoric, based on a Galilean concept of motion. Objects set up forces of attraction, and the appetite of the subject produces initiating energy forces as well. Subject-object or subject-subject relations, which result in attitudes or sentiments, are to be understood as the result of a co-motion, a meeting of the motions produced by the subject and the object. This physicalist emphasis on the dynamics of mind in collision with the dynamics of objects leaves little space for an immanent sociality.

In contrast, Smith figured the social domain within (among others) a visual and reflective rhetoric. For him, a person's understandings and sentiments form a complex set of points of observation. Smith's person is not a self-contained, sovereign actor but a bifurcated or double self, containing both an actor and an imagined observer through whom action predicates are mediated. The appetite is therefore subordinated to two

points of view, one belonging to the subject and the other to an imagined, disinterested observer whose viewpoint is constructed as if it too were
involved in the external appraisal or judgment of what is being viewed by
the subject. Through the reflexivity of the person's gaze, the imagined
observer functions as a social representative within, a "viceregent" whose
judgment is extremely influential.[20] Smith's nonabsolutist version of state
sovereignty is thus reinforced by a compatible proto-sovereignty, a
construction of an individual who is prepared for an attenuated sovereignty by his or her own acts of self-attenuation.

With his immanently socialized subject in place, Smith mounts a
resistance to a strong sovereignty model at the level of the collectivity
as well. His contribution to notions of governance are influenced more
by the forces impelling circulation and exchange than those militating
in the direction of the imposed unities and cohesions that require firm
and unchallenged models of sovereign control. Although this position
represents a significant shift from the preoccupations of Hobbes a
century earlier, it is not a radical departure from the changes in emphasis in political treatises from the 17th to the 18th centuries. With his
focus on managing an economy to secure the well-being of the population as a whole, Adam Smith addressed themes that had been blocked
throughout the 17th century because of "the preeminence of the problem of the exercise of sovereignty."[21] Certainly there were concerns
addressed in connection with the problem of wealth prior to Smith's
Wealth of Nations, but under the system of mercantilism, political
treatises, preoccupied as they were with the power of the sovereign,
treated wealth from the point of view of its functioning as a resource for
the sovereign to protect the realm, not its potential increase. In this context,
Smith's view of wealth participated in a more general departure from the
legalistic obligation of the citizen to the sovereign and moved toward an
interest in an aggregate effect, the problem of producing and maintaining
conditions for the well-being—health, wealth, longevity—of the "population."[22] As Foucault has noted, this entity, the "population" as a focus for
government, emerged in Smith's century.

One of the great innovations in the techniques of power in the 18th century
was the emergence of "population" as an economic and political problem:

population as wealth, population as manpower or labor capacity, population balanced between its own growth and the resources it commanded.[23]

Rather than neglecting sovereignty, Smith helped to shift the problematic from the originary flow of loyalty to the top, that is from sovereignty as a series of displacements, to a concern with a different flow, with the management activity of the sovereign with respect to the flows of exchanges within the social domain. The problem of sovereignty for Smith was therefore based on facilitation rather than control, on the selection of the appropriate model to maintain the flow of goods and services necessary to improve the population's condition and to maintain its vitality as a work force.

With Smith, the "social" had become the primary alibi for the "political." The very meaning of politics had shifted from the Hobbesian notion of a contract between previously wholly sovereign individuals and their general representative equivalent, the monarch, to a notion of the political arising from the social. The political had developed "a social referent,"[24] and once this happened, the problem of sovereignty became one of managing the social configuration.

With Smith, therefore, the world becomes unstuck. In place of a static, legalistic, and protection-oriented model of sovereignty, Smith articulated one congenial to the movement of things within an "art of government" concerned with the management of the relationship of persons to things. In this context, Smith's labor theory of value, based on the cost of maintaining labor power, plays the role of producing a system of calculation for that management. Moreover, the space of governance is reconstituted. It is no longer simply concerned with the maintenance of the realm as a whole but the encouragement of private ownership of the means of production. Smith's sovereignty takes up its primary locus in the society, especially in its productive venues, and the center of authority is viewed more as a steering mechanism (through the appropriate legislation) than a repository of authority.

Summarizing this change from a focus on sovereignty as the maintenance of a legalistic unity to sovereignty as the maintenance of well-being through the management of flows, Foucault refers to the development of a "governmental state," understood less as territorial extension and more

in terms of the various energies and flows produced by its population.[25]
Smith, among others, helped to produce this understanding.

Given that it was circulation and mobility rather than sovereignty and
stasis that organized Smith's approach to governance, and that his gaze
was on the social configuration rather than the ruler-ruled relationship,
he was able to notice that the exchange impulse arising out of the social
domain was surging well beyond the inhibitions constituted by the
absolutist form of sovereignty that had been theorized by Hobbes and
had remained intrinsic to the mercantilist management of wealth. Accordingly, he stressed a form of governance compatible with his notion
that a general well-being would emerge from a facilitation of the
productive capacities of the "individual." This emphasis is of course
predicated on some ideational shifts that had already come to pass,
especially on various desacrilizing modes of thought (to which Hobbes
had contributed). In short, by Smith's time, there *was* such a thing as
an "individual," whose activities could be facilitated, not only by the
state but also by other individuals.

To appreciate the emergence of this kind of individual whom Smith's
thought reflected, it is useful to recall that the self of the prior century
was more privatized than that of the 18th century. It operated within a
frame still dominated by ecclesiastical thought and practice, in which
caring for one's own salvation was largely a self-centered activity.[26]
The trajectory of the Christian devotional self was vertical, and it
tended to exclude the more horizontal preoccupation with sociability.

In Smith's century, the individual was constructed as "a sociable
person," and religious domination of the self was replaced by "a new
cult of sensitivity and friendship."[27] In place of the fear of divine
judgment there emerged a more keen sensitivity to interpersonal judgment, and the individual was less often thought of as a product of a
creator and more often as one shaped by social interaction. Accordingly, various aspects of sociability—such as conversation, a social
process highly esteemed by Smith—replaced devotion as the self-making
dynamic.[28]

Along with social interaction, social space and its dynamics must be
shaped by governance. There is a strong narrative commitment guiding
and supporting Smith's orientation toward this governance as management of flows rather than as the maintenance of a static sovereignty, a

narrative incorporating the materialist version of the history of governance noted above. In contrast with Hobbes's "mythic plot," with its discrete history of the origin of state authority,[29] Smith offers a more continuous model in which forms of governance evolve. They arise, he argues, naturally, where by "naturally" he means that they shift to provide the appropriate context for the particular mode of production in effect, a consistent linear process (as noted above). Smith thought that little governance of any kind was needed and didn't arise until property relations became complex, as in the case when people changed their vocations from hunting to herding.[30] He surmised, further, that with the growth of manufacture and trade, forces were unleashed that weakened the monarchy and strengthened the House of Commons.[31]

This materialist narrative had the effect of naturalizing Smith's preference for a form of governance oriented around facilitating trade. Even his treatment of the issue of the security function was influenced by his interest in exchange, for by "security," he meant not merely the maintenance of civil peace but also the protection of property relations and the production of a general well-being.

Although Smith's interest in commerce controlled his interest in governance, his desire to avoid inhibiting the "market" must be understood in the premodern sense. His conception of a market was not what is meant when one now refers to the global systems of exchange characteristic of contemporary capitalism. Smith's market concept was more akin to the idea of limits to the desire for goods. Indeed, given his concern with morals as a social interaction, he would have been distressed with the extent to which the global vectors along which economic exchanges now occur have loosened the bonds of mutuality.

However, although Smith did not conceive of the market as anything but the arbitrary boundaries of exchange, he recognized the significance of money in creating the conditions of possibility for uninhibited exchange. Whereas of course Marx was to later indict the money form's role in alienating value from its source in human productive activity, Smith was fixated on the encouragement of trade and primarily concerned with extracting the idea of money from old notions of hoarding and accumulating so that it could circulate in an uninhibited way, into and out of British ports. Arguing vigorously for the advantages of free trade, he stated:

Britain should by all means be made a free port, that there should be no
interruptions of any kind made to foreign trade, that if it were possible to
defray the expenses of government by any other method, all duties,
customs and excises should be abolished, and that free commerce and
liberty of exchange should be allowed with all nations and for all things.[32]

Smith was clearly and unmistakably resistant to the idea that there
could be any inhibition to the circulation of money. For him, money
was not bound up even at a symbolic level with sovereignty. It was not
a mark of wealth or national integrity, but solely an instrument to
facilitate exchange. Despite the distance of Smith's position from that
recently adopted by Margaret Thatcher, he was not without some
Thatcher-like qualms. At the level of governance, he tended to think
that the evolving forms that had encouraged commerce would also
provide liberty and security for each individual. However, "security"
here meant the protection of property and livelihood. When it came to
such a thing as national security, Smith did not share Thatcher's worries
because trade and military technology were not, in his time, dissolving
old boundaries. But he did express a deep concern about the diminution
of the "martial spirit" among citizens who are totally oriented toward
commerce. Among the bad effects of commerce he noted was that it
"sinks the courage of mankind." As his lament continued, he expressed
the opinion that when the defense of the country is left to specialists,
others with "their minds constantly employed on the arts of luxury"
grow "effeminate and dastardly."[33]

Although Smith's constructions of individual character and its relationship with the social is treated in this book at length in chapter 3, it
is important to note here the coherence of this Smithian lament with his
general view of the relationship between individual character and
collective consequences. Debates about the relationship between commercial power and the martial spirit go back to antiquity. It is certainly
the case, for example, that the Athenian-Spartan antagonism seemed to
pit a power based on commerce against one based on martial spirit, but
even the bellicose Spartans, by Thucydides' account, recognized well
the need to acquire the necessary financial resources before initiating
large-scale hostilities. As the Spartan king cautioned before the decision to declare war was made, "War is not so much a war of arms as a
war of money by means whereof arms are useful."[34] Just as in antiquity,

in modernity the relationship between commerce and defense and war is complex, and in the modern condition, "spirit" is even less relevant than it was.

It is not surprising, however, that Smith would foreground *spirit* given his tendency to construct collective relations and outcomes on models of character, on the types of motivations of individuals. Although it was arguably the case in antiquity, it is certainly the case in modernity that it is more appropriate to speak of martial tendencies than spirit. Smith recognized, as did the Spartan king quoted above, that wealth and commercial acumen is a resource for war. What he failed to recognize is that a growing commercial power becomes interested in violently shaping the world in order to maintain its trading advantages. Smith said that "the wealth of a neighboring nation . . . though dangerous in war and politics, is certainly advantageous in trade,"[35] as though the interests in one domain do not shape those in another.

However, the modern militarized state owes its bellicosity to the character of political economy and technology, not individual spirit. In this domain, as in so many others, Smith lacks insight into the contributions of form and structure to social and political consequences. In the case of the structuring of contemporary international danger, a combination of a lively business in arms production and transfers along with an interest in external pacification by nonmilitary commercial interests is as much involved in producing the issue of "defense" as are any impulses that emerge from purely "security"-oriented concerns. Indeed, *defense* is an anachronistic concept. It has been displaced by the concept of *security*, which incorporates an active militaristic practice, primarily by those industrial powers with much at stake, to regulate or protect commerce and wealth.

In the modern condition, a concern with wealth is not a softening of the martial spirit but an impulse to promote it. The "courage" imagery that Smith employs harks back to the Greek ideal of individual valor on the battlefield, but the modern "battlefield" violates the logic of this image. There is no "field" in the usual sense of the term, for the relevant domain is now the field of vision belonging to the modern surveillance satellite that distinguishes friends and foes and even prompts the firing of weapons. Warfare, or "deterrence," is now increasingly more logistical and less political. The relevant "specialists" are logistical experts

who play a role, along with the visioning equipment, in interpreting the
world for purposes of "defence." Given the speed with which weapons
and information travel, the traditional geographic inhibitions that once
formed the bases of defense and the character of the populations—whether
brave and resolute or cowardly and indifferent—within territories become
largely irrelevant. With the logisticalization of warfare has come a con-
comitant shrinking of political space, a situation that Paul Virilio has
described as "the intelligence of war that eludes politics."[36]

More important than any spirit here is the restructuring of relationships between military and political intelligence operating along with
a tendency toward adventurist global military policing that the structure
of modern commerce encourages. However, despite the increasing
irrelevance of spirit in warfare, there remain differences at the level of
national leadership that register important effects. The desire to control
deadly force remains a priority, and it asserts itself especially at moments in which national sovereignty is under stress. With this in mind,
we can return to Margaret Thatcher's concerns.

Money, Sovereignty and Modernity

If by "effeminate" and "dastardly" Adam Smith meant a reluctance
to bear arms and a generalized fear of bellicosity, Margaret Thatcher's
sovereignty orientation was neither. Her resistance to European union
was based on both her opposition to relinquishing unilateral control of
defense and war making (as her Falklands/Maldives War attests) and
her unwillingness to subsume the British economy within a wider
system of sovereign control (one, she complained, in which bankers
instead of parliaments make decisions).

Thatcher's anachronistic view of money, which emerged most recently in her resistance to the European Monetary Union, is especially
noteworthy for purposes of theorizing the sovereignty-exchange relation. For better (Smith et al.) or worse (Marx et al.), when one is dealing
with an exchangeable currency it is already not controlled by an independent mode of sovereignty. Contemporary control over national
currencies is widely dispersed. A currency's value is based on a system

of interrelationships that extend well beyond the identity/sovereign dimensions involved in the initiation of exchanges. Indeed, modernity can be understood as, among other things, a condition in which relations of capital have displaced interpersonal relations. It is, in J-J. Goux's terms, a situation of "an unprecedented rift between intersubjective relations and what function henceforth as economic relations."[37] At all levels of identity—person, family, tribal group, or nation—the meanings attached to subjectivity have paled as exchanges have become "rather abstract relations between *positions*."[38]

The significance of this rift becomes especially evident when modern capital exchange relations are contrasted with the symbolic ties between subjects that control barter relations among tribal societies. For example, among the Narringeri peoples studied by Geza Roheim, exchange relations were connected so closely with intersubjectivities that there were actual exchanges of body substances accompanying the exchange of goods. There was, for example, the custom of a father ceremoniously preserving a child's umbilical to be later passed on to a man from another tribe. With this bodily exchange, a future intersubjectivity is established. The child and children of the recipient will become "certified traders of various products exchanged between the two tribes," once they reach adulthood.[39]

United by the umbilical, the traders do not have their reciprocity deferred through money, which, as a much more abstract symbolizing instrument, depersonalizes exchange, suppressing its sovereignty dimensions by connecting abstract persons whose reciprocity is too mediated to allow for mutual recognition.[40]

To extend the comparison, an intermediate level is represented in the money forms used by the Trobriand Islanders and the North American Iroquois. The Trobriand armshells and necklaces and Iroquois wampum were media of exchange, but they were also "pledges, linked to the persons who use them and who in turn are bound by them."[41] By contrast in modern capitalist societies, money or species payments are instruments through which both subjectivities and places are dissolved rather than reinforced or formed. This dissolving of subjectivity and locationality is precisely a challenge to sovereignty inasmuch as *sovereignty* implies, in its most general sense, the authoritative control over domains and subjects. When exchange become wholly abstract, a matter

of goods destined for abstract persons in abstract positions, the rudiments of sovereignty—subjects and places—are no longer easily identifiable. It is not the case that intersubjectivity has vanished. It is the
case, rather, that the forms it takes are distantiated from the concrete
subjects affected by the exchanges. The identities of the exchangers exist
within sovereign domains and the exchanges, which link subjects across
domains, do not apply to specific subjects and are often part of a pattern
that affects the very identity spaces within which subjects operate.

In the face of this modern tendency, nationalist inhibitions, such as
those expressed in Thatcher's attempt to maintain "British money," are
increasingly inefficacious because no one sovereignty domain controls
either the exchanges or the subjectivities around which they are organized. Money, now shorn of its reference to specific subjectivities, has
been largely deprived of its sovereign vestiges, and given the recent
tendency to effect transactions electronically, money is becoming not
only more abstract but wholly dematerialized. This is well captured in
Don DeLillo's novel, *Players*, where one of the characters becomes
aware of this qualitative change in money's existence:

> He'd seen the encoding rooms, the microfilming of checks, money mov-
> ing, shrinking as it moved, beginning to elude visualization, to pass from
> paper existence to electronic sequences, its meaning increasingly com-
> plex, harder to name. It was condensation, the whole process, a paring
> away of money's accidental properties, of money's touch.[42]

Sovereignty Crises: The Different Venues

1. Language

The stresses placed on British politics as a result of the sovereignty-
exchange tensions surrounding entry into the European Union have
been manifested in a variety of domains of human practice. One of the
most exemplary and fundamental is the domain of language. The historical and everyday struggles over attaching meanings to statements
arise, as was noted above, from the condition elaborated by Lacan, that
speech involves, simultaneously, the exchange of signification and the
recognition and reinforcement of modes of subjectivity, for speech is a

phenomenon that moves from one identity to an-Other. Its ability to effect an exchange of meaning is inseparable from the extent to which there is stability in the space or context of the exchange and the identities of present and potential conversation partners.

Moreover, there is a political significance of the sovereignty dimension of discourse, which becomes more immediately evident when the technology of expression of discourse changes, as in the change from speech to writing. In addressing the impact of this shift on the sovereignty structure of language, Paul Ricoeur has noted that in the case of speech, it is the subjective intention of the author/speaker determining meaning, while in the case of writing, "the text's career escapes the finite horizon lived by its author."[43]

The speaker's loss of sovereign control over the exchange of which Ricoeur speaks here is comparable to the effect of substituting legal tender for bartering. For as is the case in exchanges of words, in exchanges involving money the substitution of representation for direct interaction produces a subversion of the identities of the exchangers, who no longer exert the same kind of force on the significance and value of the exchange.

However, the sovereignty distinction operating in the shift from speech to writing is not as simple or complete as Ricoeur has suggested. The exchanges involved in speech rest, as Derrida has shown, on something prior, on systems of inscription or writing that create the conditions of possibility for speech. It is illusory, he argues, for speakers to imagine that they control their discourse. It only appears to be wholly present to them and under their control because they are making the sounds: "The subject can hear or speak to himself and be affected by the signification he produces without passing through an external detour, the world, the sphere of what is not 'his own.' "[44]

2. The Authorship of Texts

There is a variety of technologies involved in processes of linguistic exchange, and, no doubt, the shift from voice to writing was one of the most historically dramatic. Since that development, moreover, the written text has undergone numerous contextual shifts that determine its epistemological significance, and for each of these shifts an authorship model has been involved. It has not always been the case, for example, that reading must imply a recognition of an author. As Foucault has noted, the idea of the *author* is a relatively recent and inconsistently applied invention.[45] It has been, among other things, a way of creating proprietary (sovereignty) interests in some texts. Authors are therefore sovereignty functions. They inhibit "the endless circulation of words"[46] and, as Nietzsche stated, their name on the title page dilutes the significance of the book by drawing the play of signification from a situation of unrestricted exchange into the narrow confines of the personal.[47]

Historically, the production of the author as a proprietor of a text provides an exemplary process in which to examine the sovereignty-exchange tension, and the analogy between money and language is again important in this context. Before authors could extend their reach into expanded systems of exchange, it was necessary to have a "general equivalent," and it emerged in the shape of a reformed system of alphabetization. At the beginning of the 19th century, alphabetization helped produce the European author as a participant in the economy,[48] because through *this* general equivalent it became possible to translate concepts from one language to another so that authors could participate more extensively in the exchange of knowledge.

The entry of texts into processes of exchange unleashed an accompanying process of attempts to establish sovereignty norms to control them. This process helped to produce the modern author as the proprietor who has existed in the history of copyright law. It is a history that begins in roughly the mid 18th century in Europe when authors began displacing publishers as the recognized proprietors of texts. It was not until they attained this sovereign/proprietor status that authors could then control the dissemination and reproduction of texts, to inhibit the flow of their ideas.

In the British case, Blackstone was instrumental in providing the rhetorical resources for authorial proprietorship. Writing in the mid-18th century, he developed an analogy between literary composition and private property, likening authors to owners of landed estates with a right to control passage over their grounds. He noted that when an author makes a book available to the public, it is like making keys available so that people can enter the author's private grounds. But, he added, "no man who receives a key has thereby a right to forge others."[49] The author thus retains control over the reproduction of the text.

The Lockean discourse on one's proprietorship over the fruits of one's labor and the idea that literature is the result of the act of an initiating intellect combined to legitimate this model of author sovereignty.[50] Once the idea was accepted that intellectual activity is involved in composition, a proto-sovereign model of the writing subject had to be advanced before the author-as-sovereign could emerge. This required an epistemic shift, to which Johann Herder contributed in the 18th century by helping to change the epistemology of reading. Where reading had been regarded as an act of self-recognition in which the reader tried to find his or her own life illuminated in the text, Herder substituted the view that reading involves the recognition of the intellectual activity of the writer.[51]

Other shifts in the conception of reading have had a marked effect on both the locus of sovereignty as well as the exchange value of the written word. For example, the oralization of language, which occurred when reading primers became phonetic, had the effect of shifting control over reading from the patriarchal structure of the school to mothers. Along with the phonetic primer he produced in Germany, Heinrich Stephani included directions for mothers to teach their children reading through pronunciation methods.[52] This innovation produced a new domain of subjectivity by prescribing a new body for purposes of reading. "This body has eyes and ears only in order to be a large mouth."[53] Along with this shift in subjectivity was one in spatial structure to complete the shift in the sovereignty of the reading process. In effect, the locus of authority had shifted from the school to the home. The source of reading ability, the opening into the reigning discourse network established by 1800, was therefore "the mother's mouth" operating within the confines of the home.[54]

These insights emerging from the analyses of Friedrich Kittler require scrutiny of the relationship between form and meaning. They are not available when technologies and forms are neglected, and intelligibility is constructed, as it was by Adam Smith in the 18th century, as a simple meeting between things and bodies or bodies and bodies. In Smith's view (elaborated at the end of this chapter), reading is a matter of an emotional coherence between the writer and reader. Paying no heed to either the technological forms of language or the social positions with which they are associated, Smith advised authors to adopt a rhetoric that would evoke the same emotional response in the reader as the ones felt by the writer of the text.[55]

This psychologizing of style foregrounds a medium strictly on the basis of the embodiment of persons and neglects the forms and structures that encourage differing interpretations of texts as well as the implications for differential control over meanings. Smith's psychologizing treatment of graphic writing/reading is also evidenced in his treatment of musical figuration.

3. Music

For Smith, music was strictly a mimetic art that gratifies "bodily appetites,"[56] and it does so by imitating passions.[57] Moreover, he takes his psychologizing view on the individual-music relationship to an aggregate level and promotes a harmony thematic to construct the social bond (treated at length in chapter 3):

> The sentiments and passions which music can best imitate are those which unite and bind men together in society; the social, the decent, the virtuous, the interesting and affecting, the amiable and agreeable, the awful and respectable, the noble, elevating, and commanding passions.[58]

Insofar as music is a discourse for Smith, therefore, it is expressive and imitative. In this domain, Smith was no political economist, for he discusses neither the relationship between musical forms and authority nor the political and economic implications of the spaces within which music is performed—streets versus concert halls versus drawing rooms, and so on.

Smith's narrow, mimetic/expressivist treatment notwithstanding, the history of musical listening has witnessed significant disturbances in the sovereignty-exchange interaction. One of the most significant processes of alteration was provoked by the invention of recording equipment. In his analysis of this dynamic, Jacques Attali, who does a political economy of music, points out the irony that "an invention that was meant to stabilize a mode of social organization" (to reinforce an existing structure of sovereignty), "became the principal factor in its transformation."[59] Because the initial enthusiasm for the phonograph was based on its ability to preserve, not to repeat, its first employment was in the dissemination of the voices and words of political authorities, thereby serving as "an archival apparatus for exemplary words . . . a tool reinforcing representative [sovereign] power and the entirety of its logic."[60]

However, as has been the case in so many domains of human association, exchange impulses have appropriated the invention, shifting its significance and usage away from its representational (sovereign) employment and exploiting its repetitional, and thus exchange-promoting, capabilities. The record quickly became a means for dispersing and reproducing sounds and thereby radically changed control over music (with the assistance of broadcasting facilities). Singers and publishers became less significant as control over music shifted increasingly to the record industry. Moreover, the "listener" became a different kind of subject—a consumer rather than an interlocutor—and functioned within a different kind of musical space. No longer fixed in the musical space of the concert hall as a passive recipient, the listener became a remote consumer with the equipment to reproduce the music he or she wanted.

This difference in listening resonated with changes in the social status structure. While in the domain of representation, music helped to reinforce a traditional system of prestige based on access to performance. With the shift toward repetition, which helped to produce "popular music," the class-based hierarchy, a structure for monopolizing performance, lost much of its connection with music.[61] Through the overflows generated by the exchange impulse and enabled by Edison's invention, the prior structure of sovereignty associated with music was dissolved. New structures have since developed to contain or inhibit the free flow of musical sounds, as changes in musical subjectivity (toward well-equipped consumers) and musical space have imperiled old sovereignty structures. The new sovereignty impulses now attempt to control both the spaces of musical deployment (broadcast space) and the understandings of what constitutes a listening subject (car commuter; record, tape, and disk buyer; etc.).

4. The Art Museum

For Adam Smith, painting was superior to music as an imitative art, for in general, Smith privileged visualization and, as was noted above, drew much of his figuration for social interaction from an emphasis on seeing. With painting and sculpture as with music, Smith resided within a simplistic epistemological perspective. Art is effective, for him, insofar as it is able to achieve resemblance and to the extent that it is able to *cause* pleasurable passions.[62] Thus for art as for music, Smith is not a political economist, saying little of note about the situations of its production, the locations of its display, and the control implications of its ownership and forms. One must move outside of Smith's narrow rendering of painting and other plastic arts to recognize that whatever epistemic significance the art object has in representing things and exciting emotions, its political significance is better appreciated within the same political economy framework as music.

The parallel can be drawn initially, for example, by comparing the art museum to the concert hall. The diminution of the sovereign functions maintained by old musical structures, the concert hall especially, evokes a recognition of changes in the structures involved in the play of sovereignty and exchange in the domain of art and are most significantly reflected in the changes in the function of the art museum. The relevance of the sovereignty-exchange tension to art museums is foregrounded in Karl Meyer's historical treatment of the forces that have shaped the contemporary museum. One of his chapters is entitled "The Hard Coin of Art," where he notes, "A peculiar characteristic of the art museum is its bedeviling link to the market place; no other cultural institution is so intimately involved with price movements."[63] Jean Baudrillard has remarked on this relationship more epigrammatically: "Museums play the role of banks in the political economy of banking"; they supply the "public backing" of the process of commodified art consumption.[64]

Revealingly, Meyer's chapter on "the hard coin of art" is followed by one entitled "The Sovereign Museum." He, like others who prize a noncommercially controlled approach to aesthetic appreciation, deplores the tendency of museums to become "manipulated accessories of the art market,"[65] and urges them to "strive to keep an arm's length of distance from commerce in art." However, whatever may be the sovereignty orientations of the art appreciation intelligentsia, impulses more powerful and shaping than their preferences have been at work.

Certainly the appropriation of art for purposes of legitimating aspects of sovereign authority has been the case for centuries. "Political regimes since antiquity have seen the visual arts as opportunity for legitimation and self-glorification."[66] But whatever cultural policy has existed at the level of the state, the museum as an institution has been shaped by forces well beyond those dominated by the state. Although state-level sovereigns have inaugurated some significant shaping policies, pushing the art museum in a sovereignty-reinforcing direction— not the least significant in this respect was Napoleon's influence on the French Royal Academy by patronizing painters such as David, whose canvasses were meant to glorify France [67]—by 1900 art dealers rather than state patronage had far more influence on museum collections.[68]

At present, the primary tension appears to be that between the museum as a collection and as an exhibition hall. As the former, its coherence and value is related to its representation of national (in the case of a national gallery) or civic (in the case of a city museum) pride, as well as functioning as a motivation for artistic inspiration and a research location for scholars.[69] In addition, of course, in the case of European museums, collections often represent an imperial or colonial past, downplaying the debts implicit in the collection having been built at the expense of various pre- or non-industrial societies from which aesthetic objects and artifacts have been extracted. The attempt by third-world countries to reacquire their historical treasures is, of course, also a sovereignty-oriented impulse.

However, to understand better the sovereignty implications of museum collections, one needs to turn to the question of value again and ask how such collections function as objects of value. Here Adam Smith disappoints, for he, like other classical political economists, focuses only on the labor process involved in producing objects and on simplistic, need-fulfilling models of their consumption. Smith on value is treated at length in chapter 2, but here it is important to note that the limitation of the classical approach becomes evident when one considers the kind of use made of a museum collection.

When the museum is considered as a space for a "collection," the very form of the collection aims in an identity/sovereignty direction. This is because the relationship of an object to the subject consumer in the case of collections meant for display is very different from the case of objects meant for use. Susan Stewart has explained the difference with a directional metaphor:

When objects are defined in terms of their use value, they serve as extensions
of the body onto the environment, but when objects are defined by the
collection, such an extension is inverted, serving to subsume the environment
to a scenario of the personal. The ultimate term in the series that marks the
collection is the 'self,' the articulation of the collector's own identity.[70]

Smith's failure to discern this difference is connected with his classical indifference to the role of desire and its ontological moorings as
it invests objects with significance. Smith's version of sovereignty did
not descend to the level of subjectivity and treat the significance of
objects in helping to maintain subjective coherence. This problem is
elaborated in chapter 3. Here we must go on to acknowledge that the
sovereignty impulses shaping modern museums pale in comparison
with the forces producing a trend toward the exchanges involved in
international exhibitions. This is reflected in the contemporary vocation
of the curator. "Formerly, a good curator was one who built up a
collection; today it is one who has a flair for exhibitions."[71]

The forces at work privileging exhibiting over collecting, reflected
in the curatorial vocation, must be seen in connection with the political
economy of the contemporary museum of art. Central to this political
economy is the development of the mass consumption of art and the
role of tourism in expanding the reach of this mass consumption.

As a result of these and other exchange-oriented pressures, the
museum has become increasingly a commercial entity competing to be
eligible as a stopping place in the international exchange of exhibitions.
Whatever it has accumulated or collected is now often in motion, in and
out of storage to make room for traveling exhibitions or in the process
of being packed and shipped to be part of one. The collection's "value"
within this is to be calculated more as the necessary capital to allow the
museum a place in the exchange of exhibitions than as a representation
of the sovereignty of the place where the museum is situated.

The Sovereignty-Exchange Interplay: A Summary

Having viewed the tensions that the sovereignty and exchange impulses manifest in various of modernity's venues, we are in a better

position to isolate their interactions. The first step is to recognize that we must question the purity of each impulse. As was noted above, for example, an orientation toward speech that emphasizes the exchange of signification neglects the extent to which meaning also depends on fixing the identities of the speaker and an Other to whom speech is addressed. As has also been noted, intelligibility is dependent on a fixing of the domain within which the linguistic exchange occurs. Juridical talk, geopolitical talk, and theological talk, for example, all function within cartographies, within interpretive mappings of divisions of space.

Although these identities and locations become abstract, ambiguous, and often multiple in their possibilities in the case of written utterances, there is nevertheless an ineluctably sovereign dimension resident in these intelligible linguistic exchanges as well. This is also the case with respect to other forms of exchange—goods, forms of recognition, and so forth. Insofar as a process is represented as pure exchange, its sovereignty dimension, the roles played by the identities of the exchanging subjects, and the domains within which the transactions occur have been naturalized or repressed.

In like manner, when one is focusing on aspects of sovereignty, the aspects of exchange on which a particular version of sovereignty depends tend to be repressed. Every individual and collective identity exists within a set of implicit self-Other or institution-Other relations. The way sovereignty impulses repress their exchange dimensions is analogous to the forgetting of debts. In applying this analogy to the hidden structure of institutions, Samuel Weber has argued that, in their representations of themselves, institutions do not reference the debts to various forms of otherness involved in the acts through which they are founded. "Institutions behave as if they did not carry this debt, as if the meaning they dispense was a result of their own activity."[72]

The reinforcement of an institution's sovereignty claim is therefore done by repressing the various exchanges through which its institutional identity was forged. It separates itself from its "first causes," so that its claim can remain unchallenged. This debt-denial aspect of the repression of exchange within sovereignty orientations is nowhere more apparent than in the way many modern states repress the tales of violence that its dominant groups visited on others as they territorialized their sovereignty control. Thus, for example, the claims of various parts of the "fourth world"—marginalized tribal and ethnic groupings such as Kurds, Australian aborigines, native Americans, and Hawaiians—find themselves needing to speak of such first causes to resist the dominating (ever-forgetful) form of sovereignty discourses within which the state represents itself as a single world.

In short, the sovereignty impulse resists conceptualizing its economies, acting as if its identities have been wholly self-generated at no one's expense, whereas exchange orientations operate as if the value produced is independent of the symbolically ordered identity structures and domains within which the exchanges occur.

Escaping Sovereign Repressions: Radical Gender Politics

There is one domain within which there are increasing attempts to restructure the politics of subjectivity by specifically discrediting the hegemonic institutional discourses that repress exchange and naturalize sovereignty structures, the domain of gender relations. For example, Luce Irigaray has made it evident that exchanges of desire between women have had no place within the discourse on sexuality produced by Freud, which still controls much of modernity's understanding of gender relations. Freud, she asserts, leaves women "only a choice between a sort of *animality* that [Freud] seems to overlook and *the simulation* of male models. In this economy any interplay of desire among women's bodies, women's orgasms, women's language is inconceivable."[73]

Irigaray's strategy is not simply to resist the sovereignty of the "masculinist discourse" by opposing it with a female subjectivity it fails to construct. Instead, she imagines an almost total suspension of sovereignty, a situation of "exchanges without identifiable terms, without accounts, without end."[74] However, this is rhetorical excess, for in general Irigaray's position is that against a constitution of "femininity" that draws its meaning from a male system of representation, female subjectivity is not absence but multiplicity; women "are not one."[75]

Since Irigaray's programmatic statement, many contemporary feminist thinkers have worked toward conceptions of gender aimed at undermining both the subjectivity and spatial dimensions of the dominant gender discourse. For this purpose, a primary target has been what Judith Butler calls the "masculinist signifying economy" within which the sovereignty of gender division has been produced and maintained.[76] In this vein, Joan Cocks has developed an oppositional mode of theorizing gender that ambiguates the male-female opposition by challenging the polarities on which it has been built,[77] and Griselda Pollock has mounted a challenge to the spatial strategies involved in the sovereignty model implicit in typical gender relations in her reading of art history.[78]

Action as well as signification is at issue, however. For example, in attacking the sovereignty of the masculine-feminine opposition, Baudrillard analyzes transvestism, which he sees as a way of allowing exchange to overflow the sovereign boundaries with a form of play that exploits the indistinctness of gender.[79] In its parodic acts, transvestism appropriates and burlesques feminine allure and thus *shows* the fragility and superficiality of the sovereignty frame within which ordinary seduction is understood.[80] Seduction, as Baudrillard wants to conceive it, is a form of ritual exchange, always an ironic parodying of the sovereignty frame within which the dominant form of sexuality is produced and interpreted. Reversal as a form of exchange exercises what sovereignty disallows.[81]

Kathy Ferguson mounts an opposition to the sovereignty of gender within the domain of behavior as well. She speaks of a situation of "mobile subjectivities" in which people do not occupy fixed positions but become capable of positioning. "Mobile subjectivities are too concrete and dirty to claim innocence, too much in process to claim closure, too independent to claim fixed boundaries."[82]

The domain of gender relations, as much as any, manifests not only sovereignty-exchange tensions, an interaction of mobilities and inhibitions, but also shows the need each impulse has for the other. However one may wish to efface or soften identity boundaries, the erotic exchange needs some degree of identity boundary, some degree of recognizable difference for its effective functioning. Similarly, every form of gender sovereignty requires the displacements and other interactions involved in the formation and maintenance of that sovereignty. Thus for gender relations, as for speech, exchange value arises only in the condition in which subjectivities can be posed as stations for sending and receiving. Mere circulation does not add up to value. As Goux has argued, in language, finance, and erotics, what produces value is the ability to identify the units involved in circulation and exchange. As was shown with respect to linguistic exchange above, so in the case of erotic exchange, "along with erotic force, there is the 'law' (of the other) which abstractly governs sexual exchanges and substitutions as a function of erotic 'values.' "[83]

Toward a New Formulation of Sovereignty

This charged intimacy between sovereignty and exchange, their paradoxical combination of antagonism and symbiosis, can be found in more aggregate institutional contexts, notably at the level of the state. In order to discern the effects at this level, it is necessary to seek a formulation of sovereignty and exchange that transcends the static limitations of traditional political discourses, which fail to capture the dynamics and complexities in their simple equating of sovereignty with the authority of the state.

The first step is toward a more general rendering of the idea of sovereignty, which emerges from an examination of its functioning in the variety of venues treated above. Sovereignty is a stabilized system of authoritative control. But what stabilizes it? One aspect is the firmness and continuity of its domain, the space of its authority. For example, one reason why sovereignty has been understood in such a state-centric way is because of the power, authority, and persistence of the discourse within which state sovereignty is inscribed. The apparent domain of this discourse (the geostrategic map of the world constructed in typical policy discourses), which arose as a particular answer to the question of political community, is maintained in part by the discourse's implicit claim to timelessness and universal validity as it both suppresses its specific origins and turns a blind eye toward various processes of globalization that threaten it.[84]

The geopolitical map of the world, produced by a state-centric view of sovereignty, has had significant competitors of late, all provoked by various processes of globalization in various domains, as with transnational regroupings such as the European Union. And, increasingly, the state-as-coherent-actor or unitary entity has been destabilized as various "subnational" or tribal and ethnic groups have asserted desires to reoccupy old sovereignties that preexist the current geopolitical map.

Closely related to the growing instability in what has been understood as international space is an instability in the other dimension of what stabilizes claims to sovereignty, the dimension of subjectivity. When, for example, the person-as-citizen who depends on "rights" flowing from a state affiliation is accompanied by the person-as-trader/consumer within an authority frame of a supranational economic union, the domain of subjectivity, over which states have claimed control, has become ambiguous. This has obvious implications for the stability of state sovereignty.

In addition to such pressures on sovereignty as spaces and subjectivities become reordered, there are accompanying textual changes that these dynamics encourage. As old sovereignty models break down, the ideational structures supporting them begin to dissolve or experience disturbances and reversals. Of these, one of the most significant is the traditional narrative, lodged in the history of political theory, through which the state has achieved much of its legitimacy. In arguing that "statecraft is mancraft," Richard Ashley has contributed to one such reversal. He claims that contrary to the traditional narrative—in which the state arises as the appropriate political form to house the preexisting forms of human nature, character, concerns, or modes of production—is the narrative implied in statecraft as mancraft, in which the state produces a model of human subjectivity as a legitimating device. At a textual level, modern statecraft is "an art of domesticating the meaning of man by constructing his problems, his dangers, his fears."[85]

What Ashley calls a "paradigm of sovereignty" is what I have called above a commitment to a form of proto-sovereignty, a version of human subjectivity on which sovereignty is predicated. The proto-sovereign model dominating modern state discourse is "a specific, historically fabricated, widely circulated, and practically effective interpretation of man as a sovereign being"[86] More specifically, it is a model of "reasoning man" employed to promote the illusion (central to Hobbes's sovereignty version) that the legal and coercive structures of the state are those that "reasoning man knows to be the necessary conditions of his free use of reason."[87]

In addition, part of the locational strategy used to construct modern subjectivity is temporal. "The effect of *acceleration* obtains in the sense that dangers produced through practices of statecraft, far from being indefinitely postponable into some ambiguous future, are immediately and unambiguously encountered here and now in the time of man."[88] This imbrication of space and time has also had a marked effect on the strategies that the sovereignty impulse has had to effect. In addition to basing its sovereignty claim on the dangers to reasoning man is a spatiotemporal mapping of the world in which it locates the dangers: from various locations, coming with little or no degree of warning, and so on. The state thus produces its sovereignty justification by producing both subjectivity and space within a world that is experiencing increasing disturbances to both.

An adequate formulation of the roles of sovereignty and exchange in the modern period thus requires a language within which such dynamisms can be captured, the flows that increasingly threaten sovereignty-oriented inhibitions, and the reinscriptions that occur as reactions when sovereignty-oriented reactions try to contain the flows. What should be immediately evident is that the linear narrative of Adam Smith is inadequate to such a version of force and counterforce. Smith's historical writing is treated at length in chapter 2, so what should be noted here is that his simplistic developmental story, in which appropriate institutions emerge to facilitate more abstract and complicated exchanges, is unable to encode the alternating force of flows that exceed old sovereignty constraints followed by new applications of constraints, new interpretive inscriptions.

What is precisely adequate to such a force/counterforce story is the analysis of Gilles Deleuze and Felix Guattari, who use the concepts of flows and inscriptions to capture the dynamics and complexities of the sovereignty-exchange interaction. As noted above, Goux has suggested a more-or-less unidirectional narrative of the interaction, a dynamic in which exchanges are increasingly mediated by vehicles or equivalents that facilitate circulation of things, meanings, fortunes, and so on. They are the representative equivalents that tend to overcome the control exercised by subjects over exchanges, as the process tending toward the takeover by the medium of exchange itself takes over sovereignty. Goux's narrative helps to illuminate this tendency of unchecked processes of exchange. But it fails to countenance adequately the counter-forces that either inhibit this dynamic or contain it within new inscriptions, new systems of authority and control that generate new subjects and different practices of space, new imaginative cartographies to replace the components of older sovereignties.

Deleuze and Guattari's narrative overcomes this inadequacy. It is not a Smithian, linear narrative of the unfolding of a continuous process, but an account of tendencies that counteract each other. Whereas for Goux, exchange is dominant, within the dynamic Deleuze and Guattari describe the sovereignty impulse is the dominant force. Likening the sovereignty impulse to "inscription," the fixing of authority and identity, they assert that "society is not first of all a milieu for exchange where the essential would be to circulate or to cause to circulate, but rather a socius of inscription where the essential thing is to mark and to be marked."[89] Moreover, this sovereignty dominance acts as a counterforce to inhibit flows by territorializing them.

To illuminate the interpretive impositions involved in the state's inhibitions of the exchange dynamic, Deleuze and Guattari employ the terms *codes* and *flows* in their model of force and counterforce. Referring to the precapitalist, despotic state, they speak of the drive toward inscription, a move toward interpretive containments that the state enacts because of its dread of "decoded flows."[90]

The capitalist state, they argue, depends more on an axiomatic than a coding strategy. That is, the modern capitalist state tends less to contain flows than to coordinate them. Rather than fixing and limiting, it produces or facilitates the abstractions that organize and legitimate exchanges. It encourages flows and regulates them for profit, for example, by manipulating scarcities, or absorbing overabundancies.[91]

However, the difference between the precapitalist and capitalist states should not be overstated. Although exchanges are encouraged, venerable coding impulses remain. For example, because the state, as a domain for sovereignty, operates through fixing residence, its additional activities, which go beyond its initial territorializing, must involve attempts to code all flows, and some flows are especially troublesome in that they exceed territorial boundaries either in fact or interpretation. The most dangerous of these are of course those that threaten to dissolve the state's territoriality in the process of exceeding state boundaries (at least with respect to some functions, as with the European Monetary Union).

To understand territory not as a thing, but as a dynamic, to understand "territorializing" and "deterritorializing" forces at work, one can recall, for example, the historical period in which the medieval church began to lose the ability to authoritatively territorialize the world, to code domains in relation to divine sanction. The process by which civil authorities took over this coding, often on behalf of commercial interests, amounted to a deterritorializing as the church's codes lost their grip and were followed by a reterritorializing as state-oriented coding became institutionalized. In the face of deterritorializing dynamics, forms of sovereignty assert themselves. For example, lands that lost their meaning within a theological discourse, which identifies their functioning as loci for divine bounty, were ultimately recoded as domains controlled by earthly "proprietors" that yield "products" as the fruits of labor.

This recoding has of course been markedly successful, correlated as it is with changes in the modalities of power. And although contemporary prayers still refer to some goods as God's bounty—as gifts entailing spiritual obligations—it is the market and distribution of proprietorship rather than the person-God covenant that largely determines their value. However, the state's triumph over the church has not produced an end to all coding. Flows across territorial boundaries of the state continue to threaten existing codes and to attenuate the state system of sovereignty as a whole. As money, labor forces, weapons, and scientific technology become subject to exchange dynamics that are increasingly global, the inhibitory responses by those who, like Margaret Thatcher, are defenders of old sovereignty systems become more frantic.

Moreover, the forces producing the flows, which exceed and endanger old sovereignties (and thus old coding strategies), operate within a modernity whose general characteristic has been the dissolution of geographic space. As noted above, modern exchanges privilege temporality or speed rather than site, making space what Virilio has called "chronospace." In this space, activities around the globe involve a speed of transmission of messages, weapons, money, and so on.[92] In a world based more on time than on territory, distance, in the old sense, is displaced by speed and acceleration. As a result, the inhibition of flows must involve modifying pace and trajectory rather than simply containing things. Sovereignty maintenance tactics must therefore change.[93] For example, as commercial enterprises begin drawing labor from around the globe by moving either people or production facilities, the state begins losing the ability to regulate work. As labor supplies respond to demands by becoming mobile or distantiated, sovereign entities inhibit the labor exchanges not only through legal prohibitions but also through a slowing of credentialing processes. A slowing of the paper flow has been one of sovereignty's tactics for slowing and thus managing the labor flow as well as other flows.

Another telling case of a flow threatening the state sovereignty system is the flow of scientific exchanges in the domain of space exploration. From 1972 until recently, Soviet and American scientists engaged in exchanges of information and data related to space technology. While the interest of scientists produces an impulse toward more rapid and comprehensive exchanges, state authorities, governed by the geostrategic, security dimension of the sovereignty impulse, engage in inhibitions of the exchanges. Thus a five-year exchange-of-data treaty established in 1977 was allowed to lapse in 1982 by the U.S. government, which wanted to use this as a mechanism to sanction Soviet policy toward Poland.[94] And the U.S. space administration, NASA, was continually wary of uninhibited flows of Soviet-American scientific exchange related to space technology. To inhibit such exchanges, they limited the size and frequency of symposia.

Contemporary Disturbances

Having established the frame for conceiving the sovereignty-exchange tension, what remains is to point briefly toward aspects of present global structures and processes within which the two impulses contend. In recent years, the process of *inscription*, wherein the prevailing state sovereignty structure attempts to maintain its control, has had especially to contend with two types of dynamics. One is related to the flow of capital. Adam Smith, and succeeding generations of economists, neglected the relationship between this flow and identity dynamics. But, as has been noted above, the system of exchange requires a sovereignty dimension to function, so that exchanges must always be tied to a set of identities that articulates with the flows to determine value. As one theorist with a more anthropological approach to value investments has noted, any qualitative change in the system of circulation will necessarily produce "transformations of the identity structure."[95]

For example, in recent decades there has been a change in the flows from central, industrial powers. They now export more capital than manufactured goods. This "deindustrialization of the center"[96] affects accumulations and activities at the periphery, which, in turn, impact not only on the economies there but also on the cultural frames or identity structures with which economic activities are associated.

To appreciate the impact on sovereignty structures of these changes it is necessary to recognize an ongoing dynamic that is not clearly referenced within the more static renderings of the sovereignty problematic and more economistic renderings of exchange. Adam Smith and his successors treated national units as sovereign interpretive entities, that is, as single unidirectional-acting units involved in international trade. Yet, however stable may be the names and territorial boundaries of existing national states, and the processes of official transfers of power and the recognition of their authority structure by other states and supranational agencies, every state harbors varying degrees of centrifugal force, of resistance to officially inscribed, state-oriented subjectivities.

Therefore, states always find themselves involved to some degree in attempts to maintain central control by overcoming the old affiliations that have never been fully integrated into centralized, state-controlled structures. This assertion of centralizing control takes the form not only of direct coercion but also of interpretive activity. The state engages in what Deleuze and Guattari call "overcoding," an inscription process that attempts to reinterpret old activities based on old affiliations within the state-oriented code. But such inhibition strategies become strained when changes in the structure of exchanges provoke subsumed but not wholly incorporated cultural groupings to react with new, identity-affirming activities, with attempts to "reestablish a culturally unified way of life"[97] that does not accord with the sovereignty direction of the state as a whole.

More specifically, in varying degrees, states contain a "fourth world" that has participated in the capitalist sector of the economy but has retained a resistant group identity and solidarity ready to reassert itself and threaten existing sovereignty structures when it is disturbed by demands to adjust to shifting identity spaces. This dynamic was, for example, very much involved in the disintegration of the Soviet Union and Yugoslavia. In effect, polities whose sovereign surfaces appear smooth and untroubled contain dormant resistances below the surface, which can be awakened when various unleashed forces disturb the inscription process that is responsible for smoothing the surface. Deleuze and Guattari liken the state to a great wall. In appropriating and subsuming old forces and affiliations, the state's overcoding, its territorial inscriptions through which it contains subjects within a demarcated space, "allows the old territorial inscriptions [the spatial practices of existing subsumed groupings] to subsist as bricks on the new surface."[98] However, as flows increase, the overcoding cannot always keep pace, and reassertions of dissident identity and spatial practices occur. It becomes evident that the state's debts have not all been redeemed, that the sovereignty wall has bricked-in old grievances.

Similarly, at an international level, the sovereignty system of separate states represses structures of grievance. For example, during the 1991 Persian Gulf War, U.S. President George Bush treated the conflict as if it were a disturbance in an otherwise stable and untroubled system of Middle Eastern sovereignties, and he explicitly envisioned the postwar period as a return to quiescence. But if one heeds the constitutive debts of the various state sovereignties in the region, what is apparent is that they rest on an economy of grievances. This repressed-grievance economy within the sovereignty system of the region is not apparent when one simply speaks, as did Bush and other national leaders, of the territorial integrity of each state. The grievances are built into the various territorialities. It is less the case that there are territories *with* grievances as it is that the existing pattern of state sovereignties *constitutes* territorial grievances. There is thus no quiescence or tranquility to which they could return after the war, for this "peace" exists only within the alibi of a wholly sovereignty-oriented discourse that fails to acknowledge the deep system of exchanges it represses. Just as disturbances in systems of exchange awaken grievances within sovereignty

structures by disturbing subsumed identity structures, disturbances in
the sovereignty system awaken grievances by summoning repressed
dimensions of exchange.

Conclusion

The orders of modernity both within and among the state entities on
the globe now confront new instabilities as the sovereignty-exchange
nexus is tested by new flows and ever more intense efforts at reinscrip-
tion. To summarize, a politics of sovereignty is a politics of control over
subjectivities and domains. Because stable patterns of subjectivity and
space are a function of both the regulation of things and people and the
interpretative impositions that give them meaning, sovereignty cannot
be supported simply by exhibits of raw matter, of land or flesh and
blood. The process of asserting or making sovereignty models, as well
as that of challenging them, involves active, interpretive struggles.
Struggles against what? Sovereignty maintenance involves first and
foremost the activity of creating and maintaining inhibitions, of controlling and directing flows of exchange that continually threaten extant
boundaries and subjectivities. Some threats are constant. They are
continually activated forces, propelled by self-conceptions at odds with
those within the authorized discourses of the state, and they exert a
more-or-less constant pressure against sovereignty-maintaining constraints. These come often from aspects of culture and society that are
never wholly subsumed or domesticated within the sovereignty system.
Some are episodic.

The episodic disturbances to sovereignty arrangements are various.
There are those that emerge with technological innovations, as with the
above-mentioned invention of the phonograph, which altered the shape
of musical space and reconstructed the nature of the listening subject.
In the domain of "international relations," there have been changes in
weapons technology, such as the development of all-terrain vehicles
that dissolve the earth,[99] and the development of floating and flying
arsenals that also dissolve the geographic defenses of the sovereign
integrity of nations.

Some episodic disturbances are ideational. It is these that more clearly evoke interpretive struggles, for they occur in the domain of the sovereign control over texts. As was noted above, the development of the idea that a book is a work of the genius of an author helped to alter the significance of reading and deliver sovereign control to the writer. At the level of state systems, adjustments in the perceived space of divinity as various civic versions of neo-Copernican cosmology developed, helped to precipitate the historical shift from religious to civic forms of sovereign authority.[100] Extensions of the Copernican thought system also led to the ultimate triumph of civic authority over the theological version of sovereignty by encouraging a different construction of the space of personhood. Commercial societies achieved their sovereignty justifications through the proto-sovereign construction of the individual proprietor on the earth, a successor to the brief sojourner occupying a symbolic place with a temporary, divinely sanctioned permit.

At a minimum, once it is recognized that the present global condition of sovereignty is a relatively recent and contentious set of practices rather than a naturally evolving form of wisdom, it is possible to resist theoretical frames that reify existing political arrangements. The "naturally evolving form of wisdom" model is precisely Smithian. If Adam Smith saw a struggle involved in the dynamic that was forming modern industrial society, it was one of modernity extracting itself from its past.

As a writer, Smith explicitly saw himself as a champion of science and lucidity. He opted for a civic authority not only in his statements about society as the basis for a new sovereignty but also in his style. As he made evident in his writing on writing (in his *Lectures on Rhetoric and Belles Lettres*), he was addressing a "local" audience. Commenting on the issue of lexical choice, for example, he urged the use of native rather than foreign words, and in general his rules for writing were designed for communication and lucidity—short simple syntax, avoidance of elaborate figuration, and so on. And, significantly, he modeled the relationship between the author/writer and reader in the same way he modeled the relationship between persons sharing social space in his *Theory of Moral Sentiments*. Writing, when well done, according to Smith, is an exchange of sentiments. Using the musical metaphor that dominates his notion of social exchange, he urges writers to regulate the emotionality in their style, to "lop all exuberances and bring it to that pitch which will be agreeable to those about him."[101]

However, this strategic orientation to writing would seem to locate Smith, in his relationship with his readers, as a persuader, and, indeed, his lectures on rhetoric are full of a persuasion-oriented pedagogy. But more to the point is Smith's emphasis on the reader as a member of society, whose positions emerge out of the process through which sentiments are brought into concord. Smith's emphasis in his writing is thus similar to his view of the social domain as harmony-oriented (treated at length in chapter 3). His notion of persuasion does not, for example, assume that there is a reigning ideology that must be over-turned. There is no suggestion that impertinent or ironic tropes or narrative reversals are needed to undermine an existing authority. Smith's preoccupation with lucidity assumes a natural agreeableness resident in the social domain, and he assumed that it could be accessed through the correct writing style, just as it provides the harmonious precondition for naturally emerging institutions.

Certainly there are some antisocial and specifically selfish senti-ments, which Smith recognizes in places, but for the most part his world is dominated by agreeable sentiments, and, moreover, it is held together additionally by a set of coherence-producing mechanisms that complete the forces necessary to assure social harmony. His world, in short, is one primarily based on shared cognitive and emotional orientations, and coherence is overdetermined by natural regulative mechanisms that keep the social domain well-ordered.

In Smith's views and in his style of writing, then, there is a tendency to pacify the world. For example, as has been shown, his position on sovereignty, which derives from the harmonious social order he con-structs, fails to countenance the repressed forms of unruliness that existing institutional forms and dominant interpretations cover over. A critical political treatment of sovereignty issues has required an overcom-ing of this Smithian pacification. Once it is recognized that theoretical practices affect the conditions of possibility for political practices, it becomes possible to overcome old sovereignty-oriented inhibitions and open a conceptual space for new forms of self-assertion, new modes of thinking that can contend with current, rigidly institutionalized reasons of state. Theory, when critical and self-reflective, can enable the assertion of aspects of the self and possibilities for human affinities unrecognized in dominant state-level conceits. To carry on this thinking task, more aspects of the Smith Effect must be confronted. More specifically, the Smithian story of the development of value must be assessed, for Smith's way of thinking about value, his narrative orientation, and his grammar of value remain dominant canonical modalities. Chapter 2 therefore turns to the task of dissolving this aspect of the political economy canon that Smith helped to produce.

Notes

1. The remark was made by British MP Edwina Curry on American radio.
2. Sir Geoffrey Howe, speech reported in *Guardian Weekly*, Vol. 143, No. 21, week ending Nov. 25, 1990, 6.
3. Margaret Thatcher, quoted in *Guardian Weekly*, Vol. 143, No. 19, week ending Nov. 11, 1991, 3.
4. Howe, *Guardian Weekly*, Vol. 143, No. 21, week ending Nov. 25, 1990, 6.
5. News report, *Guardian Weekly* Vol. 143, No. 18, week ending Nov. 4, 1990, 1.
6. Thomas Hobbes, *Leviathan* (London: Penguin, 1985), 217.
7. Hobbes, *Leviathan*, 218.
8. See Hobbes, *Leviathan*, chap. 13, 183-88, for this scenario.
9. Hobbes, *Leviathan*, 142.
10. Hobbes, *Leviathan*, 146.
11. Karl Marx, *Capital*, trans. Ben Fowkes (New York: Vintage, 1977), Vol. 1, 34. This use of the Marxian value analogy is inspired by a discussion in Jean-Joseph Goux, *Symbolic Economies: After Marx and Freud*, trans. Jennifer Curtiss Gage (Ithaca, NY: Cornell University Press, 1990), 13-21.
12. Goux, *Symbolic Economies*, 42.
13. Hobbes, *Leviathan*, 247-49.
14. Jacques Lacan, "Subversion of the Subject and the Dialectic of Desire," in *Ecrits*, trans. Alan Sheridan (New York: Norton, 1977), 305.
15. This point is made by Goux, *Symbolic Economies*, 55-56.
16. C. B. Macpherson, "Introduction," in Hobbes, *Leviathan*, 12.
17. See P.W.J. Riley, *The Union of England and Scotland* (Manchester: Manchester University Press, 1978) for a history of the process. Riley notes that in addition to the trade-off of trade versus sovereignty was some contention over religious issues.
18. This continuity between Hobbes and Smith is developed in Isaac Kramnick, *Republicanism and Bourgeois Radicalism* (Ithaca, NY: Cornell University Press, 1990), 7-11.

19. See Adam Smith, *Lectures on Jurisprudence*, ed. R. L. Meek, D. D. Rafael, & P. G. Stein (Indianapolis, IN: Liberty Classics, 1982), especially sections 4 and 5.

20. The notion of "viceregents within" is in Adam Smith, *The Theory of Moral Sentiments*, Glasgow Edition, ed. D. D. Raphael & A. L. Macfie (Indianapolis, IN: Liberty Classics, 1982), 166.

21. Michel Foucault, "Governmentality," *Ideology and Consciousness*, *3* (No. 6, 1979), 15.

22. Foucault, "Governmentality," 17.

23. Michel Foucault, *The History of Sexuality*, trans. Robert Hurley (New York: Pantheon, 1978). 25.

24. This expression belongs to Jean Baudrillard, *In the Shadow of the Silent Majorities: On the End of the Social*, trans. Paul Foss, Paul Patton, & John Johnston (New York: Semiotext(e), 1983).

25. Foucault, "Governmentality," 21.

26. This discussion draws from Niklas Luhmann, "The Individuality of the Individual: Historical Meanings and Contemporary Problems," in Thomas C. Heller, Morton Sosna, & David Wellbery, eds. *Reconstructing Individualism* (Stanford, CA: Stanford University Press, 1986), 315.

27. Luhmann, "Individuality," 316.

28. See Smith, *Moral Sentiments*, 23, where he recommends conversation as the main form of sociability.

29. The concept of the "mythic plot" belongs to Frank Kermode, "Secrets and Narrative Sequence," *Critical Inquiry*, *7* (Autumn, 1980), 85.

30. Smith, *Lectures on Jurisprudence*, 27.

31. Smith, *Lectures on Jurisprudence*; see pages 1-99 for the general development of the argument.

32. Smith, *Lectures on Jurisprudence*, 514.

33. Smith, *Lectures on Jurisprudence*, 540.

34. These are the words of Archidamus in Book I of Thucydides, *The Peloponnesian War*, The Hobbes Translation (Chicago: University of Chicago Press, 1989), 48.

35. Adam Smith, *An Inquiry into the Nature and Causes of the Wealth of Nations* (Indianapolis, IN: Liberty Classics, 1981), Vol. 1, 494.

36. Paul Virilio/Sylvere Lotringer, *Pure War*, trans. Mark Polizotti (New York: Semiotext(e), 1983), 18.

37. Goux, *Symbolic Economies*, 129.

38. Goux, *Symbolic Economies*, 129.

39. Goux, *Symbolic Economies*, 123.

40. Goux, *Symbolic Economies*, 123.

41. Marcel Mauss, *The Gift*, trans. Ian Cunnison (New York: Norton, 1967), 71.

42. Don DeLillo, *Players* (New York: Vintage, 1984), 110.

43. Paul Ricoeur, "The Model of the Text: Meaningful Action Considered as Text," *Social Research*, *38* (Autumn, 1971), 534.

44. Jacques Derrida, *Speech and Phenomena*, trans. David Allison (Evanston, IL: Northwestern University Press, 1973), 78.

45. Michel Foucault, "What Is an Author," in Donald Buchard, ed., *Language, Counter-Memory, Practice* (Ithaca, NY: Cornell University Press, 1977).

46. Friedrich Kittler, *Discourse Networks 1800/1900*, trans. Michael Metteer (Stanford, CA: Stanford University Press, 1990), 5.

47. Friedrich Nietzsche, *Human All-Too-Human*, ed. Oscar Levy (New York: Russell and Russell, 1964), Vol. 2.

48. Kittler, *Discourse Networks*, 70.

49. Blackstone quoted in Mark Rose, "The Author as Proprietor: *Donaldson v. Beckett* and the Genealogy of Modern Authorship," *Representations*, 23 (Summer, 1988), 64.

50. Rose, "Author as Proprietor," 56.

51. This contribution of Herder is discussed in Martha Woodmansee, "The Genius and the Copyright: Economic and Legal Conditions of the Emergence of the Author," *Eighteenth-Century Studies*, 17 (Summer, 1984), 447-48.

52. Kittler, *Discourse Networks*, 32.

53. Kittler, *Discourse Networks*, 33.

54. Kittler, *Discourse Networks*, 33. Section 1 is entitled "The Mother's Mouth."

55. See Adam Smith, *Lectures on Rhetoric and Belles Lettres*, The Glasgow Edition, ed. J. C. Bryce (Oxford: Clarendon Press, 1983).

56. Adam Smith, *The Early Writings of Adam Smith*, ed. J. Ralph Lindgren (New York: A. M. Kelley, 1967), 148.

57. Smith, *Early Writings*, 153.

58. Smith, *Early Writings*, 154.

59. Jacques Attali, *Noise: The Political Economy of Music*, trans. Brian Massumi (Minneapolis: University of Minnesota Press, 1985), 90.

60. Attali, *Noise*, 92.

61. Attali, *Noise*, 119.

62. See Smith, *Early Writings*, 135-148.

63. Karl E. Meyer, *The Art Museum: Power, Money, Ethics* (New York: William Morrow, 1979), 163.

64. Jean Baudrillard, "The Art Auction: Sign Exchange and Sumptuary Value," in *For a Critique of the Political Economy of the Sign*, trans. Charles Levin (St. Louis: Telos Press, 1981), 122.

65. Meyer, *The Art Museum*, 66.

66. Daniel J. Sherman, *Worthy Monuments* (Cambridge, MA.: Harvard University Press, 1984), 16.

67. Meyer, *The Art Museum*, 170.

68. Meyer, *The Art Museum*, 171.

69. See Meyer, *The Art Museum*, 195-96.

70. Susan Stewart, *On Longing* (Baltimore: Johns Hopkins University Press, 1984), 162.

71. Germain Bazin, *The Museum Age*, trans. Jane van Nuis Cahill (New York: Universe, 1967), 274.

72. This quotation is a summary of Weber's argument in Wlad Godzich, "Afterword," in Samuel Weber, *Institution and Interpretation* (Minneapolis: University of Minnesota Press, 1987), 162.

73. Luce Irigaray, *The Sex Which is not One*, trans. Catherine Porter (Ithaca, NY: Cornell University Press, 1985), 196.

74. Irigaray, *The Sex Which is not One*, 197.

75. Irigaray, *The Sex Which is not One*, 120.

76. See Judith Butler, *Gender Trouble: Feminism and the Subversion of Identity* (New York: Routledge, 1990).

77. Joan Cocks, *The Oppositional Imagination: Feminism, Critique, and Political Theory* (New York: Routledge, 1989).

78. Griselda Pollock, *Vision and Difference* (New York: Routledge, 1988). See especially chap. 3, "Modernity and the Spaces of Femininity," 50-90.

79. Jean Baudrillard, *Seduction*, trans. Brian Singer (Montreal: New World Perspectives, 1990), 12.

80. Baudrillard, *Seduction*, 14.

81. Baudrillard, *Seduction*, 45.

82. Kathy Ferguson, "Mobile Subjectivities," chapter 6 in *Reversal and Its Discontents: The Man Question* (Berkeley, CA: University of California Press, 1993).

83. Goux, *Symbolic Economies*, 57.

84. On this issue see R.B.J. Walker, "State Sovereignty, Global Civilization, and the Rearticulation of Political Space," Occasional Paper No. 18, World Order Studies Program (Center for International Studies, Princeton University, 1988), 772.

85. Richard K. Ashley, "Living on Borderlines: Man, Poststructuralism, and War," in James Der Derian & Michael J. Shapiro, eds. *International/Intertextual Relations* (Lexington, MA: Lexington Books, 1989), 303.

86. Ashley, "Living on Borderlines," 269.

87. Ashley, "Living on Borderlines," 268.

88. Ashley, "Living on Borderlines," 306.

89. Gilles Deleuze & Felix Guattari, *The Anti-Oedipus*, trans. Robert Hurley, Mark Seem, & Helen R. Lane (New York: Viking, 1977), 142.

90. Deleuze & Guattari, *The Anti-Oedipus*, 194.

91. Deleuze & Guattari, *The Anti-Oedipus*, 235.

92. See Virilio/Lotringer, *Pure War*.

93. This point is elaborated in Paul Virilio, *Speed and Politics*, trans. Mark Polizotti (New York: Semiotext(e), 1986).

94. Reported in Henry S. F. Cooper, Jr., "Annals of Space: The Planetary Community. I. Phobus," *The New Yorker*, June 11, 1990, 63.

95. This expression is in Jonathan Friedman, "Cultural Logics of the Global System," *Theory, Culture & Society*, 5 (1988), 447-60.

96. Friedman, "Cultural Logics," 447-60.

97. Friedman, "Cultural Logics," 450.

98. Deleuze & Guattari, *The Anti-Oedipus*, 198.

99. Virilio, *Speed and Politics*, 56.

100. See chap. 3, Part 4 in Hans Blumenberg, *The Legitimacy of the Modern Age*, trans. Robert M. Wallace (Cambridge, MA: M.I.T. Press, 1985) for a discussion of the civil struggles with religion organized around neo-Copernicanism.

101. Smith, *Lectures on Rhetoric and Belles Lettres*, 55.

2

History and Value

Introduction: Value

A dam Smith's name is associated with the problem of value as much as that of any thinker in the political or economic theory canon. Of the large number of treatments of his approach, some have dwelled on his emphasis on labor, some on his emphasis on exchange, and some on his attempts to connect the two, well or badly. For the most part, however, these analyses have operated within Smith's philosophical approach to value. They have affirmed his materialism, not only at the level of what he talked about but also at the level of his style. Lacking an analytic, philosophical distance, they have not attempted to connect Smith's textual practices with his approach to value.

The analysis in this chapter departs from the tradition in Smith scholarship by treating the intimate relationship between Smith as a writer of history and Smith as a theorist of value. Smith's historical

narratives focus primarily and explicitly on the development of exchanges and more implicitly on the development of spatial practices.
Both of these dimensions of his accounts help to construct what can be
loosely termed his *theory of value.*

In his treatment of value, as is the case in all his writing, Smith wrote
with an eye cast outward on the world. Nevertheless, his domain of
value is not so much a discovery as it is a textual production; it inheres
in his grammatical, rhetorical, and narrative practices. This analysis of
the Smithian writing modality is not simply an explication of those
practices. They are juxtaposed (as is the case in chapter 1) with alternatives that provide more politically perspicuous ways of interpreting
modernity. Smith challenged an entrenched narrative on value in order
to encourage an expanded system of exchange. The emphasis here is on
writing that challenges the narratives—Smith's among others—within
which modernity is ordinarily understood and on construals of value that
challenge the sensationalist model that dominates Smith's approach.

A lot has been said about the details of Smith's religious and ethical
proclivities and his politics but relatively little about the specific details
or style of his historical writing. The editors of the Glasgow edition of
Smith's *Wealth of Nations* address themselves to "Smith's Use of
History," but their treatment is naive, celebratory, and lacking in detail.
Their emphasis is on the way Smith uses facts to make his substantive
and philosophical points, leaving the impression that "history" for
Smith was simply a source of data.[1] However, one of the best treatments
of his politics has recognized that Smith was intensely historically
preoccupied, that his "political and religious sympathies are less important
than his historical preoccupations."[2] What must be added is that the writing
modality of Smith's "historical preoccupations" is intimately connected
with his approach to value.

To develop this connection, it is necessary to recall the idea of value
evoked in chapter 1's treatment of the sovereignty-exchange nexus.
There, it is asserted that *value* emerges precisely at the point at which
flows are inhibited. The example most relevant here refers to the
process of linguistic exchange: "To speak is not to *ex*press one's
individuality but to *sup*press it in order to participate within an institutionalized frame of intersubjectivity. A loss of individuality is compensated, then, by a gain in sociability"(MSp.9). To elaborate the point

more generally, the achievement of value requires the fixing of interpretation and, consequently, the arrest of the process of negotiating meanings. In this example, the condition of possibility for linguistic exchange requires an inhibition of the process of creating intelligibility; it is a surrender to the available system of inscription for selves—the subject positions that inhere in grammatical operations, gendered and temporal tropes that position the interpersonal significance of the speaker, and so on.

What this implies is an ineluctable connection between value and loss, for value emerges precisely at the point where interpretation is fixed, the point where a system of intelligibility ceases being negotiated. Rather than thinking of interpretation as something that produces meaning—for it is precisely what arrests the dynamic of meaning—one can say, as Arkady Plotnitsky has, that "interpretation produces value,"[3] and it does so because value emerges as a consequence of the structural limits of the process of interpretation.[4]

This way of construing the interpretation-value relation generates significant implications at two levels. At the individual level, the implications operate for the writer, who can be seen to reproduce a position on value in all those places where institutionalized systems of intelligibility are reinscribed instead of challenged. At the collective level, the implications operate at the points of clashes among social discourses. A society is always involved in an interpretive agonistics in some domains (e.g., those in which events have yet to acquire a dominant interpretation) and in an unreflective acceptance of interpretations in others. Thus, what is "real"— historically, in the present, or to be anticipated—in any society enjoys this epistemic status through an implicit prohibition of further interpretation. The "real" is then a function of, in Michel Pecheux's terms, "the discursive spaces designated . . . as logically stabilized."[5]

This observation can be sharpened by rendering it in Deleuze and Guattari's frame (elaborated in chapter 1). For them, the social domain is a place of inscription, and authorities, dreading uncoded dynamics, act continuously to overcode resistant flows, that is, to contain what is interpretively recalcitrant within an already existing authoritative meaning system. Apart from the importance their argument might have for reading the operation of sovereign power, through the very act of describing society in this way, Deleuze and Guattari have produced an anti-narrative. Rather than rendering modernity as a linear process of the achievement of value, they represent the alternating forces through which value is produced and then disestablished. What is valued can be seen therefore as maintaining its status through struggle, however quiescent things may appear.

In sharp contrast is Adam Smith's tendency toward linear historical narratives. Although Smith freed the problem of value from an old story, the mercantilist narrative of accumulation, he naturalized and fixed a new one. His storytelling therefore dissolved some objectifications but established others. More specifically, Smith's *Wealth of Nations* is a narrative or story of political and economic developments. It unfolds within his imaginative cartography, his idea of the shape of the emerging industrial world and the important locations within it. However, before turning to the details of that text, it is necessary to establish a more general position on the problem of narrative.

The Problem of Narrative

That discourse has a narrative dimension is relatively noncontroversial. What is contentious is the relationship between narrativity and events. To approach the narrative dimension of discourse first with respect to what is noncontroversial, it is generally recognized that for a narrative to exist, there must be coherent statements (sentences being the major grammatical units) within it; there must be some model of temporality governing the telling (or writing); and there must be some connectivity among the statements (some insist on "causal" but here the assumption is simply that there is some connection). Within this general model, almost all prose genres are narratives.

Another relevant position is a more controversial one in discussions about the nature of narrativity. The problem is highlighted in Hayden White's implicit separation between fictional and "real" narratives in his statement: "Narrative becomes a *problem* only when we wish to give *real* events the *form* of a story. It is because real events do not offer themselves as stories that their narrativization is so difficult."[6]

In contrast with the implication in White's statement, the assumption here is that there are no "real events" until there are narratives. Benedict Anderson's point that there was no French Revolution until print media began placing meaning-creating boundaries around the flux of certain activities in the late 18th century is telling.[7] And during the bicentennial year of the "French Revolution," the "event," which continually alters with shifts in the textual practices through which the event is constituted, underwent more rapid changes than usual. Many, especially the French, renegotiated the past to make it more compatible with the dominant self-interpretations with which they now live. Similarly, in the United States, recent professional and media attention is constructing a different "Vietnam War" than the one produced by the official discourse during the administration of President Johnson and in subsequent official and popular culture narratives right after the "fall of Saigon."

Jean-Francois Lyotard has stated the position well and contrasted it with the position that separates events from narrations:

> We habitually pose the following sequence: there is the fact, then the account of the witness, that is to say a narrative activity transforming the fact into a narrative. . . .
>
> This position on the problem of history poses a theatrical model: outside, is the fact, external to the theatrical space; on stage the dramatic narrative unfolds; hidden in the wings . . . is the director, the narrator with all his machinery, the *fabbrica* of narration. The historian is supposed to undo all the machinery and machination and to restore the excluded, having beaten down the walls of the theater.
>
> But it is obvious that the historian is himself only another director, his narrative another product, his work another narration . . . [8]

In short, in agreement with the thrust of Lyotard's position, my assumption is that there are no "events" outside of the spacing, connectivity, and the other meaning-giving dimensions that are part of producing narratives. Although there is a wide variety of narrative forms, any genre producing intelligibility—the writing of history for example—contains a narrative component, which helps construct meanings and relevance, and without which there are no facts and events. What therefore becomes worthy of analysis is the kind of narrativity involved and how it can be assessed in the context of some more general thoughts about epistemological codes—the implicit model of causality, the spatial context of the operative forces, and so on.

In the case of Smith's *Wealth of Nations*, it was Thorstein Veblen who first devoted attention to the central narratives comprising the text. This attention to narrative formed the basis of Veblen's thoroughgoing indictment of Smith's conviction "that there is a wholesome trend in the natural course of things."[9] For Veblen, this conviction betrayed a commitment to the premodern epistemological code that suggests that nature articulates the volition of the Creator, who "has established the natural order to serve the ends of human welfare" and "has very nicely adjusted the efficient causes comprised in the natural order, including human aims and motives, to this work that they are to accomplish."[10]

Smith's "natural order" is thus not a hands-on operation for the Creator. Once nature has been shaped it exists as a form of effectivity. His "nature," as one commentator has put it, is world plus compulsion and benevolent purpose. The needed conversion mechanisms are in place[11], and "the repellent egoism of men is converted into actions useful to society and species."[12]

Sensibly (albeit somewhat hyperbolically), Veblen locates Smith's arguments in a narrativity and related rhetoric, a location that would have affronted Smith, who believed that rhetoric does not belong in scientific treatises. Smith thought that his writing about political economy was summoned by the nature of the world, not produced by his literary contrivances, for his view of language is based primarily on the naming function. A proper scientific discourse for Smith is one in which the names stick close to their objects.[13] The implications of this view of language is explored more elaborately later. Here it is worthwhile to pursue Veblen's characterization of the Smithian narrative/rhetorical structure further.

Veblen noted that Smith offered more than a mere causal sequence of events guided by "a comprehensive scheme of contrivances established from the beginning."[14] The ending was also in place, at least contingently. As long as interference with the natural order of things was avoided, there would be, in the natural course of things, an outcome comprising a happy coincidence of individual, self-seeking, and collective well-being. This narrative of the natural course of things was characterized by Veblen as both teleological and "extra-mechanical" inasmuch as the sequence through which nature's forces operate has a continuity that can be interrupted; it is not a deterministic, cause-and-effect phenomenon.[15] Moreover, much of Smith's argumentative structure, according to Veblen, consists in "making the ascertained facts articulate with his teleological theory of economic life."[16] This observation can be illustrated by examining Smith's discussion of prices, where he argued that in the absence of inappropriate contrivances in policy, the value of things reach their appropriate (natural) level, for example:

> When the price of any commodity is neither more nor less than what is sufficient to pay the rent of the land, the wages of labour, and the profits of the stock employed in raising, preparing, and bringing it to market, according to their natural rates, the commodity is then sold for what may be called its natural price.[17]

The narrative elements in this passage are largely implicit. In Smith's narrative of the development of an economy, which includes the phenomenon of price, the value of a good tends toward its natural level. The elements involved in this model are human needs juxtaposed to productive labor. The 18th-century process of industrialization was the fulfillment of a destiny, for in Smith's view emerging modernity was distinctive insofar as it allowed for an unprecedented level of need fulfillment, and this was owed primarily to the development of the division of labor.

By placing labor, which is the condition of possibility for the production of an expanded level of value, above circulation and exchange, Smith closes the book on the mercantilist story and begins a new one. Most significant for purposes of the story metaphor is that it is not Smith's. As far as he was concerned, he was correcting an old error, not simply arguing for a competing interpretive frame, one with different moral and political implications. Historical writing for Smith was to function like any responsible discourse. It must either "narrate some fact or prove some proposition."[18]

Although Veblen concentrated his attention on Smith's economic narratives, no economic plot, whether Smith's teleological one or an alternative, can function without at least implicitly incorporating social and political narratives (indeed any such boundary between kinds of narratives is conventional in any case).

At a political level, Smith's *Wealth of Nations* story is a fairly explicit one. His issue, which created part of the dialogic of the text, is the seeming "antinomy between the needs of the poor and the rights of the rich."[19] Smith was clearly in favor of equity not equality, for he accepted as natural and inevitable large class divisions, seeking only to avoid the worst excesses of poverty. This would eventuate, he felt, as a natural result of the division of labor, which would produce a level of abundance sufficient to produce a reasonable standard of living for all.

There is an obvious commitment to a model of political justice hovering around Smith's political economy. Having a society of the propertied and propertyless was no problem (in a non-slave economy), for the rich person would end up being the kind of consumer that would stimulate production and thus add to general abundance. In the age of commerce, the wealthy person is therefore an advantage. However, Smith cautioned that it would be unfair as well as disruptive to allow too rapid a change in the status of one from poor to rich.[20]

But Smith had another political model, which is implicit in his treatment of space. His *Wealth of Nations* is theorized within a static and neutral (and therefore depoliticized) view of social space. The history of the development of social space for Smith is smooth and uncontentious; there simply exist public and private spaces and locales to which he refers as "neighborhoods." He is not attentive to Henri Lefebre's insight:

> If space has an air of neutrality and indifference with regard to its contents and thus seems to be purely formal, the epitome of rational abstraction, it is precisely because it has already been occupied and used, and has already been the focus of past processes whose traces are not always evident in the landscape.[21]

More generally, Smith rarely registers contentious processes. There is no apparent notion, for example, that the way people are sorted into occupations owes something to administered spatial practices, not only the encouraged system of property ownership, which was accelerating through enclosure practices as Smith wrote, but also the more subtle pressures such as expanding educational space competing with family space over the allocation of eligibilities for working. What Smith failed to register with regard to space can be discerned in other texts produced by his contemporaries—for example, the rustic landscape painting genre at the end of the 18th century in England, which though not critical, is at least expressive of the significance of changing spatiality. Ann Bermingham has shown that the representation of nature in this genre was ideological, aimed at justifying the social changes attendant to the shift from landscape viewed as the embodiment of the prestige of lineage to landscape as part of estates promising financial gain.[22] The genre demonstrates a significant change in the political significance of space, which is reflected in the interpretations imposed on land.

However, rather than noting the struggles implicit in this interpretive shift that revalued property, Smith's narrative is governed by its normative proprieties. Given the felicitous place of the division of labor in his system, he imagines the process of its formation as natural rather than political. He speaks of such things as "natural talents" and the natural motivation to exchange as the factors that sort people into forms of work. Spatial configurations and dynamics are never mentioned as part of this effectivity. And, since the difference in natural talents is not as great as many suppose, according to Smith, it is "the disposition to truck, barter, and exchange" that is most implicated in constructing the shape and divisions of the labor force.[23]

This depoliticizing impetus of Smith's narrative is simply one of the early documents in the modern history of liberal political discourse, which has emphasized distribution rather than space. Implicitly, politics for Smith has to do with the distribution of value. His political problematic involves the relative shares enjoyed by the poor, and the responsibility for producing equitability is to lie within the economy. The shares obtained by the poor for their share, within Smith's conceits, are made adequate by an unregulated economy whose productive power is partly driven, as Smith's narrative would have it, by the developing division of labor through which workers can produce an abundance and by the consumption ability of the wealthy. What looks like class antagonism in some models, then, is a symbiosis in Smith's. And, his fixation on this distributive model of politics, related to his notions of well-being and justice, is based on a comparison with his storybook version of an "African King" who, according to Smith, is less well off, given his inability to enjoy the fruits of the division of labor, than a contemporary peasant.

What kind of politics is finessed or silenced in Smith's distributive emphasis? It is, as suggested above, a politics based on spatial practices and other systems of inclusion and exclusion (e.g., the production of social identities), which are tied to the way a society constructs and administers its locations and eligibilities to participate in them. More specifically, it is a politics recognizing the power and authority implications of divisions between private and public space, industrial space and leisure space, educational space and family space (among others). Politics involves, among other things, an interplay of liberation and domination with respect to control over the boundary practices that create subjects and "space" (i.e., places that take on their significance from the practices determining their control and the normative eligibility requirements for their use).

The sundering of the spiritual space, which helped produce the modernity within which Smith wrote, permitted the liberation of certain commercial forces, but such episodes of what Deleuze and Guattari call *deterritorialization* are always accompanied by a countertendency, a "reterritorialization" wherein dominant forces are mobilized to prevent the new productive possibilities from also creating expanded human freedoms.[24] The implications of a model of political economy that is more sensitive to the politics immanent in spatial practices is addressed later. At this point, it is important to explore further the stylistic conventions that led Smith along a different narrative path than the one implicit in Deleuze and Guattari's dialectic of liberation and domination.

Smith's History

Smith addressed himself explicitly to the proprieties of writing history, especially to the proper focus. Not surprisingly, his view of the correct objects of attention of historical writing accords with his sovereignty emphasis. Just as he had emphasized an interest in the social bond and had turned his attention away from the civic bond (the relationship between an all-powerful sovereign and subjects), in his remarks on writing history he rejected a preoccupation with the "affairs of monarchs" and other "great men" and preferred an interest in what he calls "the body of the people."[25]

Smith's aim, at an analytic level, was explanation. He wished to emulate Thucydides' emphasis on causation and to resist mere entertainment. Assiduous about the problem of history, Smith, as was his wont in so many areas, did a brief history of history. And here, as elsewhere, he imposed a linear narrative on that history. He asserts that poets, whose emphases were on entertainment, were the first historians and that the writing of history then moved successively toward explanation and argumentation rather than storytelling.

Smith's history of history as well as his self-understanding of his own historical writing constitutes an aggressive denial of his own stories. Certainly he was explanatory, didactic, and argumentative, but he was also an inveterate storyteller. Although entertainment was not his focus, in many respects Smith's writing often verged toward the fictive or mythological end of the continuum of historical writing, especially because of the linear structure of his narratives.

Smith's linear narratives, his way of constructing his argument, bound up with his way of writing history has no place for the contentiousness or dialectics of action and reaction (as is elucidated, for example, in Deleuze and Guattari's analysis). His teleological, naturalizing tendency, noted by Veblen, can be situated more precisely, by recognizing that Smith's *Wealth of Nations* occupied the same discursive niche as the tradition of natural history against which Charles Darwin wrote almost a century later. Natural history, like Smith's political economy, was animated by natural theology. Darwin therefore had to write against a preexisting, naturalizing discourse to produce his new system.[26]

Among other things, Darwin was especially attentive to the pacifying and naturalizing effect of the natural history/natural theology narrative. He took "considerable pains to avoid legitimating the current social order by naturalizing it," as it was in accounts that showed it to be the result of a smooth and continuous historical process.[27] Especially significant in this regard is Darwin's omission of *man* from his text. He was sensitive to potential protest against a text that situates man in a narrative subversive to prevailing religious notions, but the absence, ironically, helps to produce the subversive effect because it countered the providential and natural theological writing, which placed man at the center of a narrative in which man's story is the result of providential guidance.[28]

Darwin's exemplary struggle with the language of his "history," which Gillian Beer has chronicled with close attention to early and later drafts of his *Origin*, enables a more critical reading of Smith's history, because it contrasts so dramatically with Darwin's and because it was precisely the kind of history that Darwin had to extract his writing from, a linear, smooth narrative with little hint of contending forces and arbitrary outcomes.

To resist Smithian-type narratives, as Darwin did, it is necessary to recognize that much of Smith's history is legendary or mythic, that is, aimed at silencing all tendencies subversive to the main, naturalizing, and legitimating story. The distinction between legend and history, developed by Erich Auerbach in his classic comparison of the narrative styles in Homer's *Odyssey* and the *Old Testament* story of Abraham and Isaac, should not be drawn rigidly, but it is appropriate for reading Smith. Stating that "the difference between legend and history is in most cases easily perceived by a reasonably experienced reader," Auerbach identifies legend as something that "runs far too smoothly."

> All cross-currents, all friction that is casual, secondary to the main events or themes, everything unresolved, truncated, and uncertain, which confuses the clear progress of the action and simple orientation of the actors, has disappeared.[29]

Not all of Smith's narrative is legend within this account. When he notes, for example, that "the art of war . . . has gradually grown up to be a very intricate and complicated science," he is engaged in relatively uncontentious historical description (even though it is highly unspecific and lacking in detail).[30] But his tale of how the division of labor is a natural consequence of talented people sorting themselves into the appropriate occupational slots, as they are carried along by a historical narrative in which abundance is, providentially, just around the corner, qualifies as legend.[31]

In such parts of the tale, Smith's discourse registers no struggles for occupational existence, no counternarratives to the unitary one he constructs. The only blemishes in his otherwise smooth surface of events derive from attempts to interfere with the natural process that will guide mankind toward abundance. In short, in Smith's legendary narrative, people end up in the occupational positions for which they are destined. The guiding piety in such a view is similar to that which constructs the narrative of Benjamin Franklin's autobiography, in which every early childhood episode is suggestive of the result, the self-made and thus exemplary American hero. Franklin, like Smith, wrote legendary history, the difference being simply a matter of genre, autobiography versus political economy.[32]

Similar to the concept of legend as it applies to plots such as Smith's is that of the mythic plot which, as Frank Kermode (after Lotman) suggests, has no "excesses or anomalies."[33] Mythic plots are eschatological plots that frequently exist alongside historical plots and "penetrate history."[34] In the case of the *Wealth of Nations*, much of the mythicization stems from the ontology surrounding Smith's text, one positing a guiding, transcendent universe with purposeful intent. Why the text is so mythicized and is thus so barren of detail is well expressed in Kermode's reading of the plot of a Keats poem: "The assurance that there is a timeless and motionless transcendental world reduces to insignificance the *faits divers* which seem to constitute the narration of ordinary life."[35]

This reference to ordinary life provides yet another insight into Smith's history. Even at the level of what appears as historical rather than mythic, Smith's narrative organizes itself around something exemplary rather than ordinary. His story of economics is strikingly linear, an aspect of the text that emerges when it is compared with a history of political economy that is attentive to ordinary life, for example, Fernand Braudel's, which is cognizant of a broader range of economies throughout the world as well as being in touch with "ordinary" rather than mythic or normatively constituted economic life. Braudel is able to discern that although with the approach of modernity society becomes a "generalized market society, this does not happen at the same time or in the same way in different regions."[36] And, more significantly, in his analysis of markets, he remarks that "there is no simple linear history of the development of markets"[37]; traditional, archaic, modern, and ultra-modern forms have existed side-by-side.

Moreover, contrary to Smith's untroubled story in which people smoothly sort themselves into places within the division of labor as a market society develops and capitalism expands, Braudel treats the resistances of a more-or-less autonomous peasant class to expanding capitalism: "I wanted to begin with inertias," he writes.[38] Noting that "mankind is more than waist-deep in daily routine,"[39] Braudel explains his working distinction between *economic life* and *material life*, arguing that the latter has never been wholly absorbed by the former.[40] Despite the rapid development of markets from the 1500s to the 1800s, it was not until the 18th century that markets affected many people. Daily material life has, even up to the present, exerted a resistance to the expanding market system.

Braudel also points out that the vaunted "division of labor," whose development Smith sketched so unproblematically, has *never* developed in a unitary way. The commercial or exchange world (of Smith's time) was a "world of hierarchies, starting with the humblest jobs—porters, stevedores, peddlers, carters, and sailors—and moving up to cashiers, shopkeepers, brokers of various sorts, and money lenders, and finally reaching merchants."[41] The process of the development of a division of labor "was at first evident only at the bottom of the pyramid—until the 19th century the top-level merchant virtually never restricted himself to a single activity."[42]

Thus, rather than the unitary, homogeneous developing system Smith suggests, capitalism, according to Braudel, is "conjunctural," developing unevenly, in fits and starts, in different ways among different groups, in short, in nothing like the mythic story sketched by Smith. Braudel offers a resistant historical narrative to Smith's, and it is made possible by his attention to the details of material life, which do not fit into the smooth, linear story Smith tells.

It is easier for us than it was for Smith to appreciate Braudel's insights, because much of Smith's legendary or mythic narrative is based on a unitary source of historicity and our postmodern imagination is constructed out of a recognition that there is no single center of history, for all previous centers of history have lost their privileged status. This has led to what Gianni Vattimo has called the "dissolution of history," in the sense of a "breakdown of its unity."[43] "This is the result of the fact that the world of mass media—which is spread out far and wide across the face of the earth—is also the world in which the 'centers' of history have multiplied."[44] Because Smith's epistemic code was connected to a unitary model of history, to dissolve this model is to put intolerable pressure on the credibility of his economic narrative. Given the contemporary lack of commitment to such narratives as, for example, Christianity's history of salvation, narratives such as Smith's, which operate under the assumption of a single center of transcendent guidance, lose their privilege.

Smith and the Problem of Value

Two dimensions of Smith's story must be understood to appreciate his approach to value. The first part is an epistemological narrative about the meeting of bodies and objects. The second is a social narration about the meeting of the individual body with the social body. As has been noted in several places above, Smith was a sensationalist. It is now time to treat the implications of this position as it affects the value of objects.

Smith had an abiding ambivalence toward sensation. On the one hand, he thought of "the external senses," as he called them, as a bounty "given us by nature" to tell us about the conditions of external bodies so that we can judge what might "benefit or hurt us."[45] On the other hand, sensation disturbs our tranquility. In his "History of Astronomy," Smith speaks of the mind's search for tranquility and harmony, which he posits as the motive for seeking parsimonious explanation.[46] Moreover, he says that the excitement produced by novel objects is dreadful.

> How much we dread the effect of the more violent passions, when they come suddenly upon the mind, appears from the preparations which all men think necessary when going to inform anyone of what is capable of exciting them.[47]

Here Smith is thinking not only of calamities but also of good fortune, for he goes on to argue that too much sudden joy is even worse than news of misfortune. In general, then, he ascribes to humans the desire to "deaden vivacity of both pain and pleasure."[48]

For Smith, therefore, sensation is the primary source of value, and embodiment is represented as a screening mechanism to dampen one's relationship with objects. Smith operates, it seems, with a simple grammar of subject-object relations. Objects constitute initiating causes—for example, they "excite our wonder,"49 and in general he uses the idea of excitement in a way that holds objects responsible for what is sensed. The subject/perceiver reacts to the initiating impacts of the objects by attempting to dampen their more extreme effects on themselves and others.

The formulation of experience and value for Smith is thus based on the encounters between an object's tendency to excite sensations and a subject's attempts to manage the effects. The implicit narrative of this epistemology should be evident: objects act prior to subjects. This narrative's relationship to value is also clear: value is generated from objects.

To achieve some distance from this Smithian narrative, we can consider what is now a well-known counternarrative, the subject-object relationship developed by phenomenologists. Maurice Merleau-Ponty's classic *The Structure of Behavior* provides an exemplar. There he precisely reverses the Smithian model, arguing that rather than seeing the object as the first cause of stimulations, it is the initiating behavior of the subject or "organism" in Merleau-Ponty's more biologically oriented discourse.

> Thus the proper form of the excitant is created by the organism itself, by its proper manner of offering itself to actions from the outside. Doubtless, in order to be able to subsist, it must encounter a certain number of physical and chemical agents in its surroundings. But it is the organism itself—according to the proper name of its receptors, the thresholds of its nerve centers and the movements of the organs—which chooses the stimuli in the physical world to which it will be sensitive.50

Merleau-Ponty's reversal of Smith's narrative is clearly antisensationalist; it holds structures of consciousness and the activity with which consciousness is complicit responsible for what is available to "sense." Merleau-Ponty is explicit in his recognition that his treatment of the structure of behavior is antisensationalist: "We have seen that the hypothesis of sensations is not justifiable,"51 he notes, after explaining that perception is aimed not toward "objects of nature" but toward intentions. And, ironically, in his rejection of Smithian sensationalism, Merleau-Ponty develops a labor theory of value predicated on the structure of apprehension: "To use a human object is always more or less to embrace and assume for one's self the meaning of the work which produced it."52

But the difference to be noted is important here. Merleau-Ponty's model of value is consonant with the primacy of the subject in the perceptual relationship. The labor responsible for significance and value is the labor of the subject, particularly the practical/intentional work of establishing a coherence among objects. In such a model, to find value is not to recover material properties of objects but to recover the aim of intentions, an aim directed not outward toward objects but inward toward the production of vital significance. Objects are not valuable because they produce sensations in a causal sense. Rather, they "play the role of occasions rather than cause."[53]

For Smith, the relationship between labor and materiality as it relates to value is dramatically different. As was noted above, in Smith's position, objects present not mere occasions for valuing but are the sensational cause of them. But more than sensationalism governs Smith's attempt to isolate materiality. His interest in exchange and his (Newtonian) scientific predilection combined to motivate him to find what was *common* to each instance of materiality. For Smith, Newton's system was "the greatest discovery that ever was made by man," and what was integral to this was the system's ability "to connect together the otherwise disjointed and discordant phaenomena of nature."[54]

The search for this material commonality was therefore to provide Smith with two coherences. The first was epistemic—it would satisfy his Newtonian emphasis on a unified and parsimonious explanation. The second was economic—it would provide a unit of measure that would free value from the purview of state authority and locate it in a broadly distributed way in the society. As Marx suggested, Smith was the Martin Luther of political economy.

The advantage of exchange was, for Smith, self-evident. It leads to enhanced levels of satisfaction. Instead of posing a fixed level of value for which states compete (the mercantilist view), for Smith "wealth" as value increases with increased exchange. At the level of thought, the production of an unfettered level of exchange required a separation of the idea of the domain of economy from the political and moral crotchets of the state.

Smith's idea of value shifts uneasily back and forth between his interest in exchange and his emphasis on production. Siding with Quesnay, who located "real wealth" in its creation, Smith focused on that which contributed to making objects available for satisfactions, but emphasized labor and paid less attention to land than Quesnay. The epistemological story remained in place. Objects satisfy senses, that is, their value derives from their material relationship to the body. But this epistemological narrative in which objects are primary is subsumed within a larger story, a story about the increased productivity that derives from the division of labor.

In the smaller epistemological story, objects (or materiality) lose some of their primacy inasmuch as Smith, as was the case subsequently with Marx, reduces objects to their subjective essence (even at times to the biological dimension of subjectivity). However, this is not the individual subjectivity or collective, cultural subjectivity that produces value through perspective. It is the subjectivity involved in making objects materially available for use in an economic way. The primary materialist narrative thus remains in place epistemologically for Smith, as it did for Marx, who insisted that the value of a commodity, in the sense of its "use value" "is conditioned by the physical properties of the commodity, and has no existence apart from the latter."[55]

In the larger story, Smith's fable is remarkably individualistic. He imagines a self-sufficient human supplying basic necessities with her/his own labor. The Smithian subject faces the world of objects alone, both as one with unproblematic needs and as a supplier. As Smith put it in his *Lectures on Jurisprudence*, "In general . . . the necessities of man are not so great but that they can be supplied by the unassisted labor of the individual."[56]

Smith's individualistic story was later to lose its place to other stories. As classical political economy gave way to neoclassical revisions, the production process was seen not as an uninhibited, expanding dynamic but as a mediated relationship of the organization of supply in the face of the demands of consumers. Thus, for example, by the beginning of this century, Alfred Marshall, who saw decisions by firms to enter into production as a key part of the process, told a very different economic story than Smith's. It was the story of the firm and its increasing productivity, not that of the individual laborer involved in an increasing degree of specialization.[57]

Although Smith occasionally turned his attention to the individual seeking "the most advantageous employment for whatever capital he can command,"[58] his story paid little heed to the social and economic organization of labor in firms. Rather, his story, like the exemplary stories in classical political economy and canonical political treatises of his time, was constructed on the basis of a juxtaposition between a state of nature in which an individual is responsible for satisfying his/her own needs and the present, "real" condition in which various reciprocities obtain. Thus Smith speaks of "that early and rude state of society" in which a laborer keeps everything [he] produces,[59] and contrasts this with the market system of exchange.

The language of Smith's historical fable is strikingly retrospective, for the primitive hunter to which Smith frequently refers is not a laborer in most senses, especially not in the sense in which people who work and people who manage work are interrelated in what Marxists call the "relations of production." Not surprisingly, Smith's discourse here is Lockian/individualist rather than Marxist. He was focused more on an origin myth in which work produces entitlement to value rather than on the value extractions involved in the social organization of work. For Smith, as for Locke, labor is not simply a concept used to understand economy; it is ontological, emerging from a form of philosophical naturalism.

As Louis Dumont has pointed out, Smith's reliance on the "early and rude state" origin myth is a "natural law argument," although Smith doubtless avoided a "state of nature" expression because of his friend David Hume's effective and influential dismissal of the idea.[60] So fixated was Smith on this pre-exchange condition story, in which he produces an individualistic relation between persons and work, that his explicit development of his position on value is highly vexed.

On the one hand, Smith baldly states in chapter 5 of *The Wealth of Nations* that "labour is . . . the real measure of the exchangeable value of all commodities," and that "the real price of everything, what everything really costs to the man who wants to acquire it, is the toil and trouble of acquiring it."[61] On the other hand, Smith's exchange orientation takes him over, and he gets wrapped up in treating the actual or what he ends up calling the "market price" of commodities, which he recognizes to be a function of other than labor contributions—the appropriation of land, the "stock," which involves capital for advances on wages and the materials for work, and the "ordinary rate of profit in [the] neighborhood."[62]

Dumont has stated the vexation clearly. In his words, *"Labor and exchange* taken together are central to Adam Smith's thought. This pair

runs like a red thread throughout the beginning of the *Wealth*."[63] He
goes on to trace Smith's heroic attempt to pull his notion of value
constantly back toward the contribution of labor in order to maintain
the identity with which he constructs economic reality, the identity
between labor and value.

Yet Smith could not ultimately extract value from the process of
exchange. His "natural state," in which he equates labor with value by
noting that the primitive producer enjoys the fruits of his labors himself,
simply would not travel into a market economy. Dumont has told the
story of Smith's struggle well. Here a somewhat different problem is
stressed. Smith's narration of the shift from the primitive condition to
the market condition, his economic history, was vexed. But at another
level, that of his smaller epistemological story, his history, as has been
noted, is uncomplicated. Objects produce satisfactions because of their
materiality, not, for example, because of the interpretive process in
which they achieve their significance (as for example in the case of a
gift, whose "value" is a function of the context of the exchange,
especially the intersubjective bond it reinforces or creates).

The Smithian subject or body faces things alone, alone in the sense
that there is no linguistic or cultural mediation between a person and
the satisfaction of value. Smith's empiricist story of value, notwithstanding its vexations stemming from his ontological commitment to
labor and his interest in exchange, is conceptually disenabling in that
it neglects the contexts in which objects take on value, and politically
disenabling in that part of context is the interpretive struggle that
determines what will control what "value" is to mean.

A Semiological Alternative

If, as was suggested at the beginning of this chapter, value is an
interpretive imposition, the analysis must turn to the modalities of
imposition. Accordingly, Smith's narrative style has been interrogated
at two levels, the first or smaller story of the subject-object relation and
the second or more general history of the emergence of value. It was
shown, generally, that Smith's position on value cannot be separated

from his sensationalist epistemology, built on an object-to-subject narrative in which an object's materiality excites a subject's sensations. This applies for Smith even in the case of an aesthetic object such as a work of art. As Smith would have it, the object excites passions and fulfills the subject's need for stimulation and novelty. Somehow, of course, genre must be intrinsic to objects as well, for Smith does not deal with the complex interpretive dynamics that determine whether, for example, a given object is food or an item of aesthetic appreciation at one or another moment.

At a minimum, a critique of Smith's view of value must treat the subject/object sensationalism on which it is based. Merleau-Ponty's reversal provides an important counterpoint, but it is not sufficiently sensitive to the syntax of the value problem. To disrupt the Smithian view more thoroughly, it is necessary not only to shift the locus of value production away from objects but also to note *how* they become valued within a syntax that relates them to other things. To appreciate how objects support valuing, we must do more than posit an initiating subjectivity. We must be able to follow the twists and turns through which narrative structures position objects. Although there is a variety of analytic discourses within which this can be shown, not the least of which is psychoanalytic, here the focus is on the semiological frame, for it has been used by A. J. Greimas to treat explicitly the narrative structure of valuing.

The first important step to take, according to Greimas, is to avoid confusing the notions of object and value. For him, the object is "no more than a pretext, a locus of value investment."[64] Here the semiotic model is close to the psychoanalytic approach to the object of desire which, even "where it proposes itself in its nakedness," is only the "slag of a fantasy," as Jacques Lacan put it.[65] Greimas proposes the example of an automobile, which is a linguistic object that exists as a set of virtualities with respect to value. It takes part in value determinations— as a means of transportation, as something related to prestige, and so on—only "thanks to syntactic trajectories established outside discursive manifestation."[66]

In separating the object from its place in a valuing process, Greimas effectively counters the empiricist/sensationalist approach of Adam Smith and others that organizes both traditional epistemology and classical political economy. Objects are not *knowable* in and of themselves; they are known by their "determinations," as Greimas puts it. From a narrative standpoint, determinations take the form of the "syntactic trajectories" for which the objects serve as supports. Similarly, objects are not *valuable* in and of themselves. Their value emerges as the endpoint of a person's aim. The "endpoint" imagery is especially important here, for the object's service as a locus of value investment operates within a syntactic and semantic structure. In the process of valuing, it serves as an end term in a relationship between the subject and the world, as "the subject's intended project" in Greimas's terms.[67]

Although Greimas here appears to work within a simple subject-object grammar, which postulates a world within which subjects seek values, he recognizes that language is not owned by individual subjects; it takes on its ability to perform within both a structure and a temporal context. The narrativization of value of which he speaks is less an individual choice than an enactment of a social code, for he notes that the value of an object for a subject emerges within a linguistic act that is not only structural but also "anchored in history."[68]

Thus for example, to understand the "hidden treasure problem" in the Pinocchio story—Pinocchio acquires, loses, and then finds again some gold coins with the help of a fairy—it is necessary, as Greimas points out, to place it historically in a Tuscan agricultural society at a time when the economy was static. There was a more-or-less "closed universe of values . . . such that for every instance of acquisition on the part of a member of the society there corresponds necessarily a loss on the part of another."[69] For example, to provide Pinocchio with a school primer, his maker/father, Geppetto, has to sell his coat. In this context a story of a found treasure is a story about the existence of value outside of the "closed universe." Of course, hidden treasure has meaning as an anti-type, for "found treasures" are opposed to produced goods, and within the ontology of classical political economy, such non-work-related experiences of value would, in Greimas's terms, "appear as anti-values or *negative values* having to do with an axiological anti-universe."[70]

What is important in this story for present purposes is that the juxtaposition is not one of economy versus myth but myth versus myth. The work-value story at the center of Adam Smith's position on value is represented materialistically by Smith but achieves its coherence only when complemented by an ontological commitment to the importance of work and a narrative that foregrounds work and makes it responsible for value, given its place in the dynamic that makes material things available for satisfactions.

The counternarration that Greimas discerns in the Pinocchio story, based on a different economic structure and a different corresponding "axiological universe," unfolds with some significantly different value-producing interpretive impulses. In the static Tuscan economy, the human subjects exist within a two-tiered universe. There is the everyday, earthly place within which value shares are limited, static, and acquired through work-related activities constrained, of course, by the norms fixing subjects' identities and the meaning of their activities. Then there is a transcendent universe that makes value possible. The finding of value places the finder not in a litigious relationship with another earthly possessor but in a spiritual relationship with a supernatural being (e.g. the benevolent fairy) who, as Greimas puts it, "plays the role of mediator between the universe of transcendent values and the immanent universe into which the new values are introduced for circulation."[71]

The Tuscans of the Pinocchio story clearly live in an enchanted world, and such stories have the effect of legitimating the worldly economy by sacrilizing the human condition, that is, by leaving one's economic fate to divine intervention. The idea of divinely inspired luck serves no doubt to draw attention away from the more local forms of domination and control over value.

In the Pinocchio story, the ontology and ethic are predicated on a spatial orientation that is medieval/sacred in construction. By contrast it would appear at first inspection that the social setting of exchange operating in Adam Smith's imaginative cartography has been entirely disenchanted. Smith's implicit geography certainly departs from the more traditional medieval spatial arrangement, which Foucault has summarized as follows:

In the Middle Ages there was a hierarchical ensemble of places: sacred places and profane places; protected places and open, exposed places; urban places and rural places. . . . In cosmological theory, there were supercelestial places, as opposed to the celestial, and the celestial place was in turn opposed to the terrestrial place.[72]

But there remain sacred moments in the Smithian space within which his value narrative unfolds. First, as has been pointed out, there is a sacred structure implied in Smith's history of economy inasmuch as he posits a transcendent, purposeful intent by a deity that guarantees harmonious results, even though the deity exists only in the form of mechanisms. Second, modernity's spatial arrangements, which were emerging as Smith wrote, retain elements of the sacred. As Foucault has noted, there has been a tendency to misperceive the normalizations and sanctifications of modern space because we have learned to resist only one form of sacrilization, the sacred cartography of the Middle Ages. Nevertheless, as he puts it,

> perhaps our life is still governed by a certain number of oppositions that remain inviolable, that our institutions and practices have not yet dared to break down. These are oppositions that we regard as simple givens: for example, between private space and public space, between family space and social space, between cultural space and useful space, between the space of leisure and that of work. All these are still nurtured by the hidden presence of the sacred.[73]

Adam Smith was unreflective about the normalizations of space that his writing reproduced. Not only did he set his "economy" outside of the effectivity of social space—his social space held an economy rather than animating it—but also his substantive references to space constituted places as innocent arenas. For example, in his discussion of the difference between natural and market prices, he spoke of the average rate of rent in a "neighborhood," as if every place has something intrinsic to it rather than being shaped by various remote forces.[74] Certainly, for example, the dynamics of political economy from Smith's age to the present have had effects on such spatial practices as being able to maintain a neighborhood, that is, a stable and relatively self-contained domain of residence and commerce. But Smith simply naturalizes places by ascribing such things as "natural rates of wages" to each neighborhood as if the effectivity exists in the place rather than as forces shaping places.

Ultimately, Smith's neglect of the cultural, social, and political practices involved in constructing space, as well as of the other contextual dimensions of value, permitted him to maintain his view that objects have value for subjects by dint of their materiality. However, as it is put by Greimas, it is the "determinations" of objects—the narrative and other meaning structures through which they are known—that have value, and, as has been shown, one of the significant aspects of the determination of objects is the imaginative cartography, the view of space within which they are recognized. The uncritical view of space found in Smith's writing can be dramatically juxtaposed to that of Foucault, whom Gilles Deleuze has called a "cartographer" precisely because he recodes and therefore remaps contemporary spaces.[75] Foucault's writing operates within a radical rethinking of social space. For example, rather than naturalizing the existing spaces of modernity, he has collapsed the spaces of the prison, hospital, school, and the like, and placed them within the domain of practice he labels "the carceral." [76] What have existed in dominant social discourses as spaces innocent of the operation of power are repositioned in his writing as part of a structure of surveillance and control.

Toward a Dematerialized Political Economy

The constructions of the body or subject, of space, and, more generally, of the interpretive impositions of meaning on bodies, things, and places are inextricably involved in what is valuable. All of these interpretive dimensions that establish value constitute the non- or dematerialized dimension of political economy. The semiotic contribution to understanding this aspect of value has been elaborated in the discussion of narrativity and value. There are two other domains of contemporary theorizing that make important contributions to appreciating the indissolubly interpretive component of valuing. One is anthropological, to be taken up shortly; the other is psychoanalytical, which in its basic conceptual formulation is strikingly similar to the conceptions animating Adam Smith's moral psychology as articulated in his *Theory of Moral Sentiments.*

An opening to this comparison is provided in Smith's text:

> The sentiment or affection of the heart, from which any action proceeds, and upon which its whole virtue or vice depends, may be considered under

two different aspects, or in two different relations: First, in relation to the
cause or object which excites it; and, secondly, in relation to the end which
it proposes, or to the effect which it tends to produce.[77]

Here we have a structural match with Freud's treatment of desire in
his "Three Essays on the Theory of Sexuality."[78] There, in the first
essay, Freud uses two "technical terms": the "sexual object," which is
"the person from whom sexual attraction proceeds," and the "sexual
aim," which is "the act toward which the instinct tends."[79] At the level
of the distinction alone, Freud's terms conform to his age's prevailing view
of the sexual instinct. The sexual instinct, like Smith's socially felicitous
form of sympathy, remains naturalized. Certain objects are believed to be
naturally attractive. Accordingly, forms of "sexual deviance" (in Freud's
terms, "perversions") were to be regarded as unnatural.

However, once the terms are in place, Freud's treatment distances him
both from Smith's model of moral sentiments and from his
contemporaries' view of the sexual instinct. Turning sharply away from
the prevailing view, Freud states, "We have been in the habit of regard-
ing the connection between the sexual instinct and the sexual object as
more intimate than it in fact is," and, "It seems probable that the sexual
instinct is in the first instance independent of its object; nor is its origin
likely to be due to its object's attractions."[80]

What is so revolutionary here? Like Smith's 18th-century version of
sensationalism, in which social objects are naturally attractive and
determine or "cause" (in Smith's words) the sentiments producing
sympathetic aims, 19th-century psychiatric theory constructed natural
objects that encouraged a proper (and thus natural) sexual aim.[81]

Although Freud continued to employ the concept of the perversion,
his argument that the sexual instinct is not controlled or produced by a
natural object effectively dismissed the idea of a perversion, because
the idea of a perversion requires the idea of a natural object from which
perversions are deviations. But more important than Freud's participation in a mentality he effectively overcame in his theorizing is the space
he helped to create for a rethinking of the relationship between desire
and the social order. Within Freud's frame, what one must imagine is
not a fixed social space filled with naturally attractive objects but a
labile structure of association whose objects attract or repel as a result

of the complex interpretive work through which the individual's relationships to objects and others are mediated as they are diffracted through society's various symbolizing practices. Moreover, the modes of consciousness that figure in the valuing of desired objects, expressed at the explicit level of discourse, undergo a series of transformations that make it difficult to recover the meanings that were responsible for the generation of the energy involved in the pursuit of them.

This is not the place to elaborate the psychoanalytic version of the workings of the unconscious. What is most important is the treatment of desiring as a process that escapes any relegation to the initiating phase of the production of the social. The psychoanalytic model rejects the Smithian subject, who is simply aimed by the natural bent of desire to felicitous participation in public space. But the problem of desire in Smith versus others must be deferred to the next chapter. Here the concern is with contributions to a dematerialized construction of the problem of value, and for this purpose the other important domain of theorizing is anthropological.

The contemporary anthropological contributions to dematerializing economy effectively begin with Marcel Mauss's treatment of the gift. Mauss showed that gift giving is governed not by the material or intrinsic value of the objects exchanged but by the social positions of the giver and receiver. What is exchanged are signs, and the fact that gift giving operates within a symbolic economy is repressed. As Mauss puts it, "The form usually taken is that of the gift generously offered, but accompanying behavior is formal pretense and social deception, while the transaction itself is based on obligation and economic self-interest."[82]

Since Mauss, various theorists have theorized society and culture as systems of sign exchange and thereby overcome the radical separation between culture and economy that obtains in both liberal/capitalist and Marxist formulations of political economy. For example, Pierre Bourdieu has emphasized how "cultural capital" is deeply embedded in all forms of exchange and how "symbolic interests" cannot be separated from economic ones. With the help of such conceptions, he is able to move from political economy to the analysis of power and authority, for the ability to hoard and control signs is at least as significant as the control over "material wealth" in the dynamics of power.[83] Similarly, Jean

Baudrillard bases his version of political economy on the sign and Georges Bataille on a model of ritual expenditure involved in processes of distinction in which the squandering of resources is central to a culturally embedded economy.[84]

Where did culture sit for Adam Smith? It would appear that it was a mere nuisance from his point of view. He treated culture more or less the way he treated any domain of normativity (e. g., in some respects, the state) that might mediate or impede exchange and the division of labor. For example, he noted that the norms of "Indostan" and "antient Egypt," which bind "every man" to follow the occupation of his father, have the effect of lowering wages and "the profits of stock below their natural rate."[85]

As has been noted, in the Smithian narrative, people generally sort themselves into occupational positions in a way that optimizes the production of wealth. And culture stands wholly outside of economy for Smith. The value of a product for persons is a function of bodies meeting things. It has also been noted, however, that Smith entertained a model of the meeting of individuals with the social body. Here, we encounter a paradox in Smith's thinking. In the domain of economy, the individual connects with the social in a strictly consequentialist way. Persons end up selecting occupational niches and engage in work strictly from the point of view of individual utilities. Insofar as consciousness enters this picture, it is consciousness of individual gain. The developing shape of the labor force in industrial society is innocent of cultural promptings. It emerges from a series of isolated individual strivings. This mythic, depoliticizing narrative not only contrasts markedly with the socially self-conscious orientation Smith has in *The Theory of Moral Sentiments* (to be treated below) but also contrasts markedly with some contemporary analyses of the historical shaping of the industrial work force.

For example, Raymond Williams is among those who tell a different story of the role that culture plays. Rather than standing in the way of labor docility and productivity, the emergence of what he calls a "culture of production" helped to shape and deliver a working class. There are, as William puts it, "indissoluble connections between material production, political institutions and activity, and consciousness."[86] Williams, like Gramsci, has emphasized the significance of the forces at work that have ideationally shaped the social milieu into the cultural support for industrial development and that have continuously reproduced the bases for a class system that supplies the relationships behind the process of capital accumulation.

E. P. Thompson's story is a more agonistic one. It emphasizes the shaping forces of antagonisms within both the ruling and working classes as well as between them. In his view, the class basis of work, as well as the structure of the work itself, has become shaped more by forms of domination and resistance than by the process of individuals striving to better themselves that Smith assumed. And contrary to the Smithian optimism about the prospects for self-improvement, Thompson's story is often one of the degradation of labor, for example, the decline of the Yorkshire woolen and worsted weavers who, like their counterparts in cotton, worked continuously longer hours for less pay as a result of being divided against themselves as manufacturers learned to manipulate the fact of their scattered venues.[87]

There have been many politically perspicuous contributions to the "culture of production" story, but for present purposes the relationship of culture to economy inherent in the value of *products* rather than of production is more central to the value problematic under analysis. Since the development of the classical political economy of Adam Smith and others, economic thinking has gradually shifted its focus to a substantial concern with consumption. Once consumption came under scrutiny, it became increasingly recognized that contrary to the classical and Marxian view that the materiality of the object met the desires for need satisfaction of the consumer, it was desire itself that produced an interpretation or determination that lent value to objects. As one commentator on the shift has astutely put it, under the new emphasis on consumption "economists increasingly understood that in their new science it was not that useful things were desired but that desired things were useful."[88]

Recall that for Marx, like Smith, the opposite position is asserted. For him, the materiality of the object, not its interpretive status, gives it value. As he put it in *Capital*, "the usefulness of a thing makes it a use value. But this usefulness is conditioned by the physical properties of the commodity and has no existence apart from the latter."[89] Once the emphasis is shifted to desire or the motivated interpretations of subjects, the value of things belongs to a different account. And as was shown above, treatments of the psychological and cultural vagaries of interpretation are inextricably bound to issues of economy.

The Production of Taste

There is a variety of conceptions under which the interpretive dynamics lending value to objects can be discussed, but among the most readily available is the concept of *taste*. Insofar as taste is a biological metaphor, it appears deceptively simple as an account of the desire of persons for objects, but the complexities mount as one assesses all the historical and structural components involved in the vagaries of taste. Consider a recent increasingly popular product, the "Swatch," a contemporary line of relatively inexpensive Swiss-made watches that come in many different colors and designs and of late have been produced in limited editions commemorating events, seasons, and other public codes. Given the relatively low cost and the combination of their coding and restriction in issue, Swatches have become collector's items, and crowds form at the Swatch counters of department stores as stamp collectors gather in anticipation of the latest issue. What, then, is a Swatch, and how does it achieve its value?

As a first approach to these questions, recall the now-anachronistic term, the *timepiece*. The dictionary eschews its social dimensions and baldly states that it is "an instrument for measuring and registering the passage of time." But even if we are restricted to this horologic aspect of a Swatch, its value cannot emerge from the facts of its ability to represent mechanically and electronically a conceptual model of temporality. To appreciate the value of a Swatch as a timepiece one must locate the historical development of the monitoring of time. There are of course many developments related to the modern tendency to monitor time in ever more precise ways, but the practices behind this tendency effectively begin in Adam Smith's century with the development of the transportation timetable. With the development of an industrial work force carried by transportation from residence to work place, it became necessary not only to order the process of moving a work force but also the responsibility of the individual to schedule precise arrivals and departures. This general development along with the growing administrative rationality of the modern state made the portable timepiece almost essential.

Therefore, to speak of a *timepiece* is to recognize implicitly many of the essential dimensions of the modern society and polity, which embodies "space-time ordering devices"[90] as the primary mechanisms through which work, governance, administration, and leisure are coordinated. The timepiece becomes valuable as such only in a society that closely coordinates such flows of people and things and that, accordingly, judges performance not simply on the basis of material accomplishments but also, and primarily, on *timeliness*.

Once the timepiece dimension of the Swatch is situated in the historically developing field of practices that summon timeliness as valuable, analysis of its value requires inquiry into social connections. The structure of the social bond is the major topic in the next chapter, but here it is important to note in a cursory way that the social is constructed not simply as a domain of functional coordination but also as a domain for the exchange of recognition. Thus, objects such as watches with functional significance also operate as signs in this exchange dynamic.

Considering first the recent emergence of the Swatch as a collectors item, it should be noted that collections can be understood as intimately involved in the identity dynamics through which people achieve recognition. The observations about museum collections made in chapter 1 are relevant here, particularly Susan Stewart's remarks about the collection-identity relationships:

> When objects are defined in terms of their use value, they serve as extensions of the body onto the environment, but when objects are defined by the collection, such an extension is inverted, serving to subsume the environment to a scenario of the personal. The ultimate term in the series that marks the collection is the "self," the articulation of the collector's own identity.[91]

Of course, in addition to the modern identity economy within which Swatches take on value as collectors items, one has to recognize aspects of the modern political economy that make it possible for some to collect things—differentials in income, storage and display space, and

so on. Not the least of the conditions of possibility for collecting are all
the historical dynamics associated with the violent triumph of seden-
tary, agriculturally based groupings over nomadic hunter-gatherers.
These latter groups also had objects with a primarily sign function
value, but their ability to collect and store was inhibited by their
tendency to be on the move.

The primary qualifications of a materialist reading of the tastes that
lend value to a Swatch are in place. It is evident that almost everything
involved in the emergence of the present, modern condition has a part
in providing the interpretive context that lends value to these particular
"timepieces." Perhaps the most important part of the context is spatial,
the condition in which media space, ranging from the relatively static
store window displays (by which Walter Benjamin marked the emergence of modernity) to the dynamic space-time venues of the printed
periodical, radio, and television, where objects are presented for acquisition. It is in these "spaces" that tastes are developed, modified, and
connected with other dimensions of social life. They provide the most
compelling domains in which to analyze the semiotic/interpretive aspects of political economy.

Although Adam Smith's approach to objects was primarily sensationalist rather than semiotic, he did have a place for culture in his approach
to value. Paradoxically, he even addressed himself to the dimension of
society based on an exchange of signs, and this perspective, treated for
the most part in his *Theory of Moral Sentiments*, sits uneasily with the
sensationalism that dominates his *Wealth of Nations*, where bodies meet
objects with very little by way of symbolic, social mediation.

Whereas on the one hand, Smith has each individual striving after
self-satisfaction, on the other hand, a consultation with his moral psychology developed in *The Theory of Moral Sentiments* (and repeated
somewhat ambiguously in parts of *The Wealth of Nations*) leads one to
believe that the Smithian self is more than a material satisfaction-seek-
ing body. It operates with an imagined spectator whose authority as an
immanent social conscience directs the self toward socially felicitous
conduct. This has led a recent commentator/analyst to argue that the
so-called Adam Smith problem—the compassion of *The Theory of
Moral Sentiments* alongside the selfishness of *The Wealth of Nations*—

dissipates with the recognition that the self has an immanent, responsible sociality, that "self-love" is not selfishness.[92]

Be that as it may, this dimension of Smith's thought is elaborated in chapter 3. Here, its relevance for the problem of value is significant. Although in many places, as has been noted, an object's materiality, refined and made available for use by labor and need-satisfying in its usable form, is predominant for Smith, in other places the object seems to be valuable because of the recognition it confers on the user. Thus, while he predicates his motivational model on individuals striving to better their condition, he ascribes to the striver a look at that "condition" from the standpoint of an Other.

Certainly, throughout *The Theory of Moral Sentiments*, Smith notes that [men] seek wealth because of the approbation it affords them.

> Nature, when she formed man for society, endowed him with an original desire to please, and an original aversion to offend his brethren. . . . She rendered their approbation most flattering and most agreeable to him for their own sake; and their disapprobation most mortifying and most offensive.[93]

Moreover, there is some evidence that the pursuit of individual gain, which Smith foregrounds in *The Wealth of Nations*, is contextualized by the valuing of approbation by the pursuer. Indeed, David Riesman has made a heroic attempt to locate Smith's political economy wholly within a reflexive sociology such that objects and wealth are valued primarily through the social positioning in the exchange of recognition they afford the consumer.[94]

But the quotations from *The Wealth of Nations* in support of this thesis are scarce and often enigmatic, and in many crucial places the theory is supported by either quotes from other Smith texts (particularly *The Theory of Moral Sentiments*) or other thinkers (e.g., Veblen and Polanyi). More-or-less clearly, the pursuit of gain creates the appeal of *action* choices for Smith in *The Wealth of Nations*, and however those actions may be viewed by the actor, who may be operating with an imagined peer or member of another class as observer, the objects themselves are still valued primarily as *things* that do not carry a complex cultural coding.

Smith well recognized that different types—that is, members of different classes—have an effective demand for different things. For example, "a very poor man may be said in some sense to have a demand for a coach and six; he might like to have it; but his demand is not an effectual demand, as the commodity can never be brought to market to satisfy it."[95] But Smith offers no logic that allows one to see how things become coded and, indeed, how demands, whether they become "effectual" or not, are summoned by the cultural coding within which objects are interpreted.

Riesman's vexed treatment of Adam Smith as a theorist of consumption notwithstanding, classical political economy from Smith onward was robustly oriented toward the production of commodities and anemically elaborated with respect to the vagaries of consumption. With the modern recognition that the value of products to consumers is often primarily a function of the social codes within which objects have significance, value and social identity become intimately connected.

As a result, to situate the value of objects it is necessary to invoke a semiological context and heed Greimas's argument about how it is the structure of determination of objects, not the objects themselves, that gives rise to value. Jean Baudrillard has summarized it well, while adding the important neo-structural concept of "social logic."

> Thus objects, their syntax, and their rhetoric refer to social objectives and to a social logic. They speak to us not so much of the user and of technical practices, as of social pretension and recognition, of social mobility and inertia, of acculturation and enculturation, of stratification and of social classification.[96]

Attuned to this social semiotic aspect of products, much of contemporary critical social theory concerned with political economy must articulate a logic of the social with a logic of the commodity. Pierre Bourdieu, who is among those who treat the semiotic sign exchange aspects of societies, has attempted just such an articulation in a treatment of "the correspondence between goods production and taste production."[97] Moreover, his analysis is particularly apposite for comparison with Adam Smith because, like Smith, he evokes the idea of a coordination mechanism.

In Smith's case, it would be appropriate to say that he put his *faith* in a mechanism inasmuch as Smith's mechanism, which coordinates individual acts to produce a felicitous social or aggregate outcome, is a result of a divine intention infused in "nature." In Bourdieu's case, the coordination is wholly secular, a feature of a social logic that has the effect of producing (and here Bourdieu is parodying the religious discourse) a "quasi-miraculous correspondence prevailing at every moment between the products offered by a field of production and the field of socially produced tastes."[98]

This social logic is not referenced in a religious scripture that speaks of a divine intention to produce a good, whether social, economic, or political but from an earthly textuality elaborated by Saussurean linguistics. It is a linguistics that develops the structural conditions of possibility for systems of intelligibility. The Saussurean logic of difference involves a series of polarities of presence and absence in sound making in the process of articulation that together build the phonemes from which intelligible utterances are assembled. It is this system of difference that Bourdieu uses to treat the articulation of produced goods and produced tastes.

As a first step to his dematerializing, symbolic approach to the value of objects, it is necessary to recognize that the "universe of products offered by each field of production tends in fact to limit the universe of the forms of experience (aesthetic, ethical, political, etc.) that are objectively possible at a given moment."[99] This is another analogy from structural linguistics, which, as elaborated for example by Roland Barthes, implies that the universe of possible utterances (*parole*) is circumscribed by the field of language (*langue*).[100] Analogously, then, the field of production of goods circumscribes the production of taste. Along with this logic is the vast field of activity in which advertising (in the broadest sense) is at the center, mediating the two fields.

There is another conceptual step involved in understanding the production of taste. It is a social logic of difference, drawn also from the structural linguistic model, and is perhaps best represented in the domain of fashion. Fashion—the changing of styles of vestment, cosmetics, and the like—makes sense only in a society where there is a contentiously charged social mobility. For example, in modern industrial societies, there is, as Bourdieu notes, an equivalence between economic power and age, but there is a gap between biological age and "social age," which is inferred from one's economic power position.

Thus, for example, the "audacities of the new bourgeoisie" hoping to displace the old bourgeoisie are given means of representation by fashion designers, who are, in turn, also involved in a struggle for prestige. In fashion design, therefore, "the newcomers to the field, young couturiers and designers, endeavoring to win acceptance of their subversive ideas, are the 'objective allies' of the new fractions and the younger generation of the new fractions of the bourgeoisie, for whom the symbolic revolution of which vestimentary and cosmetic outrages are the paradigm, are the perfect vehicle for expressing the ambiguity of their situation as the 'poor relations' of the temporal power."[101]

This is the correspondence that the social logic generates between the production of goods and the production of taste. The logic generates tastes on both sides of the divide in this case. The older economic powers, the conservative, entrenched bourgeoisie, also want a means of representation, and the older generation of couturiers and designers produce for them the vestments that allow them to distinguish themselves from the new vestimentary and cosmetic audaciousness with a specifically resistant set of clothes and "looks."

Therefore, as Bourdieu has put it, "choosing according to one's tastes" is controlled by a social logic of differentiation that emerges from the entire social, political, and economic order. Accordingly, to understand the value of the product in this domain is to read or interpret it in a way that extends that reading to the structure and dynamic of power relations within the social field.

Insofar as Adam Smith countenanced this aspect of class relations, it was not in a way that brought out this social logic, which interpretively imposes itself on objects such that they command a certain reading. In the field of economy, Smith was more attuned to one's ability to command labor, not recognition. In the field of morals, Smith was interested in the drive to command approbation, but he never clearly articulated the frames within which he analyzed this drive with his notions of value in his analyses of political economy. His focus on the drive to command respect was, rather, in the service of a moral psychology with which Smith theorized the social bond, a subject at the center of chapter 3. Here, it remains to summarize the problem of value that has been the subject of this chapter.

Summary

The main focus throughout this chapter has been on the relations between value and interpretation. It has been argued that, in general, how people "value" comes about through interpretive mediation, that the person-object and interpersonal confrontations in which value emerges are mediated by how these confrontations achieve meaning. As a corollary to this general position, it has been argued specifically that Adam Smith's constructions of value turn on *his* interpretive mediations, which are most evident in his historical narratives.

To develop the argument, however, some preliminary steps were necessary. Given the traditional (and, I argue, disenabling) approach to value, in which value provides the grounds of interpretation, the first step was crucial, for the analysis is predicated on a reversal of this relationship. It was argued that interpretation *produces* value. The reversal brought with it some additional counterintuitive corollaries, for example, that value is loss rather than gain, for it is made possible by a fixing of interpretation and therefore a suppression of contention.

The second step beyond this reversal requires a recognition of the place of interpretation within society. On the one hand, as was pointed out at the beginning of the chapter, social relations require a fixing of interpretations, for the social is a function of some degree of mutual intelligibility. On the other hand, the cost of institutionalizing some structures of intelligibility, of stabilizing some interpretations, is the suppression of creative political contention. Insofar as interpretation produces value, the stabilizing of interpretation is politically constraining.

The next step, then, is to link the contributions of thinkers/writers to the interpretive struggles within the social body, and here it has been argued that Adam Smith's historical narratives reinforce and stabilize interpretations and do so, moreover, within a model of writing that denies the writer's political role. It follows that much of the details of Smith's theory of value focused on what he spoke about—the contributions of labor, land, stock, and so on—and were insensitive to the possible interpretive complicities and resistances it contained. In general, his way of interpreting historical dynamics emphasized harmony and suppressed contention, and his way of treating space naturalized boundaries and suppressed the practices through which they are formed, policed, and resisted.

In order to resist the depoliticizing emphases in Smith's writing, which in many ways continue to support a depoliticized reading of the orders of modernity, his writing is continually juxtaposed to the alternatives above. Accordingly, Smith's sensationalism or empiricist construal of the collisions of persons and things was juxtaposed to a phenomenological and then a semiological view of values to challenge the implicit narrative of value resident in sensationalist versions.

At the level of his larger narratives, his accounts of historical developments, Smith's tendency to write linear histories was juxtaposed to the writing of those who posit more complex trajectories and thereby resist the teleological and mythic forms of legitimizing that emerge from Smith's accounts.

Once the role of Smith's stories and sensationalism within his position on value was presented and confronted, the attention turned to recent, more critical accounts of the problem of value in modernity. Here, analyses that dematerialize political economy and explicitly treat interpretive mediations are foregrounded. The foundational contributions of psychoanalysis and the anthropology of exchanges to such critical perspectives were presented as a prelude to imagining a social structure in which the exchange of signs dominates the exchange of products.

More generally, what this revealed was the tendency in Adam Smith and classical political economists as a whole to neglect the imbrication of culture and economy. When these two domains are brought together, the concept of taste achieves important recognition, and a contemporary political economy, one attuned to the conditions of the present, can be seen to revolve more around the production of taste than of things. What becomes important are the codes within which subjects are formed and interpret themselves in such a way that some "things" have value. The ground of such interpretation is a social logic that allies certain users of signs with certain producers of them.

The result of this orientation toward the social is, as was the case with Smith, to see the social domain as a function of knowledge but to base that knowledge not on the sensations that belong to embodiment but on the dimensions of bodies that emerge from interpretive struggles. This chapter thus closes with an eye on the social bond, which is the primary subject of chapter 3.

Notes

1. R. H. Campbell and A. S. Skinner, "General Introduction" to Adam Smith, *An Inquiry into the Nature and Causes of the Wealth of Nations* (Indianapolis, IN: Liberty Classics, 1976), Vol. 1. See pages 50-60 for the treatment of Smith's use of history.

2. Donald Winch, *Adam Smith's Politics: An Essay in Historiographic Revision* (Cambridge, UK: Cambridge University Press, 1978), 63.

3. Arkady Plotnitsky, "Interpretation, Interminability, Evaluation: From Nietzsche toward a General Economy," in John Fekete, ed., *Life After Postmodernism: Essays on Value and Culture* (New York: St. Martins, 1987), 127.

4. Plotnitsky, "Interpretation, Interminability, Evaluation," 128.

5. Michel Pecheux, "Discourse: Structure or Event," in Cary Nelson and Lawrence Grossberg, eds., *Marxism and the Interpretation of Culture* (Urbana, IL: University of Illinois Press, 1988), 638.

6. Hayden White, "The Value of Narrativity in the Representation of Reality," *Critical Inquiry*, 7 (Autumn, 1980), 8.

7. Benedict Anderson, *Imagined Communities* (London: Verso, 1983).

8. Jean-Francois Lyotard, *Des Dispositifs Pulsionnels* (Paris: Christian Bourgois, 1980), 170-71.

9. Thorstein Veblen, "The Preconceptions of the Classical Economists," in *The Portable Veblen*, ed. Max Lerner (New York: Viking, 1948), 241.

10. Veblen, "Preconceptions," 242.

11. Joseph Cropsey, "The Invisible Hand: Moral and Political Considerations," in Gerald O'Driscoll, ed., *Adam Smith and Modern Political Economy* (Ames, IA: Iowa State University Press, 1979), 172.

12. Cropsey, "The Invisible Hand," 173.

13. Adam Smith, *Lectures on Rhetoric and Belles Lettres* ed. J. C. Bryce (Oxford: The Clarendon Press, 1983), Lecture 3, 9-24.

14. Veblen, "Preconceptions," 242.

15. Veblen, "Preconceptions," 243.

16. Veblen, "Preconceptions," 247.

17. Adam Smith, *An Inquiry into the Nature and Causes of the Wealth of Nations* (Indianapolis, IN: Liberty Classics, 1981), Vol. 1, 72.

18. Smith, *Lectures on Rhetoric*, 89.

19. This expression is from Istvan Hont and Michael Ignatieff, "Needs and Justice in the 'Wealth of Nations,' " in Istvan Hont and Michael Ignatieff, eds., *Wealth and Virtue* (Cambridge, UK: Cambridge University Press, 1983), 2.

20. Adam Smith, *Lectures on Jurisprudence* ed. R. L. Meek, D. D. Raphael, & P. G. Stein (Oxford: The Clarendon Press, 1978), 139.

21. Henri Lefebre, "Reflections on the Politics of Space," trans. Michael J. Enders, *Antipode*, 8 (May 1976), 33.

22. Ann Bermingham, *Landscape and Ideology: The English Rustic Tradition, 1740-1860* (Berkeley, CA: University of California Press, 1986), "Introduction," 1.

23. Smith, *Wealth of Nations*, Vol. 1, chap. 2, 29-30.

24. Gilles Deleuze & Felix Guattari, *The Anti-Oedipus*, trans. Robert Hurley, Mark Sexton, & Helen A. Lane (New York: Viking Press, 1977), 34ff.

25. Smith, *Lectures on Rhetoric*, 116.

26. This part of the discussion is based on the analysis of Gillian Beer, *Darwin's Plots* (London: Routledge and Kegan Paul, 1983).

27. Beer, *Darwin's Plots*, 58.

28. Beer, *Darwin's Plots*, 50.

29. Erich Auerbach, *Mimesis*, trans. William R. Trask (Princeton, NJ: Princeton University Press, 1968), 19.

30. Smith, *Wealth of Nations*, Vol. 2, chap. 1, 695.

31. Smith, *Wealth of Nations*, Vol. 2, chap. 2, passim.

32. For a more elaborate analysis of the pious structure of Franklin's autobiography, see Michael J. Shapiro, *The Politics of Representation: Writing Practices in Biography, Photography and Policy Analysis* (Madison, WI: University of Wisconsin Press, 1988), 56-59.

33. Frank Kermode, "Secrets and Narrative Sequence," *Critical Inquiry, 7* (Autumn 1980), 85.

34. Kermode, "Secrets and Narrative Sequence," 85.

35. Kermode, "Secrets and Narrative Sequence," 85.

36. Fernand Braudel, *The Wheels of Commerce: Civilization and Capitalism 15th-18th Century, Vol. 2*, trans. Siân Reynolds (New York: Harper & Row), 1982), 26.

37. Braudel, *Wheels of Commerce*, 26.

38. Fernand Braudel, *Afterthoughts on Material Civilization and Capitalism*, trans. Patricia M. Ranum (Baltimore, MD: Johns Hopkins University Press, 1977), 6.

39. Braudel, *Afterthoughts on Material Civilization*, 7.

40. Braudel, *Afterthoughts on Material Civilization*, 18-19.

41. Braudel, *Afterthoughts on Material Civilization*, 58-59.

42. Braudel, *Afterthoughts on Material Civilization*, 58-59.

43. Gianni Vattimo, *The End of Modernity*, trans. Jon R. Snyder (Baltimore, MD: Johns Hopkins University Press, 1988), 8.

44. Vattimo, *End of Modernity*, 9-10.

45. Adam Smith, "Of the External Senses," in *Essays on Philosophical Subjects* (Indianapolis, IN: Liberty Classics, 1982), 168.

46. Adam Smith, "The History of Astronomy," in *Essays on Philosophical Subjects* (Indianapolis, IN: Liberty Classics, 1982), 61.

47. Smith, "History of Astronomy," 35.

48. Smith, "History of Astronomy," 37.

49. Smith, "History of Astronomy," 40.

50. Maurice Merleau-Ponty, *The Structure of Behavior*, trans. Alden L. Fisher (Boston: Beacon, 1963), 13. Also, at roughly mid century John Dewey and Arthur Bentley challenged the materialist sensational narrative and substituted a semiotic model of significance in which an interpreting subject plays a role in lending meaning to objects. Rather than focusing on the intentionality of consciousness, their emphasis is on "sign behavior." See their *Knowing and the Known* (Boston: Beacon, 1949).

51. Merleau-Ponty, *Structure of Behavior*, 166.

52. Merleau-Ponty, *Structure of Behavior*, 170.

53. Merleau-Ponty, *Structure of Behavior*, 161.

54. Smith, "History of Astronomy," 105.

55. Karl Marx, *Capital*, Vol. 1, trans. Ben Fowkes (New York: Vintage, 1977), 126.

56. Smith, *Lectures on Jurisprudence*, 487.

57. Alfred Marshall, *Principles of Economics* (London: Macmillan, 1907).

58. Smith, *Wealth of Nations*, Vol. 1, 454.

59. Smith, *Wealth of Nations*, Vol. 1, 39.

60. Louis Dumont, *From Mandeville to Marx* (Chicago: University of Chicago Press, 1977), 190.

61. Smith, *Wealth of Nations*, Vol. 1, 47.

62. Smith, *Wealth of Nations*, Vol. 1, 73.

63. Dumont, *From Mandeville to Marx*, 93.

64. Algirdas Julien Greimas, "A Problem of Narrative Semiotics: Objects of Value," in *On Meaning: Selected Writings in Semiotic Theory* (Minneapolis: University of Minnesota Press, 1987), 86.

65. Jacques Lacan, "Kant with Sade," trans. James B. Swenson, Jr., *October* (Winter 1989), 67.

66. Greimas, "Problem of Narrative Semiotics," 86.

67. Greimas, "Problem of Narrative Semiotics," 87.

68. A. J. Greimas, "Structure and History," in *The Social Sciences: A Semiotic View* (Minneapolis: University of Minnesota Press, 1990), 93.

69. Greimas, "Problem of Narrative Semiotics," 92.

70. Greimas, "Problem of Narrative Semiotics," 93.

71. Greimas, "Problem of Narrative Semiotics," 93.

72. Michel Foucault, "Of Other Spaces," trans. Jay Miscowiec, *Diacritics*, *16* (Spring 1986), 22.

73. Foucault, "Of Other Spaces," 23.

74. Smith, *Wealth of Nations*, Bk. 1, chap. 7, 73.

75. See Gilles Deleuze, *Foucault*, ed. and trans. Sean Hand (Minneapolis: University of Minnesota Press, 1986), 23-44.

76. Michel Foucault, *Discipline and Punish: The Birth of the Prison*, trans. Alan Sheridan (New York: Pantheon, 1977), 293-308.

77. Adam Smith, *The Theory of Moral Sentiments*, Glasgow Edition, ed. D. D. Raphael & A. L. Macfie (Indianapolis, IN: Liberty Classics, 1982), 67.

78. Sigmund Freud, "Three Essays on the Theory of Sexuality," *Standard Edition of the Complete Psychological Works of Sigmund Freud*, Vol. 7, ed. and trans. James Strachey (London: Hogarth Press, 1953).

79. Freud, "Three Essays on the Theory of Sexuality," 135-36.

80. Freud, "Three Essays on the Theory of Sexuality," 147-48.

81. For a good discussion of the implications of Freud's revolutionary separation of the sexual instinct and aim, see Arnold Davidson, "How to do the History of Psychoanalysis: A Reading of Freud's *Three Essays on the History of Sexuality*," in Francoise Melzer, ed., *The Trial(s) of Psychoanalysis* (Chicago: University of Chicago Press, 1988), 39-64.

82. Marcel Mauss, *The Gift*, trans. Ian Cinnison (London: Cohen & West, 1970), 1.

83. Pierre Bourdieu, *Distinction: A Social Critique of the Judgment of Taste*, trans. Richard Nice (Cambridge, MA: Harvard University Press, 1984), 99-168.

84. Jean Baudrillard, "Towards a Critique of the Political Economy of the Sign," in *For a Critique of the Political Economy of the Sign*, trans. Charles Levin (St. Louis, MO: Telos Press, 1981). George Bataille, *The Accursed Share*, Vol. 1, trans. Robert Hurley (New York: Zone Books, 1988).

85. Smith, *Wealth of Nations*, Vol. 1, 80.

86. Raymond Williams, *Marxism and Literature* (Oxford: Oxford University Press, 1977), 115.

87. E. P. Thompson, *The Making of the English Working Class* (New York: Vintage, 1966), 280-281.

88. Lawrence Birken, *Consuming Desires* (Ithaca, New York: Cornell University Press, 1988), 31.

89. Marx, *Capital*, Vol. 1, 126.

90. This expression belongs to Anthony Giddens in *The Nation-State and Violence* (Berkeley, CA: University of California Press, 1985). See especially chap. 7, "Administrative Power and Internal Pacification," 172-97.

91. Stewart, *On Longing*, 162.

92. Jean-Pierre Dupuy, "Deconstruction and the Liberal Order," *SubStance*, *62/63* (1990), 110-24.

93. Smith, *Moral Sentiments*, 116.

94. David A. Riesman, *Adam Smith's Sociological Economics* (London: Croom, Helm, 1976).

95. Smith, *Wealth of Nations*, Vol. 1, 73.

96. Jean Baudrillard, "Sign Function and Class Logic," in *For a Critique of the Political Economy of the Sign*, trans. Charles Levin (St. Louis: Telos Press, 1981), 38.

97. Pierre Bourdieu, *Distinction: A Social Critique of Judgment*, trans. Richard Nice (Cambridge, MA: Harvard University Press, 1984), 230ff.

98. Bourdieu, *Distinction*, 231.

99. Bourdieu, *Distinction*, 231-32.

100. See Roland Barthes, *Elements of Semiology*, trans. Annette Lavers & Colin Smith (London: Jonathan Cape, 1967), 13-23.

101. Bourdieu, *Distinction*, 233.

3

The Social Bond

Introduction: 'Manning' the Frontiers

Throughout his *Theory of Moral Sentiments*, Adam Smith isolates the stoic virtue of self-command. In his view this virtue, along with the human tendency toward a natural sympathy, makes possible an ordered society, ruled by compassion and non-selfish judgments. Like others in the history of social thought, Smith found it important to distinguish the aspects of human character that make such a social domain possible. However, such distinguishing required two forms of discrimination. Smith sought not only to isolate the aspects of the human body most implicated in collisions with other bodies in the social domain but also to determine what is significantly exorbitant, that is, to distinguish those bodies that do not qualify as human. Accordingly, he addressed himself to what has been, throughout the history of human civilization, the major boundary issue: the human-animal distinction.

As was noted in the previous chapters, Smith was generally preoccupied with boundaries, and the boundary between the sacred and the secular is the primary one on which his views impact, for his moral psychology was an explicit attempt to locate the venue of morals as social rather than sacred space. Smith's moral psychology is elaborated later, but to summarize, he posited two forces shaping the interpersonal exchanges in social space. First, there are the passions a person evinces as a result of the passions exhibited by others, and second, there are the judgments of others' actions made possible by a person's ability to adopt the perspective of an "impartial observer." Smith's model of the social was therefore not only intensely interpersonal but also a matter of direct, visual engagement.

In the domain of morals, as in the domain of economy and value (treated in chapter 2), Smith was a sensationalist. In the case of his model of the economy, he foregrounded the sensational effects of a meeting of bodies and objects, whereas in the case of morals, the sensational effects result from the meeting of bodies with bodies, mediated by observation. The sentiments that for him are the major constituents of moral apprehension are the passions produced by sympathetic bodily sensations. Since the major eligibility to participate in the moral sphere is having a body, it was inevitable that the question of the capacity for moral practices of other embodied creatures should come up for Smith. Because animals are creatures that both invite sympathetic passions and are themselves capable of them, it is not surprising that he was led to a consideration of the place of animals in the exchange of sentiments.

He brought to this consideration his characteristic, Newtonian penchant for universalizing, noting that in *all* animals, the things that cause pain or pleasure "immediately excite [these] two passions of gratitude and resentment."[1] He went on to suggest that given their ability to experience those sentiments, animals are "less improper objects of gratitude and resentment than inanimated objects."[2] But despite being "less improper," and although they are capable of feeling those sensations, animals are not "complete and perfect objects either of gratitude or resentment,"[3] because they lack one important dimension involved in the human exchange of sentiments. When there is a "concord" perceived between one's sentiments and those of another, there is a reassurance that one is being esteemed:

> What most of all charms us in our benefactor, is the concord between his sentiments and our own, with regard to what interests us so nearly as the worth of our own character, and the esteem that is due us. We are delighted to find a person who values us as we value ourselves, and distinguishes us from the rest of mankind, with an attention not unlike that with which we distinguish ourselves.[4]

Smith therefore denies animals a human moral standing in the exchange of sentiments because they are not able to make critical judgments of worthiness. Their passions do not weigh in as heavily in the human prestige system because those on whom they bestow their sentiments are not able to feel sufficiently esteemed as a result.

Two important and overlapping interpersonal economies are evoked in Smith's reference to the place of animals in the exchange of sentiments. First, he locates them as both subjects and objects in the system of exchange but devalues their sentiments. Second, in devaluing their sentiments, he locates the primary social economy to which the exchange of sentiments is connected, the exchange of esteem. In this perhaps more fundamental economy, only humans can participate meaningfully and plausibly.

Like Smith, many contemporary thinkers are drawn to a consideration of the human-animal boundary, for, also like Smith, they develop their notions of the social bond on the basis of both embodiment and a capacity that transcends it. For example, there is this formulation in Werner Stark's contemporary treatment of the social bond: "Man's uniqueness consists in his capacity to *control* his animality, a capacity which is denied to the rest of the animal world."[5] In general, both before and since Smith, theories of morality have been most often predicated on ontologies in which the essentially "human" involves both some aspect of embodiment and, paradoxically, a capacity to transcend embodiment or "animal nature."

Therefore, on two important counts, Adam Smith (and others who continue to share his ontology) is at odds with modern thought. First, because he relied on a notion of transcendence, his thinking must confront a desacrilized modernity in which the very idea of transcendence has been almost totally impeached. Second, because, as it will emerge, he also tied morals to nature and embodiment, his thinking must confront a (post-Kantian) modernity in which naturalistic forms of ethics and political legitimation have been seriously discredited.

The Smith-modernity confrontation to follow takes many forms, but there are two dimensions that must be distinguished at this point. First, the construction of the social bond requires, as has been noted, a boundary drawing that determines who or what is eligible to participate. Second, the construction of the social bond requires distinguishing certain human attributes as the socially relevant ones. Harking back to the sovereignty idea developed in chapter 1, we could say that a construction of the social bond begins with an argument for the sovereignty of the human but then moves on to a model of proto-sovereignty, an argument for the socially relevant human attributes that determine the shape of human association.

To begin the Smith-modernity confrontation, we start with the more general sovereignty issue and confront Smith's conceptual building blocks with a set of texts that take modernity a step further, into a future in which technology has dissociated both transcendence and the "natural" from their familiar contexts.

Humans, Androids, and Electric Sheep

Traditionally, when thinkers have emphasized the transcendence of animality involved in self-command, they have been thinking of an effort of will, judgment, or some wholly autonomous exercise of a human capacity. But the traditional moral thinker would lack the usual props if dropped onto Philip Dick's dystopic earth planet, early in the 21st century, for the conditions of possibility for thinking about human identity and moral conduct are altered there. Dick's novel, *Do Androids Dream of Electric Sheep*, is politicizing in a special sense. By altering the context in which human attributes function, they take on a different significance and therefore change from implacable facts about "human nature" to highly contingent dimensions of human subjectivity.

One aspect of the altered context is a result of technology. In the very first scene, Rick Deckard and his wife Iran are arguing over the settings on their "Penfields" (mood organs). In Adam Smith's universe, people's sentiments tend toward a natural harmony. Indeed, the musical metaphor so dominates Smith's discourse on the social bond that in one of his explications he has the sentiment of one in pain "beat time" with the level of sympathy [he] can reasonably expect from an observer.[6] The figuration dominating Smith's thinking is elaborated below. Here it should be noted that, in stark contrast, in Dick's futuristic universe sentiments are harmonized not naturally but through manipulation, and the music is the noise of the Penfield as the novel opens:

> A merry little surge of electricity piped by automatic alarm from the mood organ beside his bed awakened Rick Deckard.[7]

An argument between Deckard and his wife ensues when she refuses to set her Penfield at a compatible level (his is at a cheerful and energetic "D" setting and hers at a grumpy and lethargic "C"). Another major alteration in the identity structure in Dick's world is the cast of characters. In addition to humans and animals (both live and artificial), are "rogue androids." Because of a global atomic war, most of the animals are extinct, and many humans, including Deckard, own artificial ones. Owning only an electric sheep, Deckard tries unsuccessfully to get his neighbor, who will soon have two "real" horses, to sell him one. Failing that, and unable to find an affordable pet in the national catalogue of live animals or on "animal row," a string of retail outlets of live pets, Deckard decides to take a difficult assignment in his role as a "bounty hunter." This brings him into a confrontation with androids.

The androids were produced by a large corporation as part of the strategy to encourage emigration from earth's deteriorating condition. Those who emigrated did so to avoid mental deterioration from the radioactive fallout and to enjoy a better life-style, which would include the ownership of android servants, on another planet. Occasionally, however, androids would resist the docile roles for which they were invented and return to earth as dangerous killers. Bounty hunters were hired to eliminate them. Deckard's assignment is particularly difficult, for the escapees he is pursuing are an advanced model that exceed many humans in intelligence and, most significantly, cannot be unambiguously detected with the use of an empathy test that had been successful in detecting previous models.

It is the androids' lack of human empathy that sets up the complex pattern of identity relations structuring Dick's story. The people remaining on earth are involved in a fierce struggle to maintain their human identities. The primary identity threat is mental deterioration. Humans who degenerate below a particular level of mental competence are regarded as a "special," and, "once pegged as a special, a citizen, even if accepting sterilization, dropped out of history. He ceased, in effect, to be part of mankind."[8] Another significant identity threat stems from the difficulty of distinguishing androids from humans. Because androids lack empathy, they are not sympathetic to or sentimental about animals. Humans use their pet ownership to help maintain their human credentials, and if it is discovered that a pet is artificial (the threat that Deckard is facing), the rationale for the pet is obviated.

Therefore, structuring Dick's narrative is an identity triangle with humans, animals, and androids at the corners, and positive or negative valences along the sides. To disassociate themselves from androids, humans must associate themselves with animals, which are in turn disassociated from androids if they are "real." The dynamic proceeds from Deckard's task of attempting to retire rogue androids in order to be able to afford a live pet, which he wants in order to distinguish himself from androids. Apart from the identity logic in which the three different creature types are implicated is the fact that Dick's world is Smithian; the social bond is based on moral sentiments. However, in this case, there is an additional dimension, an instability in the identities that determine who or what is a worthy object of sympathetic identification. Given that humanlike and animal-like creatures have been made as well as or better than what "nature" can produce, nature can no longer be counted on to inscribe its work clearly.

The animal remains an important identity sign within the human social bond, but given both the stakes and the ambiguities of the situation, the activity involved in appropriating the sign is more feverish and disturbed than it was in the predystopian earthly condition. And, given the presence of the pseudo-human android, the animal-as-sign must play an additional role. Throughout human history (and prehistory) humans privileged their identity by distinguishing themselves from (mere) animals while, at the same time, distinguishing among themselves on the basis of relations with animals. In Dick's cruel new world, there is an additional frontier to police, and the animal must play a role in helping humans to maintain the android as other.[9]

Philip Dick's world is already upon us, for the existence of cyborgs has brought with it the kind of identity issue that his novel explores. Before treating this newer, or second frontier, however, the first one bears further scrutiny.

The First Frontier

Humanity's concern with its ontological condition may have always involved speculation about the human-animal relationship. According to Georges Bataille, evidence of this exists in the prehistoric wall paintings in the Lascaux caves. Resisting the view that the preponderance of the hunting thematic suggests the food fantasies of hungry hunters, Bataille sees the paintings as evidence of humanity's attempt to achieve separation as beings from animals.

> Resolutely, decisively, man wrenched himself out of the animal condition and into 'manhood': that abrupt, most important of transitions left an image of itself blazed upon the rock of this cave.[10]

What is the evidence for this interpretation? Among what Bataille sees in the paintings are prohibitions relating to death rituals and sexuality, and it is through this domain of normativity, he argues, that humans are distinguished from other sentient beings. Here, as in other later texts, humans recognize their animality, but something is added in the form of a troubling normativity: "The enduring animality in us forever introduces raw life and nature into the community: prohibitions exist to quell these uprisings and spread oil on the sea of insurgent animal passion and unruliness."[11] The step from animal to "man" "is conditioned upon recognizing prohibitions and upon violating them."[12]

According to Bataille, therefore, the Lascaux cave paintings are to be read symbolically rather than materialistically. They are imaginative enactments in which humans are extracting their identities from animality rather than meditations on the importance of the hunt in producing the food necessary for human survival. One detail Bataille uses in making this case for his interpretation bears special attention here, and it arises in Ridley Scott's *Blade Runner*, a film version of Dick's story. It is the presence of an imaginary animal in the paintings, a unicorn whose presence suggests that animals are being treated in terms of a relationship to an ontological concern, the relationship of a creature to truth. In *Blade Runner*, Gaff, a police detective, makes origami figures, one animal, one human with a tail, and one unicorn, which he leaves near Deckard's apartment. And, in the director's version of the film, there is a short scene with a unicorn galloping. These two unicorn representations, like the unicorn in the Lascaux caves, seems to represent an iconic meditation on human identity boundaries.

If we accept Bataille's view that the human use of animal/others has had primarily an identity-constituting function, that humans have always located animals within the discursive economies with which they distinguish themselves, it should be evident that the meanings assigned to animal-human relationships are associated with heavy symbolic investments. The borders constructed as prehistoric humans distinguished themselves from animals have therefore since been assiduously patrolled.

This has been nowhere more apparent than in the continuing fascination with monkeys and apes, who by dint of their upright postures, humanoid appearance, and social capabilities have presented the most serious challenge to the policing of the human-animal frontier. Aware of this fascination, Franz Kafka mocked humanity's efforts to distinguish itself from apes in a story in which an ape, desperate to escape its confinement, carefully studies the human behavior in proximity to its cage and, in time, "managed," as the ape put it, "to reach the cultural level of an average European."[13]

Putting it less ironically but nevertheless aptly, Donna Haraway has also noted the human preoccupation with simians:

> Monkeys and apes have a privileged relation to nature and culture for western people: simians occupy the border zones between those potent mythic poles. . . . The commercial and scientific traffic in monkeys and apes is a traffic in meanings.[14]

This trafficking has been apparent in a variety of writing genres. For example, Edgar Rice Burroughs's commercial success with his Tarzan stories is not unrelated to the boundary flirtation that Tarzan, the "ape-man," with his ambiguous background and behavior, represents. In the very first Tarzan story, Burroughs plays with the boundary in an episode in which Tarzan, behaving as an animal/predator, kills a local black tribesman and is on the verge of treating his victim as fresh meat. At the moment he is about to dine, Tarzan is apparently without the "moral sentiments" that Adam Smith and others have seen as distinctive to humans, even though Burroughs has given him the raw materials for such sentiments—various aspects of human embodiment and their associated capacities, and even added class distinctions:

> How may we judge him, by what standards, this ape-man with the heart and head and body of an English gentleman, and the training of a wild beast?[15]

The question of judgment quickly becomes moot, however, as Burroughs has immanence substitute for training. "A qualm of nausea" inhibits Tarzan, as human norms (which Burroughs seems to treat as universal) manifest themselves in the form of a counterinstinct.

> All he knew was that he could not eat the flesh of this black man, and this hereditary instinct, ages old, usurped the functions of his untaught mind and saved him from transgressing a worldwide law of whose very existence he was ignorant.[16]

Burroughs's Tarzan stories play with the human-animal boundary but maintain it nevertheless. For Burroughs, as for Bataille, the human is extracted from the domain of the animal by virtue of the prohibition.

Social science discourses, like those in the literary/commercial domain, also provide evidence for Haraway's suggestion that scrutiny of apes and monkeys is a "traffic in meanings." When it is discovered that simians appear to transgress a boundary used to maintain human distinctiveness, a new frontier is created to protect it. For example, in a recent discussion of the nature of the social link for baboons and humans, the authors grant that not only do baboons have a relatively well articulated social order but also that, like humans, their social order is "performative," they actively negotiate its structures. Once this is admitted, however, the frontier must be "manned." Accordingly, they pose the question: "When we transform baboons into active performers of their society, does this put them on a par with humans?"[17] Their answer is no. Unable to use either sociality or action-oriented linguisticality to maintain human distinctiveness, they turn to the "practical means" through which humans versus baboons perform the social and argue that, while humans have material resources and symbols, baboons have "only themselves, only their bodies as resources."[18]

This argument is more dogged than convincing. Haraway undoubtedly has it right when she says, "By the late twentieth century in United States scientific culture, the boundary between human and animal is thoroughly breached. The last beachheads of uniqueness have been polluted if not turned into amusement parks—language, toll use, social behavior, mental events, nothing really convincingly settles the separation of human and animal."[19]

The border war continues as strategies for maintaining the frontier are altered each time new evidence impeaches earlier modes for distinguishing humans from animals. The frontier shifts, but a distinction remains. Paradoxically, however, the human drive to be distinguished from animals has often required greater intimacy with them. For example, the mentality involved in maintaining the historical gulf between urban bourgeois classes and the peasantry has been based in part on the mode of intimacy with animals.

As bourgeois classes developed, especially in the 19th century, part of their distinctiveness was based on the greater degree of segregation between their living quarters and those of animals. They expressed contempt at the animal-like existence of the peasantry, who allowed farm animals into their living quarters. "The whole upbringing of the 19th-century bourgeois was based upon a notion of moral superiority to the more bestial lower classes. He had mastered the animal within."[20] However, as one historical analysis has shown, "at the same time that the urban bourgeoisie was complaining about the cohabitation of men and animals in the peasant villages, distinctions were being created between animals. Pets became very important in 19th-century society. . . . While it was considered highly improper to have piglets or hens running around in the living room, a lapdog in bed or a kitten on one's knee was something quite different."[21]

Part of the reason for this is the connection noted above, made by writers from Adam Smith to Philip Dick, between keeping pets and having good moral sentiments. "Caring for animals was thought to make people into better human beings."[22] Thus, the special value placed on owning pets, their importance in the boundary maintenance behavior of the humans who remain on earth in Dick's *Do Androids Dream of Electric Sheep*, has a continuity with the mentality of bourgeois city dwellers in earlier periods.

The Second Frontier

In Dick's novel, and in Ridley Scott's film version of the story, the altered cast of characters, notably the presence of cyborgs, "creatures simultaneously animal and machine, who populate worlds ambiguously natural and crafted,"[23] produces an immense complication for the construction of a stable and distinct human identity. And, at the same time, it underscores the extent to which the *human* identity is not simply a natural fact but an aggressive achievement involving, among other things, complex temporal strategies.

For example, in Scott's film, the androids replicate humanity's concern with temporal or historical continuity by showing a preoccupation with their past as well as their future. While the story line has the androids seeking to endure—to alter the codes that make them short-timers—it also has them seeking to manufacture a past. One android, Leon, collects pictures of someone else's past in order to manufacture a past he has not lived. Deckard, who also has photos around his apartment, expresses surprise at Leon's interest in this ersatz past. And later, Rachel, another android, displays a lot of interest in Deckard's photos, which seem to reach back over several generations. At a minimum, the issue of the photographs encourages reflection on the human-cyborg boundary by evoking a strong similarity between Deckard and Leon as collectors of photos.

Rachel is the one replicant with a manufactured memory and, because she has been kept ignorant of being a replicant, has played the dual role of an employee of the android manufacturing firm as well as its product. During a conversation with Deckard in his apartment, after she suspects she is an android, Deckard tells her that her memory is an "implant" and proves it by reciting details he could only have seen in a corporation file. The purpose of the implant was to make her think she is human. This is not surprising, for human self-understandings are organized in the form of narratives. If one compares the meaning structure of visual arts with that of human identity, as one analyst has, it becomes clear that self-knowledge and coherence require more than simply "wide-angle introspection" to "afford a coherent idea of one's personhood."[24] What must be included is a story, a "life story," for narrative plays an essential role in the development of a unified individual identity."[25]

However, as has been argued, there is that which forms identity by being integral to it—and narrative plays a part here—and there is that which forms identity by containing it and setting it apart from otherness. In the context of the social network on earth in *Blade Runner*, a narrative going back to childhood makes a self coherent by giving it temporal extension, but it has an additional significance. The fact of having had a childhood is a form of distinction with special value because of the nearness of android/others who have *not* had one.

Before the film is over, however, both dimensions of the coherence structure of the human are called into question. What does it mean to have real memories or a real past? Although this question is never explicitly raised in the film, the postmodern, dystopian world within which the action takes place—a world that is overcoded, that contains an unmanageable jumble of advertising appeals from disembodied voices along with a heteroglot of language and speech styles that threaten both self-understanding and mutual intelligibility—makes an implicit point. It is that the stuff from which memory can be made, expressed, rehearsed, and so on, is not owned by anyone. The issue of the ownership of signification has always been complex and problematic, and in the world of *Blade Runner* it is even more difficult to claim that a person can control meaning structures. Once reflected upon, it becomes evident that memory is never "natural," for codes are human inventions. Inasmuch as one cannot have a past without codes—without ways of inscribing and giving significance to it—it is problematic to say that one "has memories." *Blade Runner*'s Los Angeles of 2019, in which the very humanity of the inventors of the codes is being called into question, places an additional tax on the ownership of memory.

Where memory fails as a distinguishing characteristic of humans, so does the motivation to which it is connected—the desire to endure in the sense of having a long future. Even what seems to be the primary drive of humans to continue living is shared with androids, who develop that motivation by themselves. This shared and pervasive desire is emphasized when, at one point, one of the flying advertising vehicles promoting emigration to the "offworld" with the slogan "live on the offworld," has its sound system malfunction. The message comes out with the endlessly repeated "live on, live on, live on, live on . . ."

The failure of past and future orientations to distinguish adequately between humans and cyborgs moves in the direction of the primary deconstructive effect of the filmic story as a whole, which focuses on the identity boundaries humans use to maintain their coherence and exclusivity. What is especially important to note is that this is not the kind of problem one should consign to "science fiction," for it resonates with more contemporary identity problematics. The human-cyborg frontier that Dick and Scott explore has already been opened up. It has existed in prototypic form in the social and political discourses that have attempted to distinguish an authentic humanity from that which is manifested in modernity's increasingly instrumental modes of rationality, within which calculable and subservient forms of subjectity are in evidence. In both Dick's novel and Scott's film, the theme is very contemporary. However, rather than simply lamenting the losses humanity experiences as a result of modern technology, which is a traditional, conservative critique of modernity, Dick's novel and Scott's film deconstruct the primary opposition, that between nature and culture or artifice, with which the traditional criticism works.[26] The "manning" of the second frontier takes place in a world in which technology has all but effaced it.

Where can one turn to examine the impetus for the making of this second frontier? Just as an anthropological imagination was helpful in disclosing the identity concerns directing the constitution of the human-animal frontier, it can be effectively applied to the human-cyborg frontier. When humans have tried to distinguish themselves from animals, the primary strategy has been to locate humanity in a meaning frame in which they have a capacity that transcends the merely physical—hence the special emphasis on "moral sentiments," the capacity for which involves more than mere physicality.

However, in the confrontation with the cyborg, the strategy has been partly reversed, for cyborgs, it would seem, are machines; they have been made in contrast to humans, who are "physical." But, "the boundary between physical and non-physical is very imprecise for us,"[27] and, indeed, one of the androids in *Blade Runner* says, "We're not machines . . . we're physical." This claim is reflective of the many ambiguities that develop as Deckard tries to do his job of "retiring" androids (or "replicants," in the film version), a job he can manage only as long as he is able to maintain an unambiguous distinction between humans and cyborgs.

Deckard's practice is merely more focused than the ordinary human-cyborg policy. In a variety of domains of practice, this second frontier is being "manned." In both the novel and film version of the story, Deckard, because of his extraordinary role in the policing process (certainly not because of his cognitive complexity), is forced into reflection on what humans are and what sense their institutions make, given the special boundary problems with which they must cope.

Therefore the story, as is the case with science fiction in general when it involves the fictive production of the alien, provides an opportunity to intensify reflection on border issues. As one commentary on the genre has noted, "The story of the alien is always a story of borders and the institutional forces that try to neutralize and control those borders in the name of a certain political economy."[28] That "certain political economy" is one that Adam Smith failed to countenance because it involves an identity currency, and he consigned the identity issue to social exchanges of sympathy. In Smith's case, explicit policing was unnecessary because he made the human identity both natural and transcendent. The policing is therefore in the tropes with which he both naturalizes and sacrilizes the human condition.

Because both the novel and film eschew both the natural and sacred forms for the human identity, they tell a story in which official policy is organized around policing the identity boundaries of those eligible for citizenship status within the state. Keeping the alien/others outside human territory requires that the alien be both normatively and spatially contained. Hence, in the novel and film versions of the story, the cyborgs, who are dangerously close to humans in appearance and function, must be kept outside the territory spatially (they are an "offworld" work force) and normatively (they cannot be allowed to completely replicate humans, so they are programmed for a shortened, four-year, life span lest they learn to take on human sentiments and efface the last significant distinguishing characteristic).

Therefore, when some of them escape from their spatial alienation (they return to earth from their offworld work venue) and seek to escape their normative alienation, to effect modification in their longevity, the humans try to destroy them in order to save themselves, that is, to preserve their uniqueness. Deckard is the bounty hunter who is given the assignment to protect humanity, and his inability to maintain the motivation and perspective necessary to function in his job, to police the frontier effectively, speaks of an uncertainty that Adam Smith and others seeking *the* distinguishing human characteristics never manifested. It is not surprising that fictional genres would succeed, where much of the political theory canon has failed, in recognizing both the fictive quality of human identity and the pressures to which the fictions have been responding.

It should be evident that despite the attempts of Adam Smith and others to base human distinctiveness on some aspect of transcendence and/or "nature," what is revealed is not a definitive, universal code but a series of coding *practices*. An inquiry into the interpretation of the boundary practices constitutive of the interpretations of human nature discloses only something about the appropriation of signs, not an essential "nature." This brief inquiry therefore serves to extend the insights in chapter 2 from the importance of recognizing sign exchange as intrinsic to valuing to the importance of recognizing sign exchange in the establishment and maintenance of the social bond.

Thus, aside from the one obvious conclusion—the necessity of relaxing the usual, firm distinction between fiction and nonfiction genres—another is the necessity to relax the pressure to discover what humanity is ultimately about, to tolerate the ambiguities, as Nietzsche counseled in his remark that is especially apposite to the boundary concerns just addressed:

> Man has been educated by his errors. First, he always saw himself only incompletely; second, he endowed himself with fictitious attributes; third, he placed himself in a false order or rank in relation to animals and nature; fourth, he invented ever new tables of goods and always accepted them for a time as eternal and unconditional: as a result of this, now one and now another human

impulse and state held first place and was ennobled because it was
esteemed so highly. If we remove the effects of these four errors, we
should also remove humanity, humaneness, and "human dignity."[29]

Elevating the Social

Since the 18th century the "social" has increasingly been the alibi for
the political. As was noted in chapter 1, treatises in that century such
as those of Adam Smith on morality, economy, and law marked a
pronounced shift in the meaning of politics from the Hobbesian emphasis on the civic bond, which stressed the implied contracts involved in
rulership, to a notion of the political as custodial for the social. Accordingly, as the political began to develop a "social referent,"[30] the issue
of sovereignty shifted its focus from the legitimacy of leadership to its
responsibility for managing the social configuration, and the structure
of the social bond became an increasingly significant focus for political
theory. It was a turn toward a different "governmentality."[31]

However, despite this shift in tendency, there have remained two
sharply polar ways of treating the social. One orientation emphasizes
harmony and the other disharmony. The first conceives the person or
"body" as having tendencies that aim it in a socially compatible direction, and the second conceives embodiment as always tending toward
a dis-ease with any social arrangement. The more canonical model in
social and political theory has been harmony-oriented and has been associated with notions of moral and political impulses conceived within an
empiricist epistemology, that is, on the basis of a view that holds objects
responsible for their meaning, as was the case with Smith's sensationalism,
which not only shaped his view of value but also his view of the social
bond. His conception of interpersonal association, based as it is on a
sensationalist view of meaning, produces the social bond *as* an epistemological bond made possible because of the *common* way that objects excite
sentiments. In his model, persons know the world through sensations, and
because of both their past (sensational) experiences and their capacity for
imagination, they know what an other is experiencing when they observe
that other directly in social space.

As was noted in chapter 2, social space as Smith conceived it is uncomplicated. For purposes of understanding the social dynamic, social space is a vast theater of interpersonal perception, and the witnessing that occurs on the social stage is sympathetic (as the "brother" trope suggests):

> Though our brother is upon the rack, as long as we are at ease, our senses will never inform us of what he suffers. . . . It is by imagination only that we can form any conception of what are his sensations.[32]

An important implication of Smith's construction of the social as epistemological/sensational was its secularizing impulse. As was noted in the introduction above, in a century still haunted by a deity enchanting the world, it was a significant departure for Smith to locate the control over morals within the physical/psychological orientation of persons toward the social. But Smith's secularizing was ultimately ambivalent. His language remained largely transcendental—he figured God as the great "Author" of the universe—but his deity had retreated from human, day-to-day existence, leaving behind mechanisms that Smith, in his virtually unbounded optimism, believed to provide a structural guarantee that the self and the order would remain always attuned. However, this attunement is to be found in the tropes that organize Smith's writing rather than the world on which he imposed his thinking.

Nevertheless, heedless of his imposition, Smith looked unreflectively outward and saw another "Author," one who had left behind a "nature" with such regulative mechanisms as a socially felicitous tendency in individual human desiring. This, along with some inevitable tendencies in collective arrangements, guaranteed an order that progressed toward general prosperity and broadly distributed human contentment. This optimistic dimension of Smith's thought, although dominant, had to contend with his less sanguine view, which he seemed to achieve when he was able to abandon his mythic narrative and scrutinize the effects of inequality and poverty. Indeed, throughout his writing, there are two different textual Adam Smiths.

The textual production of Smith's more sanguine view, his harmony orientation, required a suppression of the problem of desire, a suppression that was no doubt already there in his austere Scottish imagination. He constructed human life not as an arena of excitement but as a domain of minor contentments. The world was to be accommodated not challenged, for pleasure was to exist in the absence of adversity not in the experience of emotional extremes:

> What could be added to the happiness of the man who is in health, who is out of debt, and has a clear conscience?[33]

Desire, which for many thinkers is an awful, socially dangerous engine, for Smith is relatively benign. It creates the conditions of possibility for social life and keeps it running smoothly. It is not something that rages below the apparently smooth surface of the order of things (as in David Lynch's film, *Blue Velvet*), creating ever more challenges that exemplify the costs of any order and the difficulties of ever grasping the complex dynamic producing selfhood, meaningful objects, and self-other and self-object relations. "Self preservation or the propagation of the species are the great ends which nature seems to have proposed in the formation of all animals," wrote Smith, and, conveniently, human desire is structured by those "ends," which are already fashioned in the presocial or natural condition from which humans are aimed toward their social existence: "Mankind are endowed with a desire of those ends and an aversion to the contrary."[34]

This simple, linear (and teleological) history of desire deprives it of its important social dynamic. Paradoxically, there is a possibility for such a dynamic in Smith's position. Although he never incorporates his view of the immanent sociality of the self within his theory of the production and exchange of goods, his treatment of the exchange of sympathy contains the beginnings of a complex (even contemporary) view of desire. Some social objects (other subjects), insofar as they are discerned by a self involved in symbolic communication with an imagined other, are valued not directly but through a normative, social mediation. However, this inner dynamic does not, for Smith, disturb the initial impetus of a desire that constitutes the social domain. Desire is not fundamentally at odds with the normativities of the social. Subjects are influenced in their desiring by the desiring of others, but Smith does not suggest that subjectivity itself is either formed through the dynamics of desire or brought into situations of ambivalence and contestation. Desire's initial impetus and its continued effects move primarily in the same, socially pacifying direction.

In the contemporary history of systems of thought, desire has been a central mechanism and has come to be seen especially as the primary medium through which the self is formed and the social bond is constructed. In particular, the postmodernist construal of desire, organized around reactions to Hegel's location of desire as foundational to coherent subjectivity, presents a challenge to Smith's treatment in his approach to moral sentiments.

Smith attuned the unified, coherent subject to the order, and in so doing produced ethical and political problematics within a frame in which the subject is naturally involved in a system of order-maintaining sentiments. In contrast, some contemporary thinkers suggest a more complex form of subjectivity, based on a different rendering of desire. For example, positing a subject divided from itself (Lacan) or one whose self-understandings are produced by multiple forms of exogenous power (Foucault) rather than inner aspect of "self-command," emphasized by Smith, encourages politico-moral problematics very different from those emerging in Smith's writings.

But it is not necessary to advance two centuries to situate Smith among radically different alternatives. Although Smith's construction of the self fed off the thinking of many of his contemporaries—he was influenced by Hume's account of sympathy and Rousseau's version of "natural man"—the writings (and perhaps the conduct) of one of his contemporaries, the Marquis de Sade, provides an apt comparison. This is the case not only because of the stark divergences—among other things, Sade saw cruelty not sympathy as a natural human orientation and more generally saw desire as antisocial—but also for some of the remarkable similarities. Like Smith, Sade emphasized the visual dimension of human association and figured the social bond with a theatrical metaphor.

In general, then, Smith's idea that human embodiment and the trajectory of desire it produces aim persons toward sociable "ends" and his valorization of "propagation" situate him in an almost direct confrontation with a tendency in social theory that runs from his contemporary, the Marquis de Sade, through Freud to some contemporary postmodern theorists, especially Foucault and Lacan. By reading Smith with Sade and some contemporary theorists it is possible to stage the confrontation in a way that puts pressure on the canonical tradition of epistemological realism and naturalism and its implications for ethics and politics.

The Smith-Sade confrontation is especially apposite, for Sade, like Smith, was an ambivalent secularizer. Although Sade inveighed against theology, he reasserted a theological authority in his preoccupation with transgression; religion provided the normativity he loved to hate. But otherwise, Sade departs dramatically from Smith in that he wrote against a tradition of "natural man . . . whose constituent organs function for the integrity of the whole, and whose individual integrity functions for the maintenance and reproduction of the species."[35]

Sade was not simply valorizing transgression. He was making the case, through his writing/staging, that desire is not bound up with such "natural" and cohesive functions as the propagation of the species. The acts of sodomy in his social dramas take on their significance not merely as transgressive but as nonpropagating sexual acts.

More generally, and ironically, it will emerge that Smith, whose view of writing, as has been noted, was based on a simple lucidity model—he argued that metaphors and other figures of speech are obfuscating, making "one's style dark and perplex'd"[36]—tended to perpetuate illusion. Sade, in contrast, whose writing is filled with fantastic imagery and scenarios—the epitome of a fictional discourse—aimed at accessing the real, at dispelling illusion. This Sadean "real" is a more-or-less Lacanian real, that is, it is the real of desire, a real that is not accessible to the direct vision in public space that organizes Smith's society.

For Jacques Lacan, the world of objects has no independent stability as "the real." The world provides a support for thought but it has less of a shaping effect than the productive fantasies of the subject. As he put it in one of his more hyperbolic statements, "The world is merely the fantasy through which thought sustains itself—'reality' no doubt, but to be understood as a grimace of the real."[37] Indeed, the Lacanian view is that only in fantasy, for example, in dreams, does one encounter the real of desire, whereas in waking life, when one looks directly at things, one lives in illusion.[38]

By depriving desire of its mediating function, Smith was able to construct a model of the real based on direct visualizing in social space. And by neglecting the role of his narratives in producing the harmony he thought he was discovering (just as he was insensitive to their role in constructing value), he was able to perpetuate fables of miraculous harmony while using the alibi of historical analysis. Thus, although Smith wrote in a seemingly descriptive discourse, he perpetuated illusion, while Sadean "fictions" were self-consciously constructed to supply the kind of oblique glance that dispels illusion.

Smith's Figuring of the Social Bond

How did Smith's narratives work to produce a fabulous effect? In both his discourse on moral sentiments and his subsequent treatment of political economy (in *The Wealth of Nations*), Smith constructed accommodative narratives that welcomed the new industrial society. Certainly Smith was sensitive to many of the human costs of the new order, for some of his commentaries, both within *The Theory of Moral Sentiments* and *The Wealth of Nations*, cannot help but strike the reader for their sensitivity to the negative aspects of the developing industrial age. In both texts Smith is very attentive to and moved by the plight of the impoverished. He displays a strong contempt for avarice and greed and a keen recognition of the cruelty and insensitivity displayed by the rich. And he is even sensitive to the structural contribution to human dispositions, recognizing how structured modes of encounter play a role in producing and circulating "vice" as well as more socially positive sentiments. Yet at the same time, he remains strikingly optimistic. It seems to be the case, as Robert Heilbroner noted decades ago, that the radical politics that might have emerged from Smith's sensitivity to the plight of laborers was mitigated by his overweening belief (even faith) in a rationally and benevolently designed order. Heilbroner's perceptive metaphor for Smith's faith in this design is that of the magnetic field, which has the effect of rectifying and coordinating dispositions and behaviors so that they produce collectively favorable results for both individuals and the order.[39]

However, in *The Theory of Moral Sentiments* the dominant trope expressing Smith's faith in the design is that of the "Author." In his view, the Author had designed the self, out of his benevolence, to be naturally attuned to the order. He had in effect designed a nature that would guarantee harmonious living.

> The happiness of mankind, as well as of other rational creatures seems to
> have been the original purpose intended by the Author of nature, when he
> brought them into existence.[40]

But the bitextual Smith thus leads a double theoretical life. When
describing everyday life, he frequently points to desires that express a
diverse individuality, even a somewhat centrifugal human tendency.
But at other times, his discourse is less specifically engaged with daily
life and it takes on a more normative tone, suppressing individual
difference and operating within his more mechanistic and formal rendering of an inevitable collective harmony.

When writing in this latter mode, it is a musical figuration, with
harmony as its central trope, that organizes Smith's primary understanding of passions. Whereas many have seen the passions as energies
and aims that are always to some degree in contention with the attempts
of an order to subdue them, Smith constructs the individual as one fitted
with a natural governor. He surmises, for example, that when one is
suffering and knows that others cannot be expected to develop a depth
of sympathy consonant with the passion felt by the sufferer, there is a
natural adjustment of that passion so that it is expressed at a level that
is in balance with the degree of sympathy an observer could be expected
to evince. As Smith puts it (again within a musical frame), the sufferer,
wanting the emotions in the hearts of the onlookers to "beat time" to
his own, obtains this by "lowering his passion to that pitch, in which
the spectators are capable of going along with him. He must flat-
ten . . . the sharpness of the natural tone in order to reduce it to harmony
and concord with the emotions of those around him."[41]

It is clear from the reference to "spectators" in this passage that sound
is complemented by sight in Smith's figuring of the social. Along with
the musical figuration, this passage also introduces the major organiz-
ing frame and set of tropes of *The Theory of Moral Sentiments* as a
whole, the relationship of visibility versus invisibility to the social
bond. As is well known, the grand design, comprised of the mechanisms
the "Author" left behind in "nature," which guarantee a harmonious
collectivity, is figured as the presence of an "invisible hand." Among
the consequences of this unseen guiding force is its overcoming of the
more marked effects on the poor of the rapacity of the rich. The rich are

led to moderate their rapacity "by an invisible hand to make nearly the same distribution of the necessities of life, which would have been made, had the earth been divided into equal portions among all inhabitants, and thus without intending it, without knowing it, advance the interests of society and afford means to the multiplication of the species."[42]

This view, which Smith was later to reproduce in his equally sanguine *Wealth of Nations*, constitutes a major dimension of his textual practice, his tendency to write in the form of narratives that can perhaps best be termed "mythic plots." By positing a form of transcendent guidance, Smith trivializes the details of ordinary life. Thus, ironically, while Smith shifts the center of moral reasoning to the common life and away from the formal canon, which had observed the priority of the transcendent, he reinscribes the transcendent in his "mythic plots," described in Chapter 2 as a form of narrative that perpetuates "the assurance that there is a timeless and motionless transcendent world," which "reduces to insignificance the *fait divers* which seem to constitute the narrative of ordinary life."[43]

Here, in his famous invisible-hand passage, Smith has summoned an extraworldly, authored intention to structure "nature" in such a way that it overcomes the nitty-gritty details of everyday success and failure. Epistemologically, this mode of storytelling produces a teleological rather than causally oriented history. Smith's events and situations are "extra-mechanical" (as Veblen put it). They are guided by "a comprehensive scheme of contrivances established from the beginning" to guarantee an intended, felicitous, and harmonious outcome.[44]

Given the "Design," a magnetic force field that controls the structure of association and its outcomes, a mode of desiring (musically figured) that is almost wholly compatible with social harmony, and a set of programmed social aims that guarantee well-distributed, felicitous consequences for all, the stakes of individual moral reasoning cannot be too high. Nevertheless, Smith addressed himself energetically to a moral psychology of judgment. Within this moral psychology, his understanding of the social bond involves primarily face-to-face visualization. His version of the vision-morals connection is a more-or-less democratic/populist one compared, for example, with Bentham's 19th-century version. In Bentham's model, visualization is centralized and specialized, serving as a means for the order to produce the calculations necessary for social control.

In contrast to Bentham, Smith proliferates points of observation. Whereas Bentham was concerned with the economies of pain in order to render possible policy calculations, Smith focused on the viewpoints of individuals as they sympathize with others. In short, Smith's system of thought was resistant to Bentham's heralding of the age of calculation and the formation of a process of policing identities that Foucault has shown to be one of modernity's primary political narratives.

But apart from its proliferation of points of observation, it is important to recognize the way the Smithian structure of spectatorship locates the problematic of pain. Pain is not to be collectively balanced after being perceived from a controlling center of authority. It is to be individually perceived and appreciated for its depth rather than its degree of distribution. Smith believed pain to be more intense than other sensations, or, in his terms, more "pungent." "Whether of mind or body, [pain] . . . is a more pungent sensation than pleasure."[45] Accordingly, he goes on, our sympathy with pain "is generally a more lively and distinct perception than our sympathy with pleasure."[46]

Moreover, this more distinct perception is allied to a similar privileging of what is available to the gaze, for he argues that the conception of pain from which sympathy is produced is more "lively and distinct" in the case of pain from external causes than in the case of internal causes. He states, for example, "I can scarce form an idea of the agonies of my neighbor when he is tortured with the gout or with stone; but I have the clearest conception of what he must suffer from an incision, a wound, or a fracture."[47]

Smith's privileging of direct vision is very much an 18th-century model of seeing. Living in an age of machine-generated images, it is difficult to appreciate that prior to the reorganization of vision that technologies such as photography helped to produce in the 19th century, seeing in Smith's century was mimetic or referential in conception. Smith's observers were "spectators." Technologically, the lamp and camera obscura were analogues for vision, so that Smith's world was conceived as directly perceptible in contrast with a modernity that is fragmented into separate spaces connected through mediated and abstracted forms of vision that not only produce images but also construct observers.[48]

Smith's spectators managed their own attention frames through their imaginations, for the individual imagination was, for Smith, the only mediation involved in seeing. Insofar as the Smithian spectator had a managed perception, it was a case of self-management. The Benthamite construction of vision in the next century becomes significant as a heralding of modernity, not only because of the policy function of surveillance it encouraged, but also because of the shift away from the spectator model of vision organized within a theater to a more mediated centralized administration of observation. As Foucault has noted, modern society, whose shape began to emerge in the 19th-century management of vision, is one based on surveillance rather than spectacle. "We are neither in the amphitheatre nor on stage but in the panoptic machine, invested by its effects of power . . ."[49]

When this trend toward surveillance—within which seeing in social space is an active, knowledge-oriented production of identities—is coupled with the increasing development of an observer-as-consumer whose attention must be managed, we can discern the dramatic break with Smith's century. By the latter part of the 19th century there was a new "ambulatory observer shaped by a convergence of new urban spaces, technologies, and new economic and symbolic functions of images and products" that Walter Benjamin helped to theorize.[50] An understanding of this aspect of modernity has required an appreciation not only of the mediation of vision that is lacking in Smith's construction of the spectator but also the mediating effects of desire.

Before staging the Smith versus Sade and others confrontations on the mediation of desire, Smith's neglect of another form of mediation is on the agenda, for it speaks to the problem of his treatment of pain.

Sensing versus Saying

Although Smith thought that visualization within the social domain is mediated by experience, what constitutes this Smithian "experience," which along with vision makes possible the exercise of sympathetic imagination, is personal rather than social. It treats a person's experience as unaffected by the resident social meaning systems available for the person to process that experience. It is therefore apropos to contrast Smith's position to that of Wittgenstein, who also addressed himself to the problem of imagining another's pain. Because Wittgenstein's move from an empirical to a linguistic basis for relating experience to social judgments anticipates recent approaches, the comparison provides a threshold for assessing Smith's view in the light of contemporary social theory.

Crucial to the comparison is the difference between Smith's and Wittgenstein's treatment of language. For Smith, one has experiences and then becomes perceptually and linguistically competent to regard and sympathize with the pain of another. For Wittgenstein, linguistic concords ("language games") anticipate and make possible experiences. Thus, Wittgenstein doubted the very existence of the phenomenon that Smith regarded as a "personal experience." For Wittgenstein, one's appreciation of pain is conceptual not perceptual. Or, put differently, every pain percept is made possible by a concept. As he remarked with characteristic directness (and in the persuasive second person), "You learned the *concept* 'pain' when you learned language."[51]

To say this is not to say, however, that you learned a simple designative language game in which words refer to their appropriate objects. Unlike Smith for whom language is something about objects, Wittgenstein's approach emphasizes the multiple functions of utterances beyond the simple one of naming or designating. To learn a language is not simply to learn the names of things but to learn a way of life, a set of practices that provide the context and rhetorical force for one versus another kind of utterance.

Whereas rhetorical force plays a primary role in Wittgenstein's view of language, Smith eschews all figuration and rhetoric, arguing that figures of speech are ornamental rather than determinative of significance and have the effect, as noted above, of making "one's style dark and perplex'd."[52] Heedless of the pervasive, meaning-creating force of utterances, Smith assumed that the only relevant practices shaping the significance of language have to do with grammatical proprieties. Accordingly, his discussion of language emphasizes parts of speech, and nouns, the counterparts of substances for Smith, received primary attention. So primary is the word-object relationship in Smith's approach, it structures his narration of the development of language: "It seems probable that those words which denote certain substances which exist, and which we call substances, would be *amongst* the first contrived by persons who were inventing a language."[53]

For Wittgenstein, the *how* rather than the *what* function of language is paramount. Accordingly, in the case of pain, Wittgenstein suggests that a reference to an object is irrelevant to one's understanding the meaning of it. Likening attempts to understand another's pain sensation to having a beetle in a box while assuming that the other has something in a box also, he states, "The thing in the box has no place in the language-game at all."[54]

To be able to render sympathy is not to be able to *see* some-thing or even to *imagine* some-thing, according to Wittgenstein. It is, rather, to be able to participate in a set of practices, especially the competence to use language. It means that one can, for example, invoke a characteristic grammar such as "he is in pain" at a moment that calls up not one's individual experience but rather what one *knows* about pain in the sense of being able to conceive of it within the language practices of one's culture—in Wittgenstein's terms, the language games we employ to identify and sympathize with pain.

Wittgenstein's explanation of the linguistic mediations involved in recognizing another's pain provides a critique of Smith's combination of visual and mentalistic constructions of the social bond and, at the same time, illuminates the linguistic as opposed to the psychological dimension of exchanges of meaning in human association. This shift from psychology to linguisticality is characteristic of contemporary social theory's treatment of the structure of the social bond. Exemplifying this tendency is Jean-Francois Lyotard, who constructs human interactions in terms of "language moves" or fragments of "performativity." Rather than interpersonal sympathy and a wholly mentalistic imagination, Lyotard (and other postmodernists with a linguistic view of association) heeds the rhetorical diversity within the social body, which he construes as an arena of linguistic struggle: "To speak is to fight, in the sense of playing, and speech acts fall within the domain of general agonistics."[55] This contrasts markedly with Smith's more homogeneous and thus pacific psychological view.

Smith's social body is centripetal rather than centrifugal, a view he mounts within his grammatical constructions as he homogenizes the views that selves form of others. In harmonious accord with Smith's sensationalist rendering of the meaning of sympathetic objects, which must impress themselves in the same way on perceiving subjects, is the homogenizing grammar with which he describes the harmonizing tendencies of human perspectives. Rather than a series of fragmented rhetorically oriented groups, Smith's grammar constructs such homogeneous entities as "man" and "we", for example, in his "Man, it has been said, has a natural love for society,"[56] and in his "We approve of another man's judgment," and "We expect less sympathy from a common acquaintance than from a friend."[57]

Insofar as speech enters Smith's social system, it reflects not an agonistics but the palliating force of association and communication. "Society and conversation are the most powerful remedies for restoring the mind to its tranquility."[58] The domain of language was clearly secondary for Smith. At most it could convey what was already determined by a relatively homogeneous human character.

In contrast to the tranquility that Smith attributes to conversation, modern critical theory has recognized the agonistics immanent in differences in linguistic orientations. In addition to Lyotard's recognition that an agonistic performativity rather than a commonality of self and object governs the trajectory of speech, there has been increasing interest in the political significance of genre. Here M. M. Bakhtin's insights have been influential, for he has shown how some forms of literature represent the extent to which the social body is, in his terms, centrifugal rather than, as Smith would have it, centripetal. The novel is Bakhtin's exemplar of the degree of fragmenting dynamism in the social body. It is organized around what he calls its heteroglossia, its contending voices, which pull away from and against the verbal-ideological center.

> At any given moment of its evolution, language is stratified not only into linguistic dialects in the strict sense of the word . . . but also . . . into languages that are socio-ideological: languages of social groups, "professional" and "generic" languages, languages of generations and so forth.[59]

To explore the political implications of the linguisticality of social divisions versus the homogeneity and harmony posited by Smith, we need to assess more critically the problem of pain that was so central to Smith's construction of felicitous consociation.

Pain and the Sociopolitical

For Smith, pain was unambiguous and unmediated, and he regarded it as wholly aversive. As the "more pungent sensation," however, it also provided one of the most palpable conditions of possibility for social cohesion. Insofar as knowing is based on sensation, pain as the keenest sensation provided the closest thing to certainty of knowledge. And, insofar as the social is built on a sympathetic knowledge of the other, pain becomes the primary experience on which to base the exchange of compassion, which is foundational to Smith's version of the social.

As in many areas of his thought, Smith's central concept remained an unproblematic fact or thing. Smithian pain is simply an aversive sensation. He does not, for example, bring history to bear. A historical situating of pain, if not used as mere fable to reinforce already held predilections, would reveal, as indeed a recent one has, that "the experience of pain is densely shaped or modified by individual human minds and by specific human cultures."[60]

Such investigations confirm what Wittgenstein's philosophical reflections disclosed—that "experience" requires more than embodiment and that the interpretive mediation that must supplement embodiment is not a matter of individual psychology but of meaning systems, of cultural/linguistic practices available for giving experiences meaning.

However, the Wittgensteinian insight, as Wittgenstein expressed it, represents a person's participation in cultural and linguistic practices within the depoliticized language of abilities and competences. To recognize pain or any other "feeling" according to Wittgenstein is to simply be able to invoke the appropriate language game at the appropriate time and place. Within a more politicized understanding of the social body, however, association and the exchange of meanings involves more than proprieties. Thus, for example, the historical inquiry into pain cited above predicates its analysis on the assumption that "pain inescapably engages us in struggles of interpretation,"[61] and goes on to enter that struggle to wrest control over the concept of pain away from the biomedical discourse that tends to dominate it in contemporary industrial societies.

More generally, *what* pain or any social phenomenon is acquires its degree of interpretive stability not simply as a result of a vast social concord on proprieties but as a result of the victories and defeats through which the controlling discursive spaces of pain have been established. For example, despite the continuing efforts of some religious groups, the remembered pain of martyrs, saints, and deities, which serves to unite their groups, has little effect on the administrative and ritual practices of secular society. It takes a back seat to such socially recognized forms of pain as the "mental anguish" from being denied a job, being injured, or having property damaged.

Adam Smith's treatment of pain was almost wholly secular as well, but it never descended to the level of legal disputes. It took the higher road of participating in the legitimation of a social and moral order. It is here that Smith and his contemporary, the Marquis de Sade, effectively engage. But since they never recognized each other explicitly, the confrontation must be staged.

Smith with Sade

However scandalous the Sadean system is in the context of Smith's views, many of Smith's and Sade's interests and perspectives are similar. Like Smith, for example, Sade believed pain to be the keenest sensation. Recall that for Smith, pain is a more "pungent sensation than the opposite and correspondent pleasure,"[62] and how it functions supports his epistemological sensationalism. Through the visibility of another's suffering, the observer sees (and therefore knows) that another is in pain, and this leads naturally to sympathy.

This ability for vicarious sensation is what makes possible the psychological dimension of the social bond. The normative or judgmental aspect is predicated on Smith's notion of the "impartial observer." However, despite how "pungent" a sensation pain is, Smith's construction of the self assumes a natural aversion to pain, one's own physical pain and the "natural pangs of an affrighted conscience," which would flow from the causing of pain in an other.[63]

Here the contrast with Sade is especially noteworthy. For Sade, insofar as pain is the most powerful sensation, one should seek it *and* seek to cause and witness it in another. And Smith's "pangs of conscience" for Sade are not at all natural but rather imposed. Such pangs are so-called "virtues" invented by "counterfeit divinities."[64] To the extent that one has sympathetic feelings, according to Sade (and here there is more than a hint of irony), their proper domain of employment is on oneself. As Dolmancé puts it in "Philosophy in the Bedroom," "Nature has endowed us with a capacity for kindly feelings: let's not squander them on others."[65]

Despite this divergence in their positions on the *value* of pain and the naturalness of benevolence or virtue, Smith and Sade are more or less in agreement at the level of mechanism. While the Smithian self seeks contentment and the absence of emotional vicissitudes, and especially of pain, the Sadean self seeks excitement. But within both systems, excitement or agitation comes from observing it in another. In the Sadean scenes, what may appear to be mere cruelty, when one causes pain in another, can be read as the desire by the perpetrator to identify with the pain of his/her victim in order to achieve the sexual excitement derived from imagining oneself as victim.[66] For example, the Duke in *The 120 Days of Sodom* "noticed that a violent commotion inflicted upon any kind of adversary is answered by a vibrant thrill in his own nervous system."[67]

Rather than entirely dismissing a psychology of sympathetic identification, Sade was rejecting the pious interpretation that the sentiment produced in the observer (or perpetrator) is based on a virtuous form of identification.[68] It is virtue, not passion, that is unnatural for Sade. While Smith, with his notion of natural sympathy, tries to domesticate passion, Sade seeks to liberate it: "Voluptuaries of all ages . . . passions . . . are naught but the means Nature employs to bring man to the ends she prescribes to him."[69] Sade is not simply advocating cruelty and egoistic self-interest, for there is a dialogic motive in his text; he was writing against a tradition—to which Smith belongs—that tries to domesticate desire by constructing a self with largely socially oriented and otherwise constrained passions in order to be attuned to the order.

Sade agrees with Smith in the argument that there is no such thing as a general interest; there are only individual interests. But unlike Smith, who thought that individual interests are guided by a force that naturally harmonizes them with the order, Sade saw the interests of the individual as continually opposed to the demands of the society.

In not wishing the libertine to be prevented from causing pain in another, Sade was not interested in cruelty per se but in selfhood. What delights the libertine in Sade's staged dramas is not someone's pain and suffering alone but the knowledge that he or she is responsible for it.[70] What is valued is a situation in which each can experience his or her possibilities for evoking and satisfying desire. Within such a model of value, what becomes significant is the individuality of taste, where "taste" represents not simply aesthetic sensibilities peripheral to the socially significant dimensions of the self but what most significantly defines the self. In contrast with Smith (and indeed much of the tradition of political theory), who seeks to discover that in each person which transcends individuality and thus connects each person to the social whole (e.g., Smith's "sentiments"), Sade seeks that which individualizes.

Sade contrasts with Smith in both the valence he places on pain and the ambiguities between pain and other experiences he introduces. But even more remarkable is the minute attention he devoted to it. Whereas Smithian pain is an unproblematic fact both in terms of its radical distinction from pleasure and other experiences and its details—Smith rather carelessly draws examples from torture (the rack) and medicine (the surgical incision)—Sade exposes both sexuality and pain to a searching, clinical gaze.

Nevertheless, Sade's treatment was far from scientistic. The ambiguities of the meaning of pain and the responsibilities of perpetrators and victims move Sade's primary concerns into an ethical space. This is argued persuasively in Jacques Lacan's treatment of Sade with Kant. Although there is doubtless a (Sadean) transgressive irony involved in the Kant-Sade pairing, the reading is earnest. For Lacan, Sade's interest in the vagaries of desire anticipate Freud's because of the ethical problematic implicit in Freud's treatment of the pleasure principle. Sade is significant, then, not "in respect of the catalogue of perversions," but because "the Sadean bedroom is equal to those places from which the schools of ancient philosophy took their name: Academy, Lyceum, Stoa."[71]

Why *Kant* with Sade? First and foremost, the Kantian revolution in ethics (contemporary with Sade's) is a departure from the canonical model in which moral conduct is extracted from one's natural inclinations. Ethics in the Kantian system is not derived from humans as embodied, sensual beings—either the pathological demands of the flesh evoked by the Stoic and Augustinian focus on self-mastery or the sympathetic, congenial vibrations imagined by Kant's other contemporary, Adam Smith. For Smith, the world of objects (especially other subjects) evinces socially positive passions, and this is the case because a happiness principle, "the happiness of mankind" as he was wont to put it, is built into nature by "the Author when he brought them into existence."[72]

Within this Smithian model, moral faculties are summoned by the world. In the Kantian model, by contrast, the world of objects cannot summon sentiments or evoke judgmental faculties. As Lacan puts it, "No phenomenon can claim for itself a constant relation to pleasure."[73] Since the good cannot propose itself phenomenally, it is produced, in the Kantian view, *categorically*, that is, unconditionally. The effect of the good then—its "weight" in Lacan's figuration—is not its functioning as a "counter-weight", that is, as a control or self-command against the enactment of passions, but as an "antiweight, that is to say by the subtraction of weight, for it excludes from its consideration any 'drive' or 'sentiment.' "[74] It is in this sense that the good functions as an unconditional, categorical imperative.

One would have seemed to have left Sade far behind in this antiphenomenal rendering of Kant, for is not Sade preoccupied with passions and sentiments? Indeed his libertines, like Smith's sympathetic observers, have their sympathetic sensations become excited as a result of observing the excitement in others, as in the above example of the Duke who "noticed that a violent commotion inflicted upon any kind of adversary is answered by a vibrant thrill in his own nervous system."[75] But Sadean sympathy is different from Smithian. It is not a moral sentiment but a fact about passion for Sade. This facticity, like the rest of "nature", does not provide rules for conduct.

Many readers have succumbed to the temptation to read Sadean nature as an inversion of the canonical tradition of naturalistic ethics. A neglect of the irony, reductio ad absurdum, and other tropes in Sade's writing encourages the inference that Sade was reading nature as a moral voice but one advocating the morality of selfishness rather than altruism—for example, Dolmancé's above quoted remark "Nature has endowed us with a capacity for kindly feelings. Let's not squander them on others."[76]

Another way to read Sade, however, is to pay attention to the style of the text. Like Nietzsche, Sade pursued reversals not to supplant a moral code with its reverse but to undermine the frame for producing the code. The reversals in his Gothic fictions, like those in Nietzsche's *Ecce Homo*, can be read as parodies that undermine a system of religious authority, especially its textual supports as in, for example, the use of St. Ignatius's style of writing in *Juliette* to render absurd religious conceits.[77] By deriving the reverse clues from such authorities as theology or nature, Sade is saying that they authorize nothing. As Nietzsche was to put it later, "Nature . . . has no opinion of us."[78]

Specifically, then, Sade's seeming celebration of the natural egoism in the libertine's pursuit of perversion is not a new model of human nature to serve as a basis for justifying a different order. It is an attack on Christian virtue meant to undermine the generality of the human body on which orders are based. And the aims of Sade's attacks are resident in his textual strategies.

How Sade's textual strategies work is elaborated in Pierre Klossowski's influential reading. For him, Sade's primary writing method was to set up a countergenerality to religious naturalism. This was not an alternative generalization about sensuous embodiment on which a different ethic could be based. Rather, Sade wished "to free thought from all pre-established normative reason,"[79] and he employs reversals to do it. Thus, for example, throughout *Juliette* "nature" is invoked to say the opposite of the usual ethical claims that have been derived from it:

> To be despotic is the primary desire inspired in us by a Nature whose law could not be more unlike the ludicrous one usually ascribed to her, the substance of which is not to do unto others that which unto ourselves we would not have done. . . . I affirm that the fundamental, profoundest, and keenest penchant in man is uncontestably to enchain his fellow creatures and to tyrannize them with all his might.[80]

This speech by Saint-Fond is doubled by his conduct, for the freeing of thought in Sade, to which Klossowski refers, is accomplished not simply from a philosophical discourse but from the conduct of Sade's characters. Each has different tastes, a different sensuous nature, and engages in perverse acts as an obedience to a moral imperative, that is, in accord with an ethic that breaks with any generalization based on phenomenal experience.

There is thus no *common* sense in Sade, no way to build a social bond based on a like-mindedness with sensuous origins. What is left is the need to treat the social bond without being able to rely on natural commonalities, to think of the social based not on common sense but on the recognition of the singularity of desire. Bodies are not the basis of a universal code, they are the sublimated objects of desire, in Lacan's terms, the "slag of a fantasy."[81]

Here the Smith-Sade confrontation is nearly total, for while Smith attempts to build a congenial social bond on common sense, Sade attempts to defeat the very idea of common sense. Central to this difference is that for Smith, the object of one's attention has an integrity of its own. It attracts a double seeing or vision, one look from the acting self, connected with objects through sensations, and one from an internalized, guiding self (that Smith calls "the viceregent within") that acts as a counterweight to the socially pathological or perverse. For Sade, the object of vision has no independent integrity. Its significance is shaped by the desiring of the observer. This points to a very different view of the relationship between desire and normativity from that found in Smith's treatment.

In the case of Smith, his construction of the double self, one acting and one imagined as outside the actor observing from an impartial perspective, is the primary move through which he naturalizes the self's relationship to normativity. Where (and how) is desire here? Whatever self-interested desires might pull centrifugally away from the harmonized social whole are of little moment compared to the larger desires of being within the social and of being viewed as a socially responsible person.

Therefore, the law itself, for Smith, represents primary desire and opposes or inhibits desires that could be socially unsettling, and it does this through a process of internalization. In contrast with the vice, cruelty, and desire-for-transgression that persons embody in Sade's construction of the self, are Smith's "viceregents":

Those viceregents of God within us, never fail to punish the violation of
them, by the torments of inward shame, and self-condemnation; and on
the contrary, always reward obedience with tranquility of mind, with
contentment, and self-satisfaction.[82]

In the case of Sade, desire does not found the social, and it does not
function to continually reactivate tranquil sociability and lawfulness.
Ironically, the law provides the condition of possibility for a coun-
ternormativity. Throughout Sade's boudoir scenes a *dis*passionate interest in crime and transgression is more dominant as an aim than erotic
fulfillment. This is why the Sadean scenes are effectively *dis*passionate
and boringly repetitive. Eros is governed by a lawfulness/transgres-
sion polarity, not passion or compassion. Insofar as there is a pleasure
principle in Sade, it would seem to be the satisfaction one derives from
being steadfast in fulfilling one's imperatives, not in achieving objects.
This is an emphasis that accords with the Lacanian emphasis on the aim
rather than the object of desire.

This counter-Smithian position arises out of a more profound difference between Smith and Sade on the understanding of value. Although
Smith's version of sentiments involves a complex subjectivity, for the
most part his approach to value is economistic, that is, it is negligent of
a symbolic-, identity-, or recognition-seeking impulse. Smith emphasizes the value of objects from the point of view of the labor involved
in producing them, and tends to treat their use value as a function of the
need-fulfilling properties of the object. Sade, in contrast, emphasizes
the dynamics of desire and therefore tends to dematerialize the objects
of desire. His dramas say, in effect, that one's desire for an object is
produced not from some property intrinsic to the object but from some
personal quality in the desiring production of the subject. Coprophilia,
for example, cannot easily be understood to be a function of the intrinsic
value of the desired object (or material) but rather, as he seems to be
arguing in "La Nouvelle Justine," a function of a complex web of
intersubjectivities and exchanges of desiring within which excrement
takes on value.

And, not incidental to the valuing of this otherwise valueless or
devalued shit is the enhancement it receives from the transgression
associated with coprophilia. Insofar as conventions or norms are socially valuable for Sade, it is in the pleasure to be had in breaking or

transgressing them. And, as has been noted, Sade accomplished this textually, not only with his outrageous juxtapositions but also with his narrative structure. In contrast with Smith's historical accounts in which, over time, individual activities sort themselves into coherent, socially differentiated spaces, which leaves a pattern with predominantly positive consequences (this is the primary historical narrative structuring *The Wealth of Nations*), Sade chops up his action into brief tableaux. This poses a counterdynamic to the smooth structural and temporal orderliness in naturalizing accounts of the functioning of the social order.

The difference in narrative orientation is also evidenced in Smith's and Sade's different views of the word. For Smith, the word must be faithful to the object; it must eschew rhetorical flourish, color, and passion in order to claim its only appropriate prize, accuracy. For Sade, the word is to serve in the same manner as the passion, to dispense passionate, life-affirming energy, not to achieve closure. This Sadean orientation is achieved textually. Sadean words work, as Gilles Deleuze has recognized, by compelling bodies to repeat the movements they suggest.[83] Hence the many repetitions of speeches followed by animated "pornograms,"[84] which reflect the verbal imperatives in Sade's stories.

The word and its relationship to the world thus takes on disparate roles in the Smith-Sade comparison, but this difference is more than lexical. The rhetorical dimensions are enactments of different models of social space and are connected in turn to different models of vision. As has been noted, Smithian social space is a vast open-air theater of direct vision in which congeniality or social communality emerges from the presentation of each to the other. Sade's fictive style, his sequestered theaters and dramatic tableaux, evoke a very different social space connected to a different model of vision. Sadean seeing is not the direct or mimetic model of Smithian but a mediated seeing that reflects the singularity of desire that Sade's writing conveys.

Superficially, Smithian and Sadean space are strikingly similar. They both produce their versions of the social within a theatrical metaphor, and the role of vision or viewing is central to each of their versions of social process. But in *The Theory of Moral Sentiments*, there is an absolute coincidence between theatrical and social space, as sympathies are produced while social actors view each other in the space of everyday life. Moral judgments emerge as each views the other's conduct by mediating that view through the imagined view of a disinterested spectator. Seeing is so central to Smith's conceits here that the authority problematic within which he writes is constructed with the visual metaphor. "God" is represented as the "all-seeing judge of the world,"[85] and "man" tries to approximate this judgment by transcending himself.

In sharp contrast, Sadean space, which is also theatrical, does not coincide with the social space of everyday life. Inasmuch as Sade denies the existence of an "all-seeing judge" and denies, more generally, the existence of universal moral codes—he argues that "virtues" are always merely "local" inventions—he localizes his theater in a sequestered space away from ordinary social space. The speeches and pornograms are enacted in small (off-mainstreet) theaters.

The sequestration of Sade's theaters accords not only with the view that morals are merely local matters but also with his desire to isolate the passions in order to allow the free play outside of the normal system of surveillance and criminalizing sanction. He creates a "closed economy of passions."[86] But it is not a pure economy of passions, for it is overlaid with a moral economy, one that is evoked not simply by dint of the exhortations that the ethicists of the boudoir such as Dolmancé proffer, but also through the work Sade does on the word. Barthes has put it succinctly, "Libertine morality consists not in destroying but in diverting; it diverts the object, the word, the organ from its endoxical usage."[87]

The Sadean space is therefore primarily a space of writing, which is to say, a space of imagination. The ensemble of speaker/spectators is transformed through the rhetorical motions of the speeches and bodily configurations. The theaters of imagination constructed in Sade's narrations are meant—in contrast with Smith's theatrical society—not to help reproduce the social order but to question the predominant social imagination.

While Smith homogenizes and transcendentalizes the subject with his "we" grammar (figures such as "mankind," to imply a primordial as well as destiny-driven communality of sentiment), Sade *shows* difference with a series of sexual graphemes. And *his* subjects are not homogeneous psychic perceivers but "language actors."[88] Attentive to style, Sade's novels resemble Gothic romances, but this resemblance is part of Sade's ironic posture, which emerges within the transgressive language within the plots. His textual practice works through juxtaposition both within and between statements. For example, his actor/ speakers, while in the throes of passion, combine theological and obscene expressions, loudly issuing such exclamations as "Oh, God-fuck."

In effect, Sade produced a writing organized by desire, whereas Smith's writing proceeded within the alibi of the real of the referent so that his text was insensitive to its grammatical, rhetorical, and narrative impositions. While Smith presumed to be writing in response to the world, Sade aggressively organized a world of rhetorical conflict. The collection of actors in a Sadean story represents the juxtaposition of different language practices, which, as the story unfolds, intersect and clash, producing impediments that are only overcome in forceful speeches (e.g., those of Dolmancé in "Philosophy in the Bedroom"). The series of rhetorical clashes and occasional moments of rhetorical domination and submission are doubled by the sexual encounters in which individual difference is represented as a difference in sexual tastes.

At this level, as is the case at the verbal level, more dominant sexual actors produce submission as they organize the pornograms to elicit their own pleasure and that of the others. Each separate sexual fragment or tableau, then, represents a moment in an unstable conversation, and each sexual grapheme is an arrested struggle. In the Sadean theater, then, a situation of communication (intercourse) is a temporary accord within a dynamic that offers endless possibilities for coordination among forces of resistance and cooperation at the linguistic, passionate, and behavioral levels.

What emerges from the two different theatrical strategies of Smith and Sade reaches to the depth of the motivations resident in their different textual practices. Smith's is meant to affirm the depth, permanence, and naturalness of an affirmative and felicitous social bond. Sade's is meant to dislocate and divert the permanence and naturalness of social objects and to negate the illusory affirmations of the social that exist in religious and other naturalizing discourses.

In Smith, one encounters one of the mainstream tendencies in the history of political thought, whereas in Sade what one encounters is a markedly different view of the social, which departs from the mainstream tendency to harmonize the self with the order. Although Smith saw, alternatively, both benevolent and pernicious tendencies, his main thrust was to construct the social as a scene of different selves who, in the aggregate can, by dint of their more fundamental, shared character-istics, be aimed along trajectories that smoothly blend their activities into a collective harmony.

The social for Sade is an irreconcilable problem. Social space, given the moral imperatives that define it, cannot help but frustrate any individual self and the possibility of producing ethical bonds among selves. Thus, for example, the sexual education of Eugenie in "Philos-ophy in the Bedroom" turns out to be ethical. Madame de Saint Ange's vow to "spare nothing to pervert her, degrade her" is done to "demolish in her all the false ethical notions" with which others have managed to "dizzy her."[89]

At issue here for Sade is the notion that there can be universal sentiments that naturally dictate a moral posture. "Vice and virtue," asserts Dolmancé, are "naught but local ideas."[90] Sade's position seems to be that the first condition of possibility for an ethical life is not seeking universals but rather institutionalizing tolerance, recognizing that every model of the social will have to countenance forms of otherness that will be disagreeable to the order. As Dolmancé notes in his lengthy philosophical disquisition, the law should be lenient so as to recognize the diversity of human character and especially should not blame or punish "those who, of chillier temper or more acrimonious humor, do not notice in these yet very touching social ties all the sweetness and gentleness others discover therein."[91]

Conclusion

With Sade, as with some contemporary dimensions of postmodernist thinking, the alibi of the object and the alibi of a universal and coherent subject are impeached. The "real" of both is compromised by the real of desire and the real of forces whose inscriptions are arbitrary. To follow up on both aspects of this defeat of the real of canonical political thinking as well as the ethical implications that have been derived from it, it is appropriate to turn again to Lacan and Foucault.

Sade's treatment of the self's uneasy relationship to the order is echoed in views that offer alternatives to the notion of a self that is a unified force, moving along a trajectory that must aim it in the direction of harmonizing with other selves to produce a quiescent order. If one imagines that the play of desire provoked within the self involves forces that often oppose each other, and that the order itself continually provokes aspects of desire that are resistant to it, there is an encouragement to look for other metaphors than the musical one evoked in the idea of "harmony" when attempting to think the problem of the self and the order in general and the attributes of the self relevant to ethical problematics in particular.

When one cannot rely on a stable meaning structure for objects based either on objectivity (i.e., a force emanating from objects) or subjectivity (i.e., a coherent, universal projection of subjects toward objects), one must reject a Smithian model of the sentiment or any view that tries to find a consistent relationship between embodiment and externality. What displaces these elements for understanding the achievements called *meaning* and *value* is an emphasis on the vagaries through which interpretations are established and disestablished.

In Lacan's case, these vagaries are a dynamic, operating within a linguistic figuration, of subjectivity. In Foucault's, they are the arbitrary play of forces, involving institutional, technical, and historical events, through which one system of intelligibility is encouraged at the expense of rival interpretive possibilities. The results of these different instabilities require for both Lacan and Foucault different ethico-political problematics. Insofar as both are concerned with the opportunity for self-realization within the fact of an uneasy relationship between any self and the order, what is implied is a loosening of the grip of meaning-controlling discourses in order to open a space for negotiating and problematizing the production of the meaning of the self and the significance and value of self-other/self-object relations. Within both systems, the locus of the ethico-political problematic shifts away from the long tradition in which there have been attempts to locate the subject within a fixed and authoritative version of the order (from the cosmological to the social) and toward a focus on the dynamic of self-representation.

In the case of Lacan, the Sadean influence is clear. Lacan saw Sade as one who helped to recognize that the problem of the self is not one bound up with a harmonious nature and the good life but rather one of a dynamic involving law and transgression. Recognizing that the self has an uneasy relationship to the law and the order in general, and operating out of the scene of analysis and thus out of a concern with providing the subject with an appreciation of what blocks an accord with itself, Lacan departed from the long tradition in psychoanalysis in which the self is to be reconciled with an unambiguous external reality.[92] What is to be achieved, rather, is a recognition that what constitutes the reality of the self is a process of desiring that will always be experienced as a lack and that divides the subject while producing a motive for concealing its operations. Consciousness is thus not driven toward an expanding clarity but is produced out of a host of forces whose very aims are positively in the direction of ambiguity and opaqueness.

The discourse available to the subject is therefore highly coded, and the possibility for control over the meanings of desire requires a discursive savoir faire with oneself, that is, an ability to follow desire's fugitive, discursive moves. But the publicly controlled forms of discourse create yet another form of resistance to self-discovery or effective self-representation, for the self is always already and authoritatively represented to itself within them.

Ironically, the problem of fashioning a Lacanian ethic is structurally similar to the problem faced by the Lacanian subject. Lacan's notion of a divided self that must always sit uneasily within an order that provides few discursive resources for control over self-representation gives rise to an ethic that cannot be represented within the traditional discursive frames used to locate subjects (naturally or comfortably) within orders. To approach such an ethic, one has to treat desire not as something naturally or willfully domesticated to the order but as something constitutive of a self as it clashes with the order, producing a subject with transgressive as well as accommodative aims. On this view, there can be no social or political structure appropriate to house desire, for such structures are always implicated in its production and subsequent dis-ease.

The ethic that emerges from Lacan's perspective, then, is not one of seeking a rapport between the self and the order but one of recognizing how the singularity of desire (long ago recognized by Sade) implies a fundamental nonrapport in this relationship.[93] The subject's control over desire and the elusive meanings it projects in the process must operate within a recognition of this uneasy and ambiguous self-order relationship. Precisely because of the folly of ever developing a social bond based on an epistemic certainty—either that of the object or that of the subject—a "realistic" social bond must be based on an acceptance of uncertainty and ambiguity, a lack of clarity as to what we are and what we want. John Rajchman has put it well: "In painting we would love what remains 'invisible' in the visions it offers us; in architecture what is 'uninhabitable' in the habitations it makes for us; in literature what is 'unsayable' in what it says to us."[94]

To give the subject a chance for an ethical life and to conceive a politics that cannot be a function of the discovery of a common sense, it is necessary not only to abandon the very idea of an objectively good human order whose dynamic is embedded in an optimistic narrative that foresees a future self-order harmonization but also the certainty of vision and expression on which such an order is based.

An assessment of the ethico-political implications of Foucault's investigations also requires a move away from traditional ethical and political problematics. In the Smithian construction of vision, it makes no sense to speak of "ways of seeing" or the economies of the different practices directing the gaze and producing different significances from what is seen and what is made available to be seen. Linking vision to sentiment and sentiment to individual experience provides no way to construct what Foucault has revealed as a "positive unconscious," a domain not of the immediately visible but of what is responsible for what *can* (and cannot) be seen. A focus on this latter domain makes available to analysis not what the gaze takes in but what is responsible for *producing* what is seen.

Within the Foucauldian model there is an economy of the visible and invisible. What is seen is not a function of the unity provided by a perceiving subject, as in Smith's naturalistic or sensationalist model, but is a result of what has emerged from a contention among meaning-producing forces. The prevailing structures of intelligibility represent victories and defeats as there is simultaneously a production of the seen and the said as well as the invisible and the silent.

What is afforded is a more politicized view of vision. For example, the proliferating modes of surveillance that Foucault chronicles in his history of punishment—the more visible prisons, barracks, schools, and such, and the less visible sets of archives (e.g., "population" statistics)—all represent a dramatic shift in the structures of power, which rely more on the production of individual and collective identities than the former strategies of retaliatory, sovereign vengeance.[95] And this new form of power/knowledge is continually reproduced in the prevailing discourses within the social body, for speech and modes of observation are the acts of recognition, both verbal and visual, that constitute the exchanges within the concrete domain of association.

The meanings governing the social bond are thus not immediately available to the consciousness of those whose disciplined gazes and utterances help to reproduce it. It is a bond established less through imagination and sentiment than through inscription. Within this frame, the social is a text authored by the disciplinary agencies through which subjectivities are formed and known. The interpersonal ethic that results is not one in which people involved in "the common life" participate. It is an ethic in the form of a set of identities and institutional proprieties, duties and tasks that people unself-consciously reproduce by recognizing themselves in their adoption of the prevailing social discourses within which their identities are housed.

The social bond, which Foucault's highly ethical concerns are meant to confront, is thus not one based on interpersonal recognition or the exchange of sentiments. It is a "disciplinary unconscious,"[96] a result of anonymous practices that are *self*-making. The implications for producing a more available social ethic relate, then, to a problem of disclosure under the assumption that the individual is not necessarily in control of the meanings that produce social interpretation and exchange. They are not available to the gaze, even a gaze reinforced by "experience."

Foucault's understanding of subjectivity joins with his notions of the economies of the seen and the said to distance him from Smith's harmony orientation. Departing, as in the case of Lacan, from the tradition of ethico-political thinking in which one sought to discover the "nature" or the good life and the transcendent communalities in the self, Foucault has asserted that the self is almost infinitely malleable. There is nothing stable enough in it to invest a particular expectation about the proprieties of a given order: "Nothing in man—not even his body—is sufficiently stable to serve as the basis for self-recognition or for understanding other men."[97] Within such a view, there can be no social bond that is a noncoercive epistemological bond.

Like Sade, Foucault stages this recognition. In Foucault's case, the writing is not organized as fictional scenarios but as genealogical histories that contrast markedly with Smith's mythical/teleological ones. Having rejected the validity of framing questions about the self in terms of essentials, that is, in terms of knowing what we *are*, Foucault, has produced a set of historical investigations that have the effect of dislodging essentialist and naturalizing views of the self to help disclose what we have become in the context of alternative possibilities.

More specifically, by showing that different historical ages produce different modes of subjectivity and that these subjectivities operate within discursive economies that have, as modernity has approached, increasingly aided and abetted an intensely surveilling form of power, Foucault has sought to encourage an ethic of the self as a site of resistance. As he puts it in his meditation on the contemporary problem of the subject,"Maybe the target nowadays is not to discover what we are, but to refuse what we are."[98]

This resistance is not to be constituted as mere force against force, the self versus the order. It is to operate, rather, within the frame of interpretive economies. Insofar as the self is understood within the prevailing discursive practices—political, medical, educational, and so on—the body remains docile. Foucault's ethical/political position moves against this docility, seeking to encourage an order with a less intense power/knowledge impulse, one with more tolerance or slack so that persons have the space to shape the interpretations through which the self is made. Given a modernity in which the discursive practices fixing the self have proliferated, that slack would have to be realized at a discursive level. A Foucauldian ethic would thus encourage, at the level of theory, an abatement of the quest for theorizing or seeking to discover the true self, for this "real" is a fiction perpetuated by discourses of the order. The quest for the universal or transcendent aspect of the self (*chez* Smith) on which a definitive moral psychology can be built articulates with an exercise of power that has harnessed the self to the order.

This exercise of power has intensified, in the form, for example, of an increasing interest in knowing the sexual dimensions of desire. As Foucault notes in the beginning of his investigation into the history of sexuality—essentially a history of the way in which sexuality has been problematized in various historical ages—desire is best understood not as a unifying impulse (as it is for empirical psychologists) or a more complex mode of self-realization (as it is for phenomenologists) but as something functioning in discourse, helping to constitute the body or self as an object of knowledge. The ethico-political problematic of desire is not how to contain it within an order or how to shape an order to enhance it, but how to relax the intensity of interest in it, for this interest aids and abets attempts to quarantine types of selves (those prohibited, controlled or merely watched) and types of spaces (such as "heterotopias of deviance") where boundaries are erected and movements are restricted.[99]

What is left when such knowledge quests are relaxed? Rather than following Smith's attempt to locate the socially desirable dimensions of human embodiment and the forms of imagination it directs, it is important to open up the possibility for exercising an imagination of the possibilities for the self, to show how every view of the self is one among many possibilities. Within this kind of frame, imagination becomes what desire was for Sade, something whose restlessness must be encouraged rather than contained.

Notes

1. Adam Smith, *The Theory of Moral Sentiments*, ed. D. D. Raphael & A. L. Macfie (Indianapolis, IN: Liberty Classics, 1982), 94.

2. Smith, *Moral Sentiments*, 95.

3. Smith, *Moral Sentiments*, 95.

4. Smith, *Moral Sentiments*, 95.

5. Werner Stark, *The Social Bond* (New York: Fordham University Press, 1976), Vol. 1, 7.

6. Smith, *Moral Sentiments*, 22.

7. Philip Dick, *Do Androids Dream of Electric Sheep* (New York: Ballantine, 1968), 1.

8. Dick, *Do Androids Dream*, 13.

9. In Ridley Scott's film version of the story, *Blade Runner*, the animal more or less disappears, and the identity problematic focuses almost exclusively on the human android ("replicant" in the film) identity issue. This is treated in an extension of this discussion

in Michael J. Shapiro, " 'Manning' the Frontiers: The Politics of (Human) Nature in *Blade Runner*," in Jane Bennett & William Chaloupka, *In the Nature of Things* (Minneapolis: University of Minnesota Press, 1993).

10. Georges Bataille, *Lascaux; or the Birth of Art*, trans. Austryn Wainhouse (Lausanne, Switzerland: Skira, 1955), "Preface."

11. Bataille, *Lascaux*, 37.

12. Bataille, *Lascaux*, 37.

13. Franz Kafka, "A Report to an Academy," in Nahum N. Glatzer, ed., *The Complete Stories* (New York: Schocken, 1946), 258.

14. Donna Haraway, *Primate Visions: Gender, Race and Nature in the World of Modern Science* (New York: Routledge: 1990), 1.

15. Edgar Rice Burroughs, *Tarzan of the Apes* (New York: Ballantine, 1963), 71.

16. Burroughs, *Tarzan*, 72.

17. Shirley S. Strum & Bruno Latour, "Redefining the Social Link: From Baboons to Humans," in Glendon Schubert & Roger Masters, eds., *Primate Politics* (Carbondale, IL: Southern Illinois University Press, 1991), 78.

18. Strum & Latour, "Redefining the Social Link," 79.

19. Donna Haraway, "A Manifesto for Cyborgs," *Socialist Review, 15* (March/April 1985), 68.

20. Jonas Fykman & Orvar Lofgren, *Culture Builders* (New Brunswick, NJ: Rutgers University Press, 1987), 85.

21. Fykman & Lofgren, *Culture Builders*, 78-79.

22. Fykman & Lofgren, *Culture Builders*, 79.

23. This characterization belongs to Haraway, "Manifesto for Cyborgs," 66.

24. David Novitz, "Art, Narrative, and Human Nature," *Philosophy and Literature, 13* (1989), 59.

25. Novitz, "Art, Narrative, and Human Nature," 62.

26. This argument is made in Michael Ryan & Douglas Kellner, "Technophobia," in Annette Kuhn, ed., *Alien Zone* (New York: Verso, 1990), 63.

27. Haraway, "Manifesto for Cyborgs," 70.

28. Michael Beechler, "Border Patrols," in George E. Slusser & Eric S. Rabkin, eds., *Aliens: The Anthropology of Science Fiction* (Carbondale, IL: Southern Illinois University Press, 1987), 26.

29. Friedrich Nietzsche, *Human, All Too Human*, trans. Marion Farber (Lincoln, NE: University of Nebraska Press, 1984), #111, 81.

30. This expression belongs to Jean Baudrillard, *In the Shadow of the Silent Majority: On the End of the Social*, trans. Paul Foss, Paul Patton, & John Johnson (New York: Semiotext(e), 1983).

31. This shift is described by Michel Foucault, "Governmentality," *Ideology and Consciousness, 3* (No. 6) (1979).

32. Smith, *Moral Sentiments*, 9.

33. Smith, *Moral Sentiments*, 45.

34. Smith, *Moral Sentiments*, 123.

35. The quotation is from Alphonso Lingus's introduction to Pierre Klossowski, *Sade My Neighbor*, trans. Alphonso Lingus (Evanston, IL: Northwestern University Press, 1991), xii.

36. Adam Smith, *Lectures on Rhetoric and Belles Lettres*, ed. J. C. Bryce (Oxford: The Clarendon Press, 1983), 8.

37. Jacques Lacan, *Television*, trans. Denis Hollier, Rosalind Krauss, & Annette Michelson (New York: Norton, 1990), 6.

38. This aspect of Lacan's treatment of "the real" is elaborated by Slavoj Zizek, *Looking Awry* (Cambridge, MA: M.I.T. Press, 1991).

39. Robert Heilbroner, "The Wonderful World of Adam Smith," in *The Worldly Philosophers* (New York: Simon & Schuster, 1980).

40. Smith, *Moral Sentiments*, 166.

41. Smith, *Moral Sentiments*, 22.

42. Smith, *Moral Sentiments*, 184-85.

43. Frank Kermode, "Secrets and Narrative Sequence," *Critical Inquiry*, 7 (Autumn 1980), 85.

44. Thorstein Veblen, "The Preconceptions of the Classical Economists," in *The Portable Veblen*, ed. Max Lerner (New York: Viking, 1948), 242.

45. Smith, *Moral Sentiments*, 44.

46. Smith, *Moral Sentiments*, 44.

47. Smith, *Moral Sentiments*, 30.

48. The historical narrative of vision inaugurated in the 19th century is elaborated in John Crary, *Techniques of the Observer: On Vision and Modernity in the 19th Century* (Cambridge, MA: M.I.T. Press, 1991).

49. Michel Foucault, *Discipline and Punish: The Birth of the Prison*, trans. Alan Sheridan (New York: Pantheon, 1977), 217.

50. Crary, *Techniques of the Observer*, 20.

51. Ludwig Wittgenstein, *Philosophical Investigations* (New York: Macmillan, 1953), 118.

52. Smith, *Lectures on Rhetoric*, ed. J. C. Bryce (Oxford: The Clarendon Press, 1983), 8.

53. Smith, *Lectures on Rhetoric*, 9.

54. Wittgenstein, *Philosophical Investigations*, 100.

55. Jean-Francois Lyotard, *The Postmodern Condition*, trans. Geoff Bennington & Brian Massumi (Minneapolis: University of Minnesota Press, 1984), 10.

56. Smith, *Moral Sentiments*, 88.

57. Smith, *Moral Sentiments*, 20.

58. Smith, *Moral Sentiments*, 23.

59. M. M. Bakhtin, "Discourse and the Novel," in *The Dialogic Imagination*, ed. Michale Holquist and trans. Caryl Emerson & Michael Holquist (Austin, TX: University of Texas Press, 1981), 271-72.

60. This remark is at the beginning of David B. Morris, *The Culture of Pain* (Berkeley, CA: University of California Press, 1991), 1, an analysis that *does* situate pain historically.

61. Morris, *Culture of Pain*, 34.

62. Smith, *Moral Sentiments*, 121.

63. Smith, *Moral Sentiments*, 118.

64. Marquis de Sade, "Philosophy in the Bedroom," in *Justine, Philosophy in the Bedroom, and Other Writings*, trans. Richard Seaver & Austryn Wainhouse (New York: Grove Press, 1965), 208.

65. Sade, "Philosophy in the Bedroom," 217.

66. This interpretation conforms to Freud's view of the sadistic impulse. He argued in effect that the masochistic urge takes precedence in the narrative, for the desire to inflict pain is not primary. What is primarily desired is the sexual excitement one derives from the imagination of being a sufferer. Thus one inflicts the pain in order to identify with the victim. See his "Instincts and Their Vicissitudes," *The Standard Edition of the Complete Psychological Works of Sigmund Freud*, ed. James Stachey (London: Hogarth Press, 1953).

67. Marquis de Sade, *The 120 Days of Sodom and Other Writings*, trans. Richard Seaver & Austryn Wainhouse (New York: Grove Press, 1966), 200.

68. This part of the discussion is influenced by Leo Bersani's treatment of Sade in his analysis of narrative in *Assyrian Art: The Forms of Violence* (New York: Schocken, 1985).

69. Sade, *120 Days of Sodom*, 185.

70. This point is strongly emphasized in Simone de Beauvoir's treatment, "Must We Burn Sade," in *The Marquis de Sade: An Essay*, trans. Annette Michelson (New York: Grove Press, 1953), 77.

71. Jacques Lacan, "Kant with Sade," trans. James B. Swenson, Jr., *October, 51* (Winter 1989), 55.

72. Smith, *Moral Sentiments*, 166.

73. Lacan, "Kant with Sade," 56.

74. Lacan, "Kant with Sade," 56.

75. Sade, *120 Days of Sodom*, 200.

76. Sade, "Philosophy in the Bedroom," 217.

77. This point is made in Josué Harari's essay, "Sade's Discourse on Method: Rudiments for a Theory of Fantasy," in Colette V. Michael, ed., *Sade: His Ethics and Rhetoric* (New York: Peter Lang, 1989), 143-160.

78. Nietzsche, *Human, All Too Human*, #11, 84.

79. Klossowski, *Sade My Neighbor*, 16.

80. Marquis de Sade, *Juliette*, trans. Austryn Wainhouse (New York: Grove, 1968), 317-17.

81. Lacan, "Kant With Sade," 67.

82. Smith, *Moral Sentiments*, 166.

83. Gilles Deleuze, *Masochism: An Interpretation of Coldness and Cruelty* (New York: Braziller, 1971), 17.

84. The *pornogram* term belongs to Roland Barthes, *Sade, Fourier, Loyola* (New York: Hill and Wang, 1976), 158-59.

85. Smith, *Moral Sentiments*, 130-31.

86. This is Barthes's expression: *Sade, Fourier, Loyola*, 17.

87. Barthes, *Sade, Fourier, Loyola*, 124.

88. This is Barthes's expression: *Sade, Fourier, Loyola*, 149.

89. Sade, "Philosophy in the Bedroom," 191.

90. Sade, "Philosophy in the Bedroom," 217.

91. Sade, "Philosophy in the Bedroom," 310.

92. See, for example, Jacques Lacan, "The Subversion of the Subject and the Dialectic of Desire in the Freudian Unconscious," in *Ecrits: A Selection*, trans. Alan Sheridan (New York: Norton, 1977), 292-325.

93. My interpretation of the Lacanian version of ethics is influenced by the discussion in John Rajchman, "Lacan and the Ethics of Modernity," *Representations, 15* (Summer 1986), 42-56

94. John Rajchman, *Truth and Eros* (New York: Routledge, 1991), 75.

95. Foucault, *Discipline and Punish.*

96. This expression belongs to Paul Bové. See his introduction to Gilles Deleuze, *Foucault,* trans. Sean Hand (Minneapolis: University of Minnesota Press, 1988), xxi.

97. Michel Foucault, "Nietzsche, Genealogy, History," in Donald Bouchard, ed., *Language, Counter-Memory, Practice* (Ithaca, NY: Cornell University Press, 1977), 153.

98. Michel Foucault, "The Subject and Power," in Hubert L. Dreyfus & Paul Rabinow, *Michel Foucault: Beyond Structuralism and Hermeneutics* (Chicago: University of Chicago Press, 1982), 216.

99. Michel Foucault, "Of Other Spaces," trans. Jay Miscowiec, *Diacritics* (Spring 1986), 25.

Index

About the Author

Michael J. Shapiro is Professor of Political Science at the University of Hawaii. His recent publications include: *The Politics of Representation: Writing Practices in Biography, Photography, and Policy Analysis* (University of Wisconsin Press, 1988); *International/Intertextual Relations*, coedited with James Der Derian (Macmillan, 1989); and *Reading the Postmodern Polity: Political Theory as Textual Practice* (University of Minnesota Press, 1992).

ARNOLD'S GENERAL STUDIES

General Editor: M. C. MORGAN

What is a Novel?

MALCOLM BRADBURY

 **Edward Arnold** (Publishers) **Ltd.**

© Malcolm Bradbury 1969
First published 1969
SBN 7131 1573 4

ARNOLD'S GENERAL STUDIES

Already published
VISUAL ART   B. A. Killeen
ATOMS AND ANCESTORS   F. B. Welbourn
SCIENCE IN SOCIETY   R. L. M. Synge

In preparation
STATISTICS   D. M. Urquhart
SOME MORAL PROBLEMS   Kenneth C. Barnes
POLITICS AND ECONOMICS   Richard Bailey
RACE RELATIONS   Philip Mason

Printed in Great Britain by
WESTERN PRINTING SERVICES LTD, BRISTOL

General Preface

General studies as a subject in Sixth Forms or Technical Colleges now hardly needs champions but it does need suitable material. Young adult students, whatever their abilities, are conscious of their limited knowledge in many fields and of the folly of trying to discuss or write on topics they may be ignorant of. They want information.

This series of booklets is designed to give essential information in a number of specific areas and at reasonable length. Each booklet, written by a specialist, discovers the bones of its subject and aims to stimulate thought and imagination. Each is open-ended in that it invites questions and leads on to some of the most perplexing problems in the subject. Throughout each booklet there are 'signposts', by way of bibliographies and other suggestions, which can help the interested student to pursue any topic in greater depth.

The booklets are so bound that they are reasonably durable—but they can also easily be dismantled and the pages punched to form part of a student's own folder or file in which he can expand and illustrate the material given here and agree or disagree with it.

The General Editor and the Publisher welcome comments and suggestions for further topics.

To David Farrer

Contents

Acknowledgements

Much of the material in this book was worked out for and with the students of the First Year Novel Course at the University of Birmingham. I should like to express my gratitude to them, and also to my colleagues in the teaching of the course. Above all to one colleague in particular, David Lodge, a very fine novelist and a very fine critic.

Norwich, 1969

CHAPTER ONE

The Novel Today

The novel is a more or less modern form of literature—we usually reckon it to start with CERVANTES' **Don Quixote** (1605–15)—and not one you will find in all the cultures of the world. Narrative is almost as old as time itself; even written narrative has a long history. But the particular form of narrative we have in the novel—the long invented story in prose with a realistic emphasis and very much the original and individual product of one man's experience and imagination—has never been universal. Still, in our own culture it has been one of the central forms of literary practice for the last 250 years; and it remains so today. It sustained homebound women and literate servants in the eighteenth century; it formed matter for communal family reading in the nineteenth; it has filled leisure hours and long train and plane journeys in the twentieth, and despite the competing claims of film and television we still continue to read and be fascinated by it. So in our culture a considerable number of novels are written, published, bought or borrowed and, one hopes, read every year—novels satisfying all kinds of taste at different levels of seriousness. If we were asked, we might find it hard to explain why we should spend time reading something that is a tissue of lies, or why we should be impressed by interpretations of people, society and life that are produced by individuals who aren't professionally or scientifically trained to deal in these matters. But in its mixture of imagination and realism the novel has long engrossed us, from level to level—as simple narrative for its own sake, as a complex interpretation of experience, as a complicated play of art. And despite the growth of expertise in what are called human sciences, despite the new forms of art that have emerged, there are few real signs that it is stopping doing so. This original, empirical species of writing still holds its power. Of course the novel we know now is not quite the novel as it was in the eighteenth or even the nineteenth century. It is, after all, a structure of experience; and as society, ideas and experience have changed and the very content of the human mind has altered, so novels have

7

changed too. Yet the sequence remains; and the broad form has
had a kind of institutional continuity. At times it has been pronounced dead, but it certainly is not. The novel is a loose and
changeable form, and that perhaps has ensured its survival, its
power to go on doing what it has always done: describing and
exploring the culture of its society—and making it.

THE PLACE OF THE NOVEL TODAY

When the novel emerged, it *was* very novel: the product of a
new cultural environment produced by two basic things—a new
medium and a new audience. The medium was the commercial,
available printed book that followed on cheap paper, movable
type, growing literacy. The audience was a rising class of urban
tradesmen with fresh interests and values. The novel brought in
new ways of seeing life, and therefore extended the arts both
technically and socially. It emerged, then, as a popular narrative
form—dealing with fairly familiar experience, in fairly familiar
language. So it was, as one critic has put it, the 'burgher epic'.
And ever since it has tended to exploit that basic fascination that
narrative can have for its own sake, to appeal to broad audiences,
to draw on popular mythologies, to confront fairly recognisable
and ordinary experience. It has also tended to identify with new
tendencies or rising classes and to change with new modes of
publishing. More than many forms of art, it has often thriven
close to the line where literature and sub-literature meet, and
been pulled toward simple storytelling, journalism, polemic or
moral tract. But it has also made itself serious and complex, and
has been proved one of the most variously resourceful of all art-
forms.

Today there is a new revolution of the media and the audience;
once more a matter of technological coinciding with social change.
But now the technological change is *away* from print—toward
electronic media (radio, films, television) which are, again, undergoing large commercial application to obtain their maximum use.
The social change is the growth of something like mass-society—
a much less stratified, but much bigger and more uniform, society.
It tends to receive its communications and its culture rather
passively from a common centre, and this is why the mass-media
are so important (and indeed why *they* are one of the forces making
our experiences more uniform). These media have certainly
partly ousted the novel from its cultural centre. For not only can
they often present narrative more effectively—a story can be presented more quickly visually than verbally, with more immediacy
and less exposition. They have also taken over some of the novel's

documentary qualities—its ways of telling us about other parts of society, or what makes it work, or how people we know or places we live in might appear in other eyes, or what forces are affecting our lives. The rise of mass-circulation journalism at the end of the last century also affected the novel, but there we can see clearly how the novel responded. It did so rather as painting responded to photography; both by borrowing and reacting against the new techniques and so proliferating new ones of its own. This seems to be happening again in fiction; the rapid visualism of the media is being borrowed, and also being withdrawn from. The novel is not in short ceasing to function. After all, it does retain certain advantages over radio, television and film. Books have their own inbuilt convenience. They are easily carried and stored, easily retrieved for further consultation, and they can be consumed by the reader at his own time and his own speed in the place of his choice. And from the writer's point of view, the novel is the most controllable form of narrative. It is more individualistic, more personal, more open to the writer's distinctive mind and art. Written language is a very precise instrument; and unlike the film or TV script it is not handled by influential intermediaries but transferred to the reader with the minimum of interference.

Similarly, the novel is also responding to and being changed by the new audiences of the post-war world. It is becoming less clearly segmented into highbrow, middlebrow, and lowbrow; it is answering to new tastes and styles. No doubt it has suffered somewhat from the decline of the old middle-class reading public and the relative decline in the status of books. Earlier in the century a novelist could acquire a vast celebrity, a star status. Novels got a large proportion of the space devoted to the arts in newspapers and magazines; and a famous figure like Arnold Bennett could make an author's reputation with a newspaper mention. The novelist today certainly lacks the remarkable influence and power, the sense of helping to form the culture of society and the taste of the reader, that was felt by a Laurence Sterne, a Charles Dickens, an Anthony Trollope, an Arnold Bennett. That was already beginning to fade in the early part of this century, when the division between the 'serious' novelist and the 'popular' one began to sharpen. Today, probably, the popular novelist finds the market somewhat harder than he did, though the bestseller is still a remarkable commercial proposition, and a novelist like Ian Fleming can earn not only startling sales but startling interest from readers. Novels are probably still normally read by the middle-classes, but the growth of the paperback has altered the market too. It has made novels available to a broadened public, particularly to the young. The longer time spent in education—some of it spent actually in studying novels or the novel—has also helped the more serious novelist: his sophisticated audience has increased, though it may also have become much more abstractly interested in literature.

None the less, the career of the novelist today is perhaps not quite as attractive as it was. Compared with Sir Walter Scott or George Eliot, he is not likely to make large profits from his work, nor often to be taken quite so seriously. The modern novelist is probably therefore likely to feel the contemporary limitations as well as the advantages of his form, as a medium of expression, as an instrument for influence, and as a medium of success. In England, at least, he may find his career a shaky one. So he may well not write novels alone, but also television scripts and film scenarios, or poems and plays. As a result of all this, it would seem true to say that we are not in one of the great eras of the novel at the present time—not in England, though the situation seems different in France and the United States. But even so, the number of novels published annually continues to rise; important and gifted novelists do continue to appear on the scene; the general level of competence is enormously high; and the novelist still has a sizeable audience.

What is the present state of the form? In 1968, 31,420 books were published in Britain. Of these, 2,094 were novels. Most of these novels (not all by English writers) appeared in the form of one-volume hard cover books c. 75,000 words long and costing somewhere near 25s. each. In addition, many novels published earlier reappeared in paperback reprint, usually after a one-year or two-year timelag; while many novels of the past, of 'classic' status, were also reissued as hardbacks or paperbacks. These forms of publication, and this length of novel, have not always been conventional. In the past, novels were frequently a good deal longer. And they commonly appeared either in an expensive three-volume format, or else in some kind of serial form. For instance, a famous eighteenth-century work, Laurence STERNE'S **The Life and Opinions of Tristram Shandy, Gent.,** appeared in nine thin volumes between 1760 and 1769, the venture only being concluded by the death of the author. A hundred years later, Charles Dickens was publishing many of his novels in short serial instalments of about 32 pages, only later gathering the whole up into a book. Each of them could change the story according to the responses he got from his readers. Besides being shorter and more self-contained, the modern novel is relatively inexpensive compared with most forms of past publication: and it is made the more available by the free library system (the nineteenth-century circulating library had of course to be paid).

Among last year's novels there were various sorts and levels of fiction, many of them ventures in familiar sub-genres—romance-novels or love-stories for various audiences; crime and detective stories; science-fiction novels; historical novels; works of semi-pornography. Only a proportion of these books—including, of course, some in the above categories—attempted to do more than cater for fairly familiar needs of the audience. Only this proportion will seek to explore more or less fully the nature and feel of human experience, the moral logic and complications of the kind of life they have chosen to deal with, the deeper texture and moral complication of society, or the very structure of the novel-form itself. But these are the potential survivors—and it will normally be these that the reviewers in the serious newspapers and weeklies will try to pick out, as they sort through the piles of the ten or twenty novels appearing that week in search of the four or five they feel worthy of review. So, in the course of a year, perhaps no more than 500 of the total number of novels will ever receive a proper review. Of these, in turn, a very small number indeed will be selected for special attention. An even smaller number will crop up again when literary critics start writing surveys of the modern novel or the fiction of the 1960s. The reviewers are important middlemen in the fortunes of the novel, and inevitably they make mistakes—because the line between competence and brilliance is always hard to draw, because they work under conditions of haste, because there are so very many novels. There is a second court of appeal: the readers themselves. Many novels will acquire a clique reputation among certain special groups —ranging from small groups like the friends of the author, to larger ones like a particular intellectual, generational or class community. TOLKIEN'S **Lord of the Rings** cycle, for instance, gained a great reputation among many younger readers and has been brought back into critical attention as a result.

As this suggests, the selecting out of reputations is a long-term process and in many ways an extremely chancy one. It is to a point a cultural phenomenon, deserving sociological study. Often a novel will crystallise a fashionable attitude, a taste, a temper of mind, among a particular group at a particular time, rather as the mini-skirt did. The general excitement of ten years back about the Angry Young Man is a clear case of this. But, more than the mini-skirt, novels do have it in them to reveal much of the meaning of a fashion or a temper; they report their own content and can be more fully analysed. This aspect of novels is always important, not only in the fiction of the present but in the fiction of the past. It is of course only when a novel is genuinely exploratory that its interest becomes *more* than a matter of sociological fascination . . . becomes, in a full sense, a matter for literary criticism. Even so, criticism can always be very profitably aware of the social and cultural origins of novels. The popular response to novelists is often a very significant indicator of taste and of the interests and obsessions of a culture. For novelists can throw into relief those details of a society which particularly interest those who live in it. Novelists often articulate myths highly relevant to the society— like the meritocratic myth of success embodied in John BRAINE'S **Room at the Top**. Or they catch the language of a tone or moral temper; this was an essential part of Ernest Hemingway's success. Or they draw into fiction parts of the society which seemed previously to be submerged, as Alan SILLITOE did with **Saturday Night and Sunday Morning**. Or they offer an image of man as he sees himself to be now—as in Albert CAMUS'S **The Outsider**. Or they manage to give a kind of common co-herence to a new audience, a new cultural group, as J. D. SALINGER did with adolescents in **The Catcher in the Rye**. All of these are relevant parts of a novel's significance and meaning.

The post-war novel in England has not been remarkable for its revolutions of form; but it has conducted a fairly intensive ex-ploration of the way we live now. While a few novelists, like Lawrence Durrell, Iris Murdoch and Samuel Beckett, have been conspicuously experimental, many others (Kingsley Amis, John Wain, Colin MacInnes, Alan Sillitoe, Angus Wilson, for instance) have been more concerned with exploring new kinds of social experience and new ways of looking at our situation. Iris Murdoch once observed that there are really two kinds of novel: the crystal-line, which concentrates on refining and even on schematising the plot; and the journalistic, which concentrates on the chance happenings of life and on responses to immediate truths. She points out that both elements are needed in a novel: a sense of myth and a sense of actuality. In a contemporary novel, a novel of our own time, the reader is often most drawn by that sense of actuality, because it illuminates his own environment and experience, and instructs him in his own world. But *all* novels, even the most detailed ones, involve a conscious making, a play of art. If the current English novel has chosen to emphasise the element of actuality rather than the element of fictiveness, then there are perhaps two main reasons. The first is that we have seen a marked change in our world since the war, and we have had to explore new ways of seeing and knowing it. The second is that we live so soon after the great experiment of the modern novel early in the century: an experiment, by writers like Henry James, James Joyce and D. H. Lawrence, so large and radical that it is difficult for the modern writer to feel he can go further. None the less, there are increasing signs that the novel is moving toward a new era of formal experiment in England, as it already has in the United States and in France: experiment less remarkable than that of the early 'modernist' writers, but still a way of examining the nature of modern experience not only by detailing it but trying to find a fictive structure relevant to it.

THE CRITICISM OF NOVELS

The novel has a double obligation, as Iris Murdoch says; it must know and explore the world outside itself, and it must also explore within itself—its language, its structure, its form. And if, as readers, we are to understand the nature of the novel, we must likewise be able both to immerse ourselves in the actuality of particular novels and to stand further back and look at the nature of the form, in its resources and its complexity. We must, ourselves, be able to appreciate the intensity of experience in this particular work of fiction, and also to be able to see its art—and compare it with the art of other novels in order to see it more completely. The activity of literary criticism has always sought to ask questions relevant to both kinds of response. Part of its purpose is to ask specific questions about the particular work we are interested in—*this* poem, *this* play, *this* novel—and to enter into it as a distinctive and unique imaginative experience. But another part of its task is to stand back and compare—to ask broad and general questions about the nature of the form, its history and tradition, and its social meaning and significance. The central activity of criticism—the imaginative response to the individual book—can only develop properly through the making of comparisons and connections, and that means having some sense of the general attributes of the art-form which the writer has taken as his means of expression. For the writer, the making of a novel is a fairly lonely activity—an attempt at ordering his own distinctive experience and vision in a right and satisfying way. But all novels exist in some relation to their precedents, and every writer has some sense of the tradition of the form—or at least of the stock of practices he can draw on. For the critic, standing outside, any novel, however individual, will belong to the tradition and the shared community of the novel, though it may also change these.

Criticism ranges, then, between the broad and the specific questions—between *what is a novel?* and *what is this novel?*—and the purpose of this book is to explore the ways in which we can talk about both these questions. I have started with the broader and harder questions first. Not that this is always the best approach in criticism; but a book dealing with the novel generally must contain an implicit 'poetics'—that is, an assumed view of what a novel is and a language for talking about what parts go to make up a novel's whole. For criticism is not only a response to books, but a way of learning to talk about books, to find an adequate language for expressing our experience as readers. The obligation on criticism is to be inclusive, which means not to let its theory get ahead of its practice, so that it can only talk about one kind of novel or one kind of poem. So I have tried to conduct my argument hereafter with two things in mind—first, that there are certain general questions and quandaries about the novel which need airing; and secondly, that every novel of serious interest that you read invites not just a description but an imaginative response, an appreciation of the distinctive life and art that has gone into it. The purpose of this book is to help with a general critical approach to *all* novels— not just the ones I shall go on to refer to or discuss. These I have picked out largely from novels usually regarded by critics as serious and important, because they more than any will suggest something of the variety of fictional method and the vast resources of the novel form. But what I have said can be applied to other novels that are not discussed here—for every novel is a contribution to this most complex and varied of the literary forms.

CHAPTER TWO

Defining the Novel

Of all the literary forms—poetry, drama, the novel—the novel is the hardest to define, and probably the most difficult to discuss effectively in criticism. For this there are various reasons. The novel in England began in the eighteenth century—a period in which classical definitions were strong in other forms—with a strong impulse against formal definition. From the start, there was a stress on the novel's originality, on its defying the traditional literary conventions or at least reforming them radically. Hence the appropriateness of the very term *novel*. Secondly there is the problem of the novel's sheer size—its bulk in terms of its length and the variety of experience it can contain. As Percy LUBBOCK says in his **The Craft of Fiction** (1921): 'As quickly as we read, [the novel] melts and shifts in the memory; even at the moment when the last page is turned, a greater part of the book, its finer detail, is already vague and doubtful.' And thirdly there is the fact that criticism in the past has usually taken poetry and drama to be the two respectable and worthwhile forms; it is only fairly recently that it has really been granted that novels can have the complexity, self-consciousness and seriousness of the other two. Consequently most criticism has exercised itself on poems and plays, and when it has turned to novels it has often chosen to make use of the critical techniques developed for poems and plays.

NOVELS VERSUS POEMS AND PLAYS

A lyric poem we can examine closely, word for word. The novel is much less susceptible to this kind of analysis. We can (and there are many successful and fascinating examples of this)* examine particular passages of the novel's prose in close detail, acquiring a sense of the resources and power of the individual writer. But when it comes to the analysis of the total structure, that overall design of which these passages are only a particular part, then we find the task difficult and the terminology (plot, character, description and so on) weak. Critics of the novel must not only be attentive to those qualities of mood, imagery and verbal intensity

* For instance, in F. R. Leavis, *The Great Tradition* (London, 1948).

we talk of when we discuss a lyric poem (itself, of course, as much of an organism as a novel, but more open to analysis because we can hold onto the whole as we talk of the parts). We must also define the fullness of the novel's design as it exists progressively; we must analyse the sources of momentum and energy which are produced by the sheer spatial extension of the book. We can effectively reveal the workings of the single paragraph; we can suggest its relation to the larger action; but when it comes to talking about that action and the large and full world in which it is conducted we often find ourselves in difficulties. Moreover, the novel's peculiar closeness to life, its concern with the immediate, the here and now, the feel of place and time, also creates difficulties. We can see a poem within its fictional frame, within its convention. But the language of the novel tends to be much less heightened, closer to ordinary usage. It appeals much more to our immediate and familiar experience of people, of places, and of the feel of life generally. It often insists on the reality of what it describes; even though the form is also capable of extreme poetic and stylised effects.

Hence the novel is a complex structure that is much more extended than most poems, dealing with a wider range of presented life, appealing to the reader with a much greater variety of approaches, and above all stating its conventions and its intentions with much less clarity. A poem normally reveals its character to us pretty readily; we know right away that a poem is what it is. It has its own distinct and recognisable conventions, metrical, rhythmical, typographical, formal. And it usually suggests fairly quickly, by layout and tone, what *kind* of a poem it is, with a distinctiveness impossible to fiction. We recognise the design of a sonnet, and have an immediate general awareness of the sort of sentiment and thought this type of poem can contain. Even with more extended poems, like the epic, there are conventional devices (an invocation to the muse, say) for suggesting its general character and its heroic nature. Of course there are, particularly in modern poetry, many attempts to break down the forms: mock-epic, e.g. BYRON'S **Don Juan**, or even anti-epic, e.g. ELIOT'S **The Waste Land**. With drama, too, there is a distinctive form of presentation—actors, stage, an audience with a sense of theatrical ritual—which also puts a formal frame around the work. Novels lack these clear conventions, and that is why the form is so hard to define.

WHAT IS A NOVEL?

The question is one critics have found particularly difficult to answer, for reasons already suggested. Its language is prose—the language we speak in, argue in, write in. So there is little about a novel's presentation to distinguish it directly from any other printed book. It is often hard to tell it apart from history, biography, reportage or sociology, on the techniques and structures of which it very often draws (for instance Henry FIELDING very deliberately calls his most famous novel **The HISTORY of Tom Jones**). It is of course fictitious, like poetry and drama, though it sometimes deliberately plays down its fictiveness. Beyond that there is little to distinguish it by: to say how it works, what shape it will take, what effect it will seek to produce, what relation this novel has to others. This unformalised quality of the novel is something it may explore and exploit—the fact that it has a good deal in common with ordinary speech, or with reportage; the fact that it is particularly able to follow out in detail the happenings of everyday experience; the fact that the structure is intrinsically loose enough to let the slow, disorderly skein of that experience work itself out, unfold itself as in life. When we start reading a novel, we can have little real foreknowledge of what kind of events and insights the novelist is going to explore, or what kind of relationship with the author and with language we are entering on. The novel lacks the sharp sense of generic quality other forms have; it also tends to exploit the lack.

This mixed character of the novel, and its openness to wide variation, has been used in all sorts of ways. One of the earliest English novels, Daniel DEFOE'S **Moll Flanders** (1722), exploits the potential literalness and factuality of the novel's prose:

> My true name [the novel begins] is so well known in the records or registers at Newgate, and in the Old Bailey, and there are some things of such consequence still depending there, relating to my particular conduct, that it is not to be expected I should set my name or the account of my family to this work; perhaps, after my death, it may be better known; at present it would not be proper, no, not though a general pardon should be issued, even without exceptions and reserve of persons or crimes.

> It is enough to tell you, that as some of my worst comrades, who are out of the way of doing me harm (having gone out of the world by the steps and the string, as I often expected to go), knew me by the name of Moll Flanders, so you may give me leave to speak of myself under that name till I dare own who I have been, as well as who I am.

Real places, present dangers—though this is fiction, it is clearly presented as fact, with a perpetual appeal to the true, the actual

and existing. It is set in a contemporary world and not in an
illusory or 'invented' universe. Even the fiction of the name of the
central character has to be placed as the concealment of a real fact.
The authenticity gained by placing the story in the real and known
world is also supported by the language. That, too, is recognisably
ordinary and literal—very much the language of a fairly ordinary
person assumed to be telling her own story in the form of a re-
collection, and embodying her matter-of-fact view of the world.
By no means all novels are as 'factual' as **Moll Flanders**; nor do
all novels exploit the relation of art and life like this. But the important thing is that here, in this early novel, we have a kind of
literalness never before achieved by any other art-form. There is
a deliberate avoidance of the established conventions and techniques of heightening we associate with other kinds of literature.
Instead, the book conveys the feeling that the structure of this
kind of literature must come from those structures and perceptions
by which we, as ordinary men, see, record and order our natural
experiences, and this means a heavy stress on the particularity
and detail of life.

On the other hand, if we take another fairly early English
novel—this time Laurence STERNE'S **The Life and Opinions
of Tristram Shandy, Gent.** (1760–67)—we find a totally different
way of exploiting the medium. Sterne's novel is built upon the
joke that a fiction is precisely a fiction, and he tantalisingly exploits
the situation of his storyteller, Tristram, to mock the conventions
and the literalness the form can possess. His author's preface and
the dedication appear in the middle of the novel; he misses out a
chapter, and then recites its contents later; he makes persistent
comedy out of the writing situation, the reading situation, the
publishing situation, the contrast between the time of the events
told and the time it takes the reader to read them ('is it not a
shame to make two chapters of what passed in going down one
pair of stairs? for we are got no farther yet than to the first landing,
and there are fifteen more steps down to the bottom; and for
aught I know, as my father and my uncle Toby are in a talking
humour, there may be as many chapters as steps . . .'). Sterne's
novel is already a protest against such generic conventions as the
still-new form could assume—for instance, many eighteenth-
century novels begin with the birth of the hero, so he begins his,
ironically, with the hero's conception. It is also a reminder that
literalness is a literary *illusion*. And novels like Defoe's should not
mislead us into thinking that the language of fiction is less highly
charged than that of poetry, or that novels are without distinctive
conventions, structures, and powers to create an intense fictiveness

—a fictiveness not always used as mockingly as Sterne uses it. Novels may often be lifelike; but to appreciate them we must never forget that they are not life. They invent life and create it, controlling and providing and using every detail of what is invented. And they invent it through language—which means that the final terms of what is written are always controlled by the writer; and that a fiction is a making.

But it is because novels can invent in so many ways, and are open to so many kinds of structure and order, that we find it hard to define the form. In his book **Aspects of the Novel** (1927), E. M. FORSTER popularised the definition of a French critic which is vague enough to be possible. A novel is, he says, 'a fiction in prose of a certain extent'—and he adds that the extent should be not less than 50,000 words. This distinguishes the novel from the poem and play, from the short story, and the work of non-fictional prose. It also, perhaps, hints at other marked features of novels. For if length is important then this implies a certain largeness of structure; if prose is important then that suggests a range within which language can be used; if fiction is important it stresses that the factuality must finally be permeated with invention and control. Actually, though, there are quite a lot of works that meet Forster's definition and still are not usually considered novels—mediaeval prose-romances like Malory's Arthurian stories, moral allegories like John BUNYAN'S **Pilgrim's Progress**, moral satires like SWIFT'S **Gulliver's Travels**. Even in the nineteenth century, novelists like Nathaniel Hawthorne and Henry James distinguished between novels and romances, and knew when they were writing the one or the other. So HAWTHORNE insists, in a preface to **The House of the Seven Gables** (1851), a neo-Gothic work about a curse working through the history of a New England household:

> When a writer calls his work a Romance, it need hardly be observed that he wishes to claim a certain latitude, both as to its fashion and material, which he would not have felt himself entitled to assume, had he professed to be writing a Novel. The latter form of composition is presumed to aim at a very minute fidelity, not merely to the possible, but to the probable and ordinary course of man's experience. . . .

This suggests that a considerable element of 'fidelity' and realism is an important part of the definition of a novel. Yet in the twentieth century we have seen dispute going on at the opposite pole—with, for instance, Truman CAPOTE'S **In Cold Blood**, the heavily-researched story of an actual murder in Kansas which might have been called non-fiction had Capote not insisted it was a novel (on the grounds that it finally pursues a standard of aesthetic rather than factual relevance). So, despite Forster's suggestion, the novel remains hard to recognise; but it is surely between these two poles—that of romance and that of non-fiction —that it stands.

In fact a certain recognition of the realism of the novel is essential to defining it. Romance in prose surely predates what we mean by the novel; it is really only after the novel clearly emerges with a self-aware existence, a conscious generic identity, that we can think of it as a form and as a tradition. That happens certainly after 1605, when CERVANTES reacted against mediaeval romance with the comic deflations of **Don Quixote**, which had the satirical purpose of bringing about 'the Fall and Destruction of that monstrous Heap of ill-contrived Romances, which, though abhorr'd by many, have so strangely infatuated the greater part of Mankind' (including, of course, the deluded Don himself). In fact, the novel really needs a degree of historical and sociological, as well as literary, explanation. It is as a form associated with certain fairly modern ways of knowing and understanding life, and we normally connect it with the rise of scientific empiricism and the social dominance of the bourgeoisie. It is associated with the historical triumph of written prose as an instrument for empirical analysis, reportage, and linear argument; it belongs with an un-mystical and unheroic way of looking at the world. As two recent critics, Robert Scholes and Robert Kellogg, comment, in their book *The Nature of Narrative* (1966), the novel is an empirical kind of narration: 'It requires for its development means of accurate measurement in time and space, and concepts of causality referable to human and natural rather than supernatural agencies.'

In view of all this, perhaps the best definition of the novel is still the one attempted by Henry FIELDING in his preface to **Joseph Andrews** (1742), when he tried to suggest the nature of the still new form emerging from the traditional genres. Employing the language of the old neo-classical poetics, he called his book 'a comic epic in prose'. That sounds rather contorted, but it drew in all the elements he felt relevant to a definition. The novel was an epic because it worked through a variety of episodes, rather than through the tight, exact action of a tragedy; it could therefore follow more closely the contingencies of life. It was a '*comic* epic' because though it was large it was also light, not confining itself to sublime or serious experiences, and because it ranged through all the classes of society and their different kinds of manners. It was in prose and could work by a loose associative process. But it was still a stylised form, a realistic *myth*, an invention of tone and structure, rather than a direct copy of real life. Fielding's definition may be oblique, but it does emphasise most of the important things that we can say in definition of the genre.

The Realism of Fiction

The bias of the novel toward realism has at different times been seen as the novel's good fortune and the novel's embarrassment. To some novelists the whole point of the form was that it allowed the exploration of all life's details and richness; to others—a notable example is the group of novelists gathered around Henry James, Joseph Conrad and Ford Madox Ford—there was a persistent danger in yielding up the art of fiction to what James called 'clumsy Life at her stupid work'. But in fact the realism of the novel, its referential and empirical aspect, has come to mean so many different things to so many different readers that it is worth looking more closely at some of the various ways in which novels can be realistic.

REALISM OF DETAIL IN NOVELS

In its simplest sense, realism means that exactness and fullness of rendering, that detail of life, which is one of the things we associate with fiction. The novel, more than any other form, possesses the power to appeal to our sense of recognition; to make us feel that that was how it was, that was how it felt, that has the ring of true experience, that is just what it looks like. In his novel **Phineas Finn** (1869) Anthony TROLLOPE has a comment on the disasters for which the poor novelist gets rebuked: 'He catches salmon in October; or shoots his partridges in March. His dahlias bloom in June, and his birds sing in the autumn.' The capacity for exactness and accuracy of observation, for the gleaning of true and relevant detail, is something we immediately appreciate in contemporary novels, and something we find instructive and historically illuminating in the novels of the past. In some novels, such observation seems a good deal more incidental than in others, and even within a highly-controlled book a novelist can seem to pause to take particular pleasure in detailing something he knows very well. But in every case the observational power has to be something more than a capacity to catch the facts or render the impression; it is, inevitably, an *interpretation*.

22

This is a short scene in Kingsley AMIS'S novel **Take a Girl Like You** (1960), where the central character, a young and rather innocent schoolteacher named Jenny Bunn, is taken out to dinner by a boyfriend, Patrick Standish:

> A peep in the glass showed her that the red wool sheath dress, though not new, was doing its job, making the best of her bust without being too ostentatious, and the backswept hair with medium earrings gave the right sort of grown-up look. And she had got through the restaurant part quite decently, asking Patrick to do the choosing for her—a good tip from *Woman's Domain*—and getting rid of nearly all the raw fish and sort of meat fritter and rather sharp wine without hankering much after a gravy dinner and a cider. She had managed the cutlery all right, too, by just keeping her head and working inwards from the outside. . . . .

This is the sort of scene Amis does particularly well, and his abilities as a modern chronicler of detail are one of his great attractions as a novelist. The scene is packed with specific detail— how Jenny looked, what she ate, how she ate it. It is also packed with specific emotions—how the way she looked mattered to her, what she made of what she ate, and why she ate it in that way. It also contains a precise awareness of contemporary social manners. But what is given is interpreted—not just by Jenny, but by the novelist working with and through her. It is he who establishes the base of rather down-to-earth lower middle-class language that realises Jenny's observations and attitudes: a language that is partly hers but also slightly detached from her, so that the reader can acquire all the preferences and assumptions and subtleties of tone that will make not only this scene but the whole book work. Throughout the book, in fact, Amis sustains a tone that half-appreciates the sort of internal language going on in Jenny, and half-distances it so that he can 'handle' her as a novelist (we would need to read the whole novel to know how much Amis's reference to Jenny's reading *Woman's Domain* is ironic). Amis's realism of detail is, in fact, a very important part of his novel, since it is part of a generally realistic attitude which prefers ordinary things to extraordinary ones, the visible to the invisible, the world of society and manners to, say, the private world of the inner psyche that might interest another novelist. The whole novel turns on the question of how much Jenny should change her manners and moral attitudes when she encounters a new and more modern set; should she sleep with Patrick? So the realism of detail is part of a total system of persuasion by the novelist, indicating that you must

take the world as it is. But of course the world 'as it is' will differ
from novelist to novelist: even from novel to novel in the work of
the same writer. C. P. Snow's novels also require his characters
to make realistic choices, but the frame of choice is totally differently created; it functions in a world of public and scientific as well
as private events, equally detailed—but according to a different
pattern of perception.

There is another, rather different, kind of realism we associate
with the novel: the power it has to convey the vivid energy that
exists in things or experience, the force and feel of life. One writer
we particularly associate with this vividness of rendering is
D. H. LAWRENCE, in such passages as this, from near the
opening of **The Rainbow** (1915):

> So the Brangwens came and went without fear of necessity,
> working hard because of the life that was in them, not for want
> of the money. Neither were they thriftless. They were aware of
> the last halfpenny, and instinct made them not waste the peeling
> of their apple, for it would help to feed the cattle. But heaven
> and earth was teeming round them, and how should this cease?
> They felt the rush of the sap in spring, they knew the wave
> which cannot halt, but every year throws forward the seed to be-
> getting, and, falling back, leaves the young-born on the earth.
> They knew the intercourse between heaven and earth, sun-
> shine drawn into the breast and bowels, the rain sucked up in the
> daytime, nakedness that comes under the wind in autumn,
> showing the birds' nests no longer worth hiding. Their life
> and interrelations were such; feeling the pulse and body of the
> soil, that opened to their furrow for the grain, and became
> smooth and supple after their ploughing, and clung to their
> feet with a weight that pulled like desire, lying hard and un-
> responsive when the crops were to be shorn away. . . .

Lawrence's way of getting what he called 'the living moment' and
'the vivid relation . . . at that quick moment of time' is obviously
not just by a direct detailing, and not by that language of literalness
and truth we saw in **Moll Flanders**, but by a lyric and rhythmic
intensity in the telling. When he creates a particularly vivid
moment (a classic example would be the scene with the pheasant
chicks in **Lady Chatterley's Lover**) it gets its vivacity not just
from the specific matter of the scene but from Lawrence's sense of
the general fullness of existence, what F. R. Leavis calls his
'reverent openness to life'. So, here, the specific facts of the
Brangwens' ways of farming in this place at this point in
history (nineteenth-century Nottinghamshire), all clearly given, are

assimilated into cycles of nature and cycles of feeling; they are part of an overall creation of life as a rhythm and a flow, into which individual situations and even individual identities merge. It is only through the givenness and actuality of situations that, for Lawrence, life can exist. But this particular individual identity, this particular historical time or social place, while it is the essential condition of vivid experiencing, must take its part in a total rhetorical pattern.

Most novels use in some way the capacity fiction has to yield itself up to the detail of particular moments. Amis's and Lawrence's are two of the very many ways in which this can be done: in Amis's case the emphasis falls upon the actuality of detail, in Lawrence's on its neo-symbolist relevance or what James would call its 'illustrative' quality. In other writers the stress might fall upon external social detail, the external appearance of characters; or on internal psychological awareness. It may be the novelist, primarily, who observes; or it may be his substitute, one of his characters. The important thing is that this is part of the high *specificity* of fiction, its way of making round and solid many of the things with which it deals. It is part of the novel's tendency to give its characters specific names, specific psychic structures, specific historical and social locations. The fullness, the individuality, the complicated surrounding conditions of experience are part of the matter of novels. It means that the patterns of causation and motive in novels tend to be complex ones; that novels have a way of including the accidental and the contingent, or of making their existence out of moments and events. Perhaps Iris Murdoch was saying the same thing in a different way when she commented that the novelist is a describer rather than an explainer. Certainly a lot of the meaning of novels lies in what is rendered and given, rather than in what is rationalistically interpreted. So what Robert Louis Stevenson called 'the besotting particularity of Fiction' seems to be an attribute of the form. However, it would be dangerous to assume that this particularity means that novels are only a stringing together of such moments. A novel of very high specificity can have an extremely *shaped* structure—as with Henry James, say—while another can have a fairly loose and undogmatic one, e.g. TOLSTOY'S **Anna Karenina**. Nor need a novel based on a plethora of incident and episode be, in the end, more realistic than one which is not; the famous digressive principle of **Tristram Shandy**, or the loose associative principle of development in Virginia Woolf's novels (a distinctive form of 'stream-of-consciousness') are highly artificial and patterned 'systems' of particular moments. A realism of

particularity is certainly not all we mean when we talk of the
realism of the novel.

REALISM OF STRUCTURE IN NOVELS

One consequence of the 'particularity' of fiction is that we often
read novels for their parts—for characters, places, and scenes—
rather than as total structures. Structure, the broad pattern of
disposition of the total material, is normally rather harder to talk
about—a point to which I shall return later. Here I wish to discuss
the argument, common in criticism, that the realism of the novel
can be identified with its structure itself. For instance, in an essay
called 'Manners, Morals and the Novel' (collected in *The Liberal
Imagination* (1950)), the American critic, Lionel Trilling, argues
that the novel is 'a perpetual quest for reality, the field of its research being always the social world, the material of its analysis
being always manners as an indication of the direction of man's
soul'. He suggests that the novel is the literature of a shifting and
a bourgeois society; and that its way is to examine money, snobbery,
status and class, and establish what is appearance and what reality.
It is fascinated by the detail of life, but also questions it. So the
destruction of illusions and the establishment of a more precise
reality provide the structure or myth of the novel. In fact not all
novels take this form, only most European ones in the eighteenth
and nineteenth centuries. (Trilling rather embarrassingly admits
that 'the novel as I have described it has never really established
itself in America' because of its lack of national social density and
established manners.) Still, his case that one of the main themes of
fiction is a quest through society for reality does help explain a
great deal about the classic form of the novel. Accepting the density
and reality of the social world, and attempting to find a structure
for conveying it, the classic novels show individuals moving through
the social web seeking their own personal, moral and public
identity.

In FIELDING'S **Tom Jones** (1749), the hero, Tom, is of
uncertain birth and hasn't a fixed place in the order; so he moves
freely through many parts of society, rural and urban, high and
low—making himself, testing abstract principles against his own
standards and desires, coming out as a representative of a moderate,
realistic goodness. In Jane AUSTEN'S **Emma** (1815), Emma
Woodhouse is a too-romantic heroine who makes all kinds of social
mistakes; she has to learn that these are finally *moral* mistakes,
and when she does she marries the one character in the novel, Mr.
Knightley, who unites the social *and* the moral virtues. In George
ELIOT'S **Middlemarch** (1871), the characters are embroiled

both in a complex social web, that of an English provincial town, and a considerable social change, that of the First Reform Bill of 1832; in their different ways they are shown making or not making something of their lives in this shifting environment. In each case, a kind of virtuous scepticism—or realism—is an essential part of the author's vision. The enquiring disposition of the novelist (and his or her most favoured characters) is in support of an individual, empirical examination of social and mental conventions, to see if they adhere to experience and actuality. In many cases, this involves an appreciative love of the material world, of manners, social traits, particular individuality—a realism that recognises that the detailed stuff of society and the detailed habits of people matter. But it also involves, in many cases, the parody or destruction of a false myth, a romanticised view of the situation—and the substitution of a 'realistic' myth. This involves scepticism or irony, as in Jane Austen. In this brief ironic passage in her last novel, **Persuasion** (1818), we can see that irony working both lovingly and sceptically:

> She [Anne Elliot, the heroine] now felt a great inclination to go to the outer door; she wanted to see if it rained. Why was she to suspect herself of another motive? Captain Wentworth [whom Anne loves] must be out of sight. She left her seat, she would go; one half of her should not be always so much wiser than the other half, or always suspecting the other of being worse than it was. . . .

The irony is internal to Anne, though the screw is further turned by the novelist; part of Anne's motive *is* to get a glimpse of Captain Wentworth. A more extreme example of this sceptical realism is Gustave FLAUBERT'S **Madame Bovary** (1857), with its double irony. On the one hand, the heroine's romantic fantasies of love are sceptically mocked as unrealistic by the novelist; on the other hand, they are also used to expose just how *inadequate* her dreary French provincial environment really is.

Trilling's case has to exclude a whole body of major works—many of the best American novels, like Nathaniel HAW-THORNE'S **The Scarlet Letter**, Herman MELVILLE'S **Moby Dick**, Mark TWAIN'S **The Adventures of Huckleberry Finn** and so on, and much modern writing. That damages Trilling's argument, but it should not destroy it altogether. The novel does move between realism and romance if only because the realistic myth of one society or one period becomes another's *romantic* myth, opening up the next stage of scepticism. The novel as

Trilling describes it is itself open to deflation from the stand-point of a latter-day realism. In late-nineteenth-century realism, often called naturalism, a determinist and environmentalist emphasis emerges—it doubts the power of the individual to determine his own existence, as society becomes large, abstract, machine-like. So in Emile Zola, Theodore Dreiser, Thomas Hardy and others, man becomes the object of pressure from external forces—from society, fate, or processes of industriali-sation or urbanisation—and realism then becomes the discovery of the individual's inability to determine his fate. Or else the novelist comes to suggest, as in the work of D. H. Lawrence, Marcel Proust or Virginia Woolf, that the only truly real realm of existence is within man's own consciousness. So novelists tend to become increasingly sceptical about the idea of society as a web of manners and morals informing human life; or about the indepen-dence of individual existence; or even about the capacity of novels to create myths at all. This further 'demythicising' emerges particularly in the novels of what we call 'modernism'—that radical remaking of fiction that was brought about by writers like Henry James, Joseph Conrad, Marcel Proust, James Joyce and Thomas Mann. In **Ulysses** (1922), for instance, James JOYCE employs a vast ironic contrast between a traditional heroic-epic view of experience and a modernly realistic one: he builds the novel on the frame of Homer's *Odyssey*, playing this off against the fortunes of three characters in the Dublin of 1904 to show the loss of myth or meaning in history. Cervantes and Henry Fielding had employed mock-heroic for the purposes of comic realism, but Joyce works to a much more depressing and despairing conclusion.

A convenient instance of the depth of modern realist scepticism is to be found in Joseph CONRAD'S **The Secret Agent** (1907), one of the most ironic novels ever written. It is a novel without what fiction usually has, a hero or heroine; so all we can identify ourselves as readers with is the author's ironic distance from every single one of his characters—an irony that, as Conrad said, 'would enable me to say all I felt I would have to say in scorn as well as in pity'. It is a novel without a coherent society, set in a London that is only a veneer of order and civilisation, 'a monstrous town more populous than some continents . . . a cruel devourer of the world's light'. It is a novel without a plot, in the sense that its events have no final coherence and are presented from a stand-point of remarkable obliqueness. It creates a world in which no character can discover truth or set himself free. Though the world is anarchistic, the anarchist characters are absurd and simply manifest human nature 'in its discontent and imbecility'; the idiot Stevie who draws pointless circles is the most sympathetic figure; while Minnie Verloc, who does win freedom by killing the husband who has brought about Stevie's death in a pointless bomb explosion, finds only freedom's dreadfulness: 'She had become a free woman with the perfection of freedom which left her nothing to desire and absolutely nothing to do. . . . And she did not move. She was a woman enjoying her complete irresponsibility and endless leisure, almost in the manner of a corpse.' Conrad destroys every possible centre of human value that seems to emerge momentarily in the novel; and so realistic scepticism and mistrust become a total and annihilating vision, reinforcing Minnie Verloc's view that 'life doesn't stand much looking into'. In **The Secret Agent** Conrad passes far beyond that loving appreciation of social reality that Trilling sees as part of the novel's realism, while he continues with the tradition of realistic scepticism. He questions the very possibility of heroes, of a society that can be given meaning and put into significant relationship with men, of a human quest for discovery, of a designed plot—traditional assumptions of earlier realism. And in doing that he questions the very idea of fiction itself, as an order or a myth.

The novel—and realism—as Trilling defines these things do not die out in our century. But they are qualified, and that is a reminder that realism is like reality—that is, not an *absolute*, but a mode of perception, which is subject both to historical change and to subjective interpretation. And novels tend to draw their notions of what is realistic from prevailing and influential views of what orders human experience. (The views of Darwin and the social determinists of early sociological thought lie behind naturalism; the views of Freud and Jung lie behind the realistic psychological novel, the novel of consciousness; the views of Heidegger and Sartre lie behind many of the modern novels which heighten realistic contingency into a philosophy of the absurd.) Certainly the novel does have an inevitable bias towards realism—because it uses the most literal of literary languages, prose; because it tends to emphasise the authenticity of individual and personal experience; because it tends to deal in human relationships; because it does not really have a predetermined form (as tragedy does) but can let the form emerge. But its realism can be expressed so variously that we can speak of realism as a changing attribute of the form, not as a definition of it. Those definitions of the novel which stress the novel's closeness of reference to life, its preoccupation with individuals and society, its attentiveness to what James called 'the awful mixture of things' are just —but not complete. Realism can involve structures of great formal complexity:

the controlled, aesthetic structuring which Henry James calls 'form' which emerges out of the specificity, or the fictive self-questioning of works like **Tristram Shandy, Ulysses** or **The Secret Agent.** For though the novel may uniquely give details of daily life and personal experience as no other art-form can, it is always in the end a structure in language, working through rhetorical persuasion and linguistic designing and making. It is to this aspect of the novel that I now want to turn.

CHAPTER FOUR

The Fictiveness of Fiction

There are a fair number of novels that are novels about the novel. *Tristram Shandy*, we have seen, is one. This is a passage from another, André GIDE'S **The Counterfeiters** (1926), which contains the character of a novelist, Edouard, who is writing a book called *The Counterfeiters* which contains the character of a novelist:

> 'Is it because the novel, of all literary *genres*, is the freest, the most lawless,' held forth Edouard, '. . . is it for that very reason, for fear of that very liberty (the artists who are always sighing after liberty are often the most bewildered when they get it), that the novel has always clung to reality with such timidity? And I am not speaking only of the French novel. It is the same with the English novel; and the Russian novel, for all its throwing off of constraints, is a slave to resemblance. The only progress it looks to is to get still nearer to nature. . . .'

Edouard's protest is partly the justification for Gide's novel, partly an event *within* it, to be taken on a level with all the other events. But by making the writing of a novel part of his own action, Gide is doing, but very explicitly, what most novelists do: keeping the reader's attention focused upon the storyteller and his mode of working as well as upon the story he tells. For Gide, this involves a very conscious split between form and content. Edouard says he wants to put everything in his novel (in fact he means everything he sees, knows and learns in his own life) and 'stylise it into art'. This is something of a philosophical dilemma, since Gide presumes that novelists somehow have a material you can start with, and the real effort is one of giving form to it. In fact, since they have to invent the material as well, the formal process starts earlier—in the initial perception of reality, or of what constitutes the stuff of a particular novel. We might almost say that the technique of the novel begins long before the author starts writing a word of his book, in the primary acts of selection about what is to be told and what ways will be needed to tell it.

FORM AND CONTENT

But why does Edouard/Gide protest about the novel's way of

'clinging to reality'? He is complaining about the fact that most novels of the past seem to have copied life without exposing the artificiality of their doing so. We have already seen some of the ways in which the novel is equipped to get this effect, the way in which it can hide the artificiality of its process. That effect is, we have seen, partly the result of the literalness of prose, that realism in it which enables the novel to 'rival' reality. Because of its high powers of reference, fictional prose is able to become 'invisible' in a way most literary languages cannot. And because it is capable of being discursive, of describing rather than explaining, it can also give a very high degree of authenticity to its subject. When, as part of the expansion of scientific and empirical views of the world and of matter, the seventeenth and eighteenth centuries extended the resources of written prose, making syntax less contorted and denotation possible through plainness of style, they gave language a command over the circumstantial which the novel took up. This enabled writers to place things firmly in time and space, in a logical but not a forced sequence. It gave language, in fact, the property of truth. Ernest Hemingway's instruction to himself as a writer—'Write the truest sentence that you know'—emphasises this: truth and reality can lie not only in things themselves but in the way of writing a sentence about them. All of this means that a novel can make us forget that what we are reading is a total invention in language, and not an account or copy of a prior reality. It is a normal part of the story-telling function of novels to insist upon and sustain this realistic illusion, the illusion that these events really happened and are being told. But novels do this to various extents. The reader is often constantly shifted between taking language as 'invisible'—a direct vehicle of meaning, a tool of description—and taking it as a self-conscious manipulation of the relation between words or sentences and things. We are made aware of a matter 'told' and we are made aware of the way of the telling.

That is why criticism often distinguishes between the *form* and the *content* of a novel—even to the extent of suggesting, in some cases, that a novel can be all 'content' and no form. That has been said of *Moll Flanders,* on the grounds that the novelist builds in no means of evaluating his material. In fact, the distinction is dubious, since all linguistic structures must have a form of some kind. However, that form can be more self-conscious in some books than in others. In many of the novels we read—ordinary westerns or detective-stories or love-romances—there is a minimum of self-conscious form. On the other hand, many novels we take seriously, particularly the great modern novels, have 'form' in conspicuous quantity; they have a manifest display of technique. Yet even in novels which constantly draw attention to their technique of fictiveness, there often remains a distinction between what is 'told' and the way of the telling. Despite the complicated technique of *The Counterfeiters*, for instance, we are still asked to believe that the book is telling the 'true' story of Edouard. In other novels, the emphasis on technique is so great that it subsumes *all* its narrative matter; the self-conscious means of telling leave no material untouched. That was the case, as we saw, with *The Secret Agent*. In a book like *Ulysses*, Joyce goes further; each stage of the telling has a technique which enacts what is being told. However, it would be misleading to suggest that conspicuous experimentalism is the only way for a novel to have form. For a novel to be presented fully, it is usually necessary for the novelist to heighten our degree of attentiveness to the language, the devices used, or to the narrative speaker. Of course he does this not only to make a display of consummate artifice, but to order and master his vision and to produce his desired effects.

In fact, the novelist's desire to intensify the fictiveness of his fiction may come from the pursuit of many different literary ends. He may be seeking to intensify the realistic illusion, to strengthen the literal feeling of the narrative. Or he may be after a greater sense of *life*, a sense of its complexity and immensity. On the other hand, he may be after effects of a rather opposite kind. He may want us to feel the sense of art as an order beyond and outside life. Or he may want to stress the fact that novels are fictions—unreliable and unverifiable inventions, works of absolute artifice which can only *pretend* to get down life or order it. In the twentieth century, we have moved toward a symbolist view of art which emphasises its unreality: the fact that it is an interpretation imposed *on* the world and not an interpretation *of* the world. Much of the twentieth-century obsession with form and technique, and its way of making the artist 'a spectator at the birth of his work' (Max Ernst), comes from the sense that there is no objective reality a novel or any work of art can state. Yet we should not forget that novels have long emphasised their fictionality and inventiveness; and that this is something that has always been part of the resources of art.

THE PRESENCE OF THE NOVELIST

One way of expressing the element of fictiveness in fiction is to say that novels often enact the problems of their writing, the conditions under which the story can be told, as they go along. In *Tristram Shandy*, Sterne does this by constant suggestions that

he is both brilliant and incompetent: 'Holla!—you chairman!—
here's sixpence—do step into that bookseller's shop, and call me a
day-tall critic. I am very willing to give any one of 'em a crown to
help me with this tackling, to get my father and uncle Toby off the
stairs, and to put them to bed.' The writing of the novel is one of
the events enacted by the narrative—even to the point of con-
fessing how difficult it is to tell it right or keep it going. More
often, though, we have the introduction of the author into the
narrative in a different guise. Tristram Shandy is a comic author-
substitute, and he is not exactly seeking to inspire confidence. But,
often, the presence of the novelist is introduced precisely to give
a sense of confidence and command—a feeling that the novelist is
wise and knows everything. So William M. THACKERAY comes
into **Vanity Fair** (1848) and stresses his authorial privileges:

> If, a few pages back, the present writer claimed the privilege of
> peeping into Miss Amelia Sedley's bedroom, and understanding
> with the omniscience of the novelist all the gentle pains and
> passions which were tossing upon that innocent pillow, why
> should he not declare himself to be Rebecca's confidante too,
> master of her secrets, and seal-keeper of that woman's conscience?

This effect is called by the critics 'the intrusion of the authorial I',
and is often condemned on the grounds that it breaks up the
illusion, that it tells instead of shows, and that it violates point of
view. In fact, in Thackeray's case, it actually intensifies the illusion,
by making the novelist seem to know everything, by suggesting
his close intimacy with every motive and every detail, by suggesting that there is a final objective reality which the novelist
can get at and establish.

In **Howards End** (1910)—a social-moral comedy which explores and criticises the division of England between its businessmen
and its intellectuals, between its materialism and its spirituality
—E. M. FORSTER also intervenes, in this passage about
Margaret Schlegel, his main character:

> To Margaret—I hope this will not set the reader against her—
> the station of King's Cross had always suggested Infinity. Its
> very situation—withdrawn a little behind the facile splendours
> of St. Pancras—implied a comment on the materialism of life.
> Those two great arches, colourless, indifferent, shouldering be-
> tween them an unlovely clock, were fit portals for some eternal
> adventure, whose issue might be prosperous, but would cer-
> tainly not be expressed in the ordinary language of prosperity. If
> you think this ridiculous, remember that it is not Margaret who

is telling you about it; and let me hasten to add that they were
in plenty of time for the train. . . .

The passage has often been complained about, or quoted as an
example of Forster's Thackeray-like technique. In fact Forster
intrudes in a rather different way. He is not trying to move on the
action, or to editorialise (as Hardy often does by introducing
gnomic utterances about fate), but to make a delicate adjustment
to the tone of the telling. He is softening, by a genial narrative
voice, a thought that might seem pretentious if given directly to
the character. At the same time, the passage puts him particularly
close to Margaret, who in fact represents many of the values that
he wants to emerge out of the narrative. His intrusion also emphasises that the telling *has* a tone. Margaret Schlegel, who marries
Mr Wilcox, a practical businessman, wants to 'connect the prose
and the passion'. So, too, does Forster—who has to mediate all
the way through the novel between the ordinary language of
prosperity (the language which deals with the materialism of life
and its ordinary necessities: like catching trains) and the language
of eternal adventures. He has to find a tone somewhere in between
the narrative of life in time, or fairly ordinary prose, and the
narrative of life by value, which is more normally poetry. His
answer lies in a genial comedy which can shift from one to the
other and even play each off against the other (as the passage shows).
That tone must be clearly conveyed to the reader; so Forster
breaks, fairly gently, into the narrative to show his comic command
over the book.

Henry JAMES objected to this sort of procedure, on the grounds
that it caused a 'breaking-up of the register', a violation of point-
of-view. His objection is sometimes misunderstood by critics,
who suggest that he was opposed to the use of the omniscient
author. A reading of one of his best novels, **The Portrait of a
Lady** (1881), with an eye on how the narrative is presented will
quickly show how wrong that view is. This is how the novel
starts:

> Under certain circumstances there are few hours in life more
> agreeable than the hour dedicated to the ceremony known as
> afternoon tea. There are circumstances in which, whether you
> partake of the tea or not—some people of course never do,—the
> situation is in itself delightful. Those that I have in mind in
> beginning to unfold this simple history offered an admirable
> setting to an innocent pastime. The implements of this little
> feast had been disposed on the lawn of an old English country-
> house, in what I should call the perfect middle of a splendid

summer afternoon. Part of the afternoon had waned, but much
of it was left, and what was left was of the finest and rarest
quality. . . .

The objective narrator is established from the start, the voice of
social comedy of manners and of an appreciative connoisseurship.
But the point of the novel is that the novelist seeks to set his
central character, Isabel Archer, free to act—rather as Ralph
Touchett seeks to set her free by leaving her his fortune. Of course
she is not free, because she is a fictive invention; but the novel has
a compositional trajectory which creates this sense of freedom—
from things, from limiting social contexts, from the novelist
himself, only to narrow it down again as Isabel finds that she is
bound (and as James reasserts his dominance again). James's
critical point was that it is necessary to create, not only an authorial
voice, but a sense of form, of a vital organising principle. That
means bodying out the essential points of growth in the novel; in
the case of *The Portrait of a Lady*, this was for James the character
of Isabel herself, whom he distinguished out as being the 'essence'
of the novel, the starting point in relation to which all other parts—
including the narrator—had to be appropriate. So the way in which
we are most aware of the presence of the author is not as a voice
but as a maker of the total shape or structure as a composition.

We can perhaps most clearly see this 'sense of form' at work in
one of our most 'aesthetic' novelists, Virginia WOOLF. In what
is probably her best novel, **To the Lighthouse** (1927), there is
no direct authorial narrator at all. Instead the action is presented
by a 'stream-of-consciousness' flowing through the characters and
beyond them into a kind of abstract narrative. It is a book in which
we are highly aware of the abstract form. The novel tells of a few
simple events. Sometime before the First World War, a family
goes to its holiday house in Scotland and, on the evening in which
we catch them, plan a trip to a nearby lighthouse. The trip
does not take place next day, but ten years later. In the interim,
Mrs. Ramsay, the central character and the focus of the family,
has died; the War has taken place and other characters have been
killed; a pair of lovers have broken up. For most novelists, these
events would be the story; but Virginia Woolf pushes all that into
the background. She cuts out two basic slices of time: the evening
before the planned trip, and the actual journey, dividing these with
an interlude which puts all these more major events into a kind of
parenthesis. The trip is completed, and so, simultaneously, is a
painting which Lily Briscoe, an artist, has long been working on.
The novel not only *has* an aesthetic, an experimental form; it is

also about an aesthetic completeness, the finishing of a painting
and the rounding off of a fictional pattern. The implication is that
events, by themselves, have little meaning; nor do individual
identities; nor does the structure of an individual life—Mrs.
Ramsay, who emerges as important, dies halfway through the
book. But pattern, design and form do have meaning and significance, and can have structure and completeness. A painting is
finished and the book can end.

NOVELS AS VERBAL INVENTIONS

There are many and various ways of letting the light of fictivity
into novels. But what all of these do is to remind us that the
novel is, by nature, a particular and distinctive form of *discourse*.
That is to say, a novel is a verbal invention, and everything it contains has been determined and controlled by language. The writing
out of a novel is the creation of a structure, derived from the
properties of language, the properties of life as the novelist per-
ceives and selects them, and the properties of form as the novelist
starts projecting it in order to give his work a satisfactory coherence.
What it normally invents or represents is a society, a human community of people, in a given time at given places; and this means
that we can usually test the writer's invention against our own experience in certain ways. In this respect novels usually have a kind
of verifiable reality, which becomes part of the common reference
that exists between reader and writer. That reality will always be
different in every novel, of course, and our relation to it will be in
every case different. That is because every novel is a *made* thing.
It is not mechanically made; hence the complexity of the very
idea of form. For most novelists who have written about the
creative process have stressed on the one hand that form is a kind
of natural, imaginative growth of their material, *and* a carefully
controlled process of design. In some novels there is an emphatic
attention given to that control or design, an elaborate formal concern or a conspicuous experimentalism. This is of itself no particular guarantee of intrinsic quality, no automatic Good House-
keeping Award; nor, on the other hand, is it a wilful violation of
the novel's real nature. It is simply a heightening of a propensity
of the novel. For fictiveness is a part of fiction; the fictive act is a
process of making and shaping. Hence novels without a highly
manifest form still *have* a form—since all fiction must.

CHAPTER FIVE

The Structure of Novels

When a novelist writes a novel, he creates a new and distinctive universe. It has its own institutions, its own citizens, its own patterns of relationship and systems of kinship, its own moral and social values by which people live, its own sense of what is important to them. It may resemble the real world in many respects, and may appeal to a common recognition of society, reality, humanity; but it is a world made of *language*. In most novels (there are exceptions) what is invented is a society, often of considerable reality, with a specified historical and geographical place, consisting of a group of people, small or large, in a given situation or sequence of situations—a group of people with their own manners and customs, their own expectations, desires and needs. The institutions and customs of this society often play a large part in the action, forming lines of conduct, moral dilemmas, and so on. Through them a large part of the action works, the conventions and limitations are set up. Out of this community come the marriages with which Jane Austen's novels so often end, the codes of female virginity on which Samuel Richardson's novels depend, the ladders of class up which so many fictional heroes—from STENDHAL'S *Julien Sorel* in **The Red and the Black** to John BRAINE'S *Joe Lampton* in **Room at the Top** —fight their way. This society is what the novel usually leads us through—by making us follow a sequence of actions relevant to it, illuminating it, by creating a developing logic which often has an historical validity or a mythical dimension (a *plot*).

But, still, this is a 'made' world; and so the writer must persuade us into it. He must set up, every step of the way, a system of internal probabilities that make that world consistent and logical within itself. All that is in it has to be selected as part of the total effect; and the writer stylises it, shapes it, imposes special emphases for the sake of control, design, development. For example: Jane Austen clearly deliberately concentrates and makes narrow her social world, holds it within the frame of the experience of a particular small class (generally the rural gentry) in order to intensify her moral and ethical world, to win a close analysis of conduct and values. But Charles Dickens creates a world that is usually very broad, geographically and socially, a world that contains many classes and communities, and so creates an atmosphere not of moral precision but of broad moral generosity. Each world is distinct from the other, has different logics of working and is observed with different perceptual assumptions.

Every novelist constructs and conventionalises his own world: in general (he has familiar interests and techniques we recognise from novel to novel) and in particular (each of his novels is different, creating new conventions and communities and solving new problems). Nor does he make all his decisions, know all his answers, before he begins to write his novel. Every novel, being a new start, creates new needs and methods. A writer will usually know a good deal about the world of a particular novel before he begins to write the finished text; but it is only in the writing that significance, connection, inter-relationship truly begin to exist. So, as he writes, the writer is always working out his logic and sequence, solving problems of presentation, seeking to persuade the reader in a continuous and consistent way. He has to create a sense of unity. And this unity will come from two places, though they are totally interlinked. The first is the unity that comes from sustaining the consistency of the world within the novel, making event and behaviour probable while keeping it in development. We talk about this kind of unity by words like 'plot' or 'narrative development'. But then there is the unity that comes from making the language and pattern of perception, the whole persuasive structure and organisation, consistent and developing. For the novelist must devise a *tone*—a relationship with the reader which enables him to perceive and share that universe, to respond to it with certain attitudes, certain sympathies and repulsions. We talk about this kind of unity by words like 'technique' or 'form', or else by words emphasising that it also involves matters of evaluation, like 'irony'. These two things—which can never finally be separate from each other in the writer's mind—are at the heart of his creative process. And this means that always, at every point in the work, the novelist is inevitably creating not only *what* we read, but *how* we read it.

HOW NOVELISTS PERSUADE

The making of a novel is the making of a world in language, and it is a persistently developing world. It normally consists of a devised succession of events, in an organised structure which involves the writer in all sorts of acts of choice and selection, of incident and language, to the end of provoking recognitions and responses in his reader. The writer has to persuade us into accepting the laws of, the terms of, the expectations proper to, those principles of development and exploration by which the whole work becomes a structure. When we start to read a novel, we start at once to take our bearings. We become aware (consciously or unconsciously) of certain choices the writer has made, which give us the terms for understanding this particular world, and which condition the onward motion of the narrative. We begin to *expect*; we start to be persuaded. In a minute, we shall see, in looking at the openings of four different novels, specifically *how* we are likely to do this. But generally our expectations begin to form in two basic ways. We start to have expectations about the logic of the story: for instance, that its main concern will be with the life of one individual and will probably culminate in a certain way (in a moment of insight, a success or failure in a desired relationship, a death, for instance); or that its concern will be with the life of a community rather than with one man, and will culminate in some social illumination; or whatever. We will, if we are experienced readers, start to gather the kind of story we are reading: this is a psychological novel, a comic novel, a romance novel, a symbolist novel. But we will also start to have expectations about the 'form', about the management of the telling. Where has the novelist located his 'point of view', and what is his attitude to the narrative? And how is he creating the logic of evaluation, the system of preferences embodied in the novel? For certain words, certain acts, certain characters will seem to have the support and favour of the novelist, while others will be given the force of his criticism.

Most of these things are matters of choice for the novelist, and we must consider the choices as deliberate, because they are committing. They form the essential way in which the novel *means*. For, as we have seen, what the novelist invents or 'represents' he also organises, from start to finish, with every word, sentence, paragraph and chapter that he writes. He must always be mediating his tale to us, and in a serious novel he is recognisably making significant and crucial choices in doing so. As we have seen, this is not to say that a novelist must always know his entire novel before he begins it; or that once we have read the beginning we can sit down and work out the end. The writer learns in the process of writing, and finds his own limitations and possibilities. But Henry James, in his 'Preface' to **The Portrait of a Lady** (1881), probably gives the best description of the writing process as I am suggesting it. He points out that one starts writing a book with the feeling that certain things are of the 'essence' and others of the 'provision'; some are central, others more incidental, more 'illustrative'. As readers, we too must feel our way toward this essence. This means not only that we must form attitudes and begin feeling our way ahead, but put the various expectations we are acquiring into some sort of relation. For instance, two novels may have a similar formal technique; but in one it is apparent that maintaining the consistency of that form is a major concern, while in another the writer may be willing to be inconsistent about it, since it is of the 'provision' rather than of the 'essence'.

So we pick up a novel, begin to read, and at once sense that certain essential choices have been made by the novelist already. He has perhaps decided to give his story a firm historical location and draw on our sense of historical verisimilitude; or he has blurred the historical setting to give a sense that these events are less local and dated than timeless and eternal. He has put the centre of the story in one man's life, or found it in a community where many men meet. He has chosen to tell the story in the first person; or the third; or in some mixture. He has chosen to present himself as a storyteller involved, in some way, in the action; or as a man standing right outside it in a position of independence; or he has appointed some invented personage to do the telling for him; or he confesses to having made it all up *as* a story. He has so placed himself as storyteller that he stands at the end of the sequence of events he is going to tell, and reveals his knowledge of the ending at the beginning; or he puts himself in the middle of the story as one not knowing how it will end. He has chosen to start off his narrative with the birth of a hero (so probably focussing the book in the importance of individual destiny, so probably making a world in which individual experience and judgment of life is primary); or he has chosen to record an historical process that spans generations, so probably making a world in which individual life is less important than the totality toward which individual lives contribute. The variables here are enormous, but once the writer has chosen his way—to start the action here, to see it through these eyes—he has fixed a good deal of the line of growth of his novel. For from them a logic flows, not only a logic of technique and tone but a total system of development: in other words, a structure.

Thus, as I have said, the novelist is considerably committed by these choices made at the beginning: committed because every decision about order, sequence, and angle of vision is a profound part of the story's meaning. For instance: if a novelist undertakes at the beginning to tell his story as a chronological sequence—starting at the first point of time relevant to his action, and carrying on until he reaches the last—he will end up with a totally different version of the universe, of the relationships and meanings that exist within it, the way in which it can be perceived, than if he had chosen to move the story backwards and forwards in time (as William Faulkner often does) or if he were to shift from event to event in some 'timeless' continuum (as sometimes happens in Virginia Woolf or William Golding). If he undertakes to tell the story through one single 'consciousness', that assumes a very different view of this particular created world, this novel, than if he undertakes to tell it through many. To take an example: Emily BRONTË chooses to tell **Wuthering Heights** (1847) through two 'centres of consciousness'. There is Lockwood, who tells the story to the reader; then within his story is reported another, that told by the servant Nelly Dean about the earlier relationship of Heathcliff and Cathy. This may seem cumbersome, especially since Emily Brontë has to go to some odd lengths to maintain consistency in this—she has to arrange events so that Nelly Dean is dusting away in a corner every time a significant development in the Cathy-Heathcliff story takes place. At times she actually lets the logic slip, something a devout follower of Henry James would find unforgivable. But on the whole she chooses to sustain it, deliberately, since it makes the story much more 'heroic' to have these events placed in a remembered past than to have them in the narrative 'present' of the book. The novelist is not *mechanically* bound by such logic—as E. M. Forster once observed (in *Aspects of the Novel*), the novelist will often want to shift point of view occasionally to bounce the reader into a new perception—but he must have a self-created logic or sequence for which he is responsible. In these terms, every novel is its own world, its own distinct and created universe, with its own *way* of persuasion, derived from the obligations of mediating this particular tale. We may think sometimes that Jane Austen's novels are all alike; they are not. Each persuades us in a different way, calling up somewhat different expectations and values, appropriate to the workings of this particular narrative and solving the problems that are alone its problems. And so it is with all novels.

PERSUASION AT WORK: FOUR OPENINGS

Here are the first paragraphs of four novels from different writers at different periods. As we read them, there are three things we might usefully watch for:
(a) *the point of view*. This refers to expectations about technique.

What is the relation of the narrator to his story? Is it told in the first or the third person? How many 'consciousnesses' are used and in what sort of relationship?

(b) *the tone of the telling.* This is close to the first, but refers to the way the story is evaluated. What is the attitude of the narrator to the story he is telling through these technical means? What is his attitude toward the reader? What relationship with him is he creating?

(c) *the projection of future developments.* This refers to expectations about sequence and order, and hence about the logic of the story. What social and moral worlds are being created? What kind of information is conveyed, and in what order? What sense of what is to come does it arouse in the reader?

OPENING NO. 1

I was born in the northern part of this united kingdom, in the house of my grandfather, a gentleman of considerable fortune and influence, who had, on many occasions, signalised himself in behalf of his country; and was remarkable for his abilities in the law, which he exercised with great success, in the station of a judge, particularly against beggars, for whom he had a singular aversion.

My father, his youngest son, falling in love with a poor relation, who lived with the old gentleman in quality of housekeeper, espoused her privately; and I was the first fruit of that marriage. During her pregnancy, a dream discomposed my mother so much, that her husband, tired with her importunity, at last consulted a Highland seer, whose favourable interpretation he would have secured beforehand by a bribe, but found him incorruptible. She dreamed she was delivered of a tennis-ball, which the devil (who, to her great surprise, acted the part of a midwife) struck so forcibly with a racket, that it disappeared in an instant; and she was for some time inconsolable for the loss of her offspring; when, all of a sudden, she beheld it return with equal violence, and enter the earth beneath her feet, whence immediately sprung up a goodly tree covered with blossoms, the scent of which operated so strongly on her nerves, that she awoke. The attentive sage, after some deliberation, assured my parents, that their first-born would be a great traveller; that he would undergo many dangers and difficulties, and at last return to his native land, where he would flourish in happiness and reputation. How truly this was foretold, will appear in the sequel.

As we read these two paragraphs, what bearings do we take? The following comments are not intended as exhaustive, but simply suggest some of the signals we might pick up.

The novel clearly begins as a first-person narration; by a character who is assumed to be setting down the story as a written narrative, and who addresses the reader in his narrative role ('How truly this was foretold, will appear in the sequel'). He appears to be placed at the end of the sequence of events to be told; and hence to know their outcome, which, from his tone, does not seem to be terribly unfortunate. His 'consciousness' appears to be the central one, and so presumably most events will somehow be reflected through him and affect him. To begin with, his tone seems straightforwardly factual, telling external events in a rather detached way and in orderly sequence of 'and then . . . and then . . .' But it seems to be touched with a certain note of comedy, both as regards these events (particularly the dream) and the way he treats them (the 'attentive sage'). He also seems to have a degree of ironic detachment toward his family and himself: which may be part of the comic tone, or may reflect a more profound distance. The events he tells, he tells *as* events; there is no sense that he is making them up. He therefore presents himself to the reader in a fairly reliable, truthful way, and also as above all a figure interesting to readers because of what *happened* to him, rather than for what he thinks or how he feels. The novel starts out in a small, family community to which the speaker shows no signs of being particularly attached; it is not placed particularly clearly in geography or time. It starts with the hero's birth, though what is significant about it, in these two paragraphs, is not that it is an important social event, or an important consequence of anybody's emotional lives, but that it is the start of something. But of what?

I think that, on the strength particularly of the dream, what we expect are adventures. Indeed the dream—it may or may not be reliable, but that is the point—seems to prefigure the novel. Moreover the adventures, however terrible they may be, seem likely to have a happy outcome. The association of the hero with the devil has a certain ominous ring, but this is softened by the return of the tennis-ball as a goodly tree. We don't have to interpret the fable even in the way the 'attentive sage' does to recognise at least one thing about it; it is the traditional fable of comedy, or of one kind of comedy. There is a familiar narrative type which is comic, deals with a not particularly virtuous hero who sets out on adventures, meets various misfortunes on his way, but finally returns to his place in the society which he has temporarily upset; that is the picaresque novel. Here the hero starts out with some of the conditions that might be appropriate to that sort of narrative; slightly dispossessed socially, the son of a not particularly good marriage as far as social advantages are concerned. This may or may not be such a novel, but the novelist raises the notion of the species, to use it later as he wishes. Indeed he deliberately sets up a principle for the action, by the use of the strange and comic dream, which he could use in various ways; to prove that the sage's interpretation is correct, to show that the dream comes true but in ways the sage could not envisage, or to show it all to be completely wrong, to an ironic effect. But at least this involves a deliberate arousing of expectations appropriate to the beginning of a narrative: a parable of the story, to be read along with the story. It is, in fact, a cliffhanger, an encouragement to continue to satisfy a sense of order and design which gives the feeling that the entire novel is itself ordered and designed, has a shape that starts with an individual's birth, continues through his experiences, and concludes positively and roundly before the 'act' of storytelling starts.

All this, it seems to me, one can surmise on the strength of having read no more than these two paragraphs. But if we met these in a book, we would have more information. We would have the title and the author, the visible size of the book, to help us further; we would probably know when it was written. I have suppressed that information because, if we try to guess when the passage was written, there are more questions we can ask. On the evidence of what has been said already, and on the grammatical and stylistic usages, the literary and aesthetic conventions employed, we might well make a fair attempt at dating the passage, setting it in the historical sequence of the novel. To stress, very briefly, a few points: it is an externalised, eventful mode of narration; it takes the birth of a hero as a signal start for a story, that birth being stressed in its social aspects somewhat and its adventure aspects even more; it promises to be an individual and empirical narrative, examining life from one man's experience of it; it reminds us of a picaresque form for the novel, whether or not it actually goes on to provide it. (The author, title, and date of publication are given at the end of this chapter.)

OPENING NO. 2

Emma Woodhouse, handsome, clever, and rich, with a comfortable home and happy disposition, seemed to unite some of the best blessings of existence; and had lived nearly twenty-one years in the world with very little to distress or vex her.

She was the youngest of the two daughters of a most affectionate, indulgent father, and had, in consequence of her sister's marriage, been mistress of his house from a very early period. Her mother had died too long ago for her to have more than an indistinct remembrance of her caresses, and her place had been

supplied by an excellent woman as governess, who had fallen
little short of a mother in affection.

Sixteen years had Miss Taylor been in Mr. Woodhouse's family, less as a governess than a friend, very fond of both daughters,
but particularly of Emma. Between *them* it was more the
intimacy of sisters. Even before Miss Taylor had ceased to
hold the nominal office of governess, the mildness of her
temper had hardly allowed her to impose any restraint; and
the shadow of authority being now long passed away, they
had been living together as friend and friend very mutually
attached, and Emma doing just what she liked; highly esteem-
ing Miss Taylor's judgment, but directed chiefly by her own.

The real evils indeed of Emma's situation were the power
of having rather too much her own way, and a disposition to
think a little too well of herself; these were the disadvantages
which threatened alloy to her many enjoyments. The danger,
however, was at present so unperceived, that they did not by
any means rank as misfortunes with her.

Sorrow came—a gentle sorrow—but not at all in the shape
of any disagreeable consciousness.—Miss Taylor married. It
was Miss Taylor's loss which first brought grief. It was on the
wedding-day of this beloved friend that Emma first sat in
mournful thought of any continuance. The wedding over and
the bride-people gone, her father and herself were left to dine
together, with no prospect of a third to cheer a long evening.
Her father composed himself to sleep after dinner, as usual, and
she had then only to sit and think of what she had lost.

The event had every promise of happiness for her friend. . . .

This time the narrative is in the third person, though still
focused on one single character (as opposed, say, to a community,
a society or a landscape). This raises a different field of expectations from the first person narrative; it gives the character a
different place in the novel's universe. We can envisage all sorts of
reasons for the author's making this choice, but they will be
reasons of a different order from those affecting a first person
narrative. Perhaps Emma is not the central character, or is one of
two or more central characters; perhaps she is less important to the
story than her society or environment; perhaps the novel demands
a literal realism best enforced by the novelist as speaker; perhaps
she *is* the central character, but there are tactical reasons for
seeing her through an independent vision. At any rate, this will
be a less personal and empirical novel than the last. If, as seems
likely, the person who is telling the story is the novelist (as

opposed to an invented narrator who is himself or herself a character), then the persuasive control of the story can be broadened. Still, there are many different kinds of novelist-narrators. What is this one like? And placed in what relation to the character this passage is about? Is the action being presented through the consciousness of the character (this is still possible with third person narrations, as we shall see in Opening No. 3)?

At the beginning of the passage, it is fairly clear it is not. It can hardly be a thought in the mind of Emma Woodhouse that she is 'handsome, clever, and rich': that is seen from outside. Moreover, the 'real evils' of paragraph four are explicitly not perceived by Emma. Indeed, the general mode of presentation is hardly enactment within the character's mind, but rather summary description, a catching up on certain primary events which happened before the narrative present of the story. Yet as we move into that narrative present, we move a good deal closer to Emma; and when we reach the fifth paragraph, where that 'present' really begins, the relationship of narrator and character grows a little less clear. The sentence: 'The wedding over and the bride-people gone, her father and herself were left to dine together, with no prospect of a third to cheer a long evening' could be part of Emma's 'mournful thought'; so could what follows it. They are less clearly matters of independent authorial report. But why then does the novelist begin more distantly and then move closer? And why does she give, over four preceding paragraphs, so many events in summary, not dramatising them but simply telling them?

The narrative present, the dramatised part of the action, starts on the day when Emma, nearly twenty-one, loses her friend and experiences grief—really for the first time. Emma is comfortably placed and contented and seems to have long been so. But this is treated with a technical distance which also embodies a certain degree of moral scepticism. All the things that are told us about Emma lead toward one conclusion: that Emma has been spoiled. Her father is indulgent, her mother long dead, her governess has also been her friend. She has a happy disposition, which seems admirable and approved of. But she has two moral faults: she is wilful or selfish, and she is vain. The faults are explicitly stated in paragraph four, where the author's moral surveillance becomes frank; but the element of questioning is there in the tone from the start. Indeed the tone seems one that simultaneously celebrates Emma's happiness *and* establishes a sense of its moral risks. In the very first sentence, Emma Woodhouse *seemed* to unite the best blessings of existence. The tension is then developed by various moral doubles; her father is 'affectionate', which is good,

and 'indulgent', which may well not be; while she and Miss
Taylor live together 'as friend and friend very mutually attached',
which is good, and 'Emma doing just what she liked', which is
probably not. If the reader is to gather this, there must be a very
precise stating of the moral signals, a very careful control; and in
fact the novelist selects each apparently documentary detail to
build up a totally consistent impression, then supported with an
explicit statement of the disadvantages that 'threatened alloy' to
her enjoyments. At the same time, this functions as a part of the
narrative present also. For if the description of the past establishes
the basis of friendship between Miss Taylor and Emma, and
hence the grief she feels now at the marriage, it also locates the
kind of grief. After all, the marriage has every promise of happiness
for her friend; why should Emma grieve? In life, of course, there
would be all sorts of reasons for her to do so; but already, after
reading five paragraphs of the novel, we have surely been conditioned to question it. Emma had 'rather too much her own way';
and here is an illustrative instance. In short, in a few relatively
undramatic paragraphs the novelist has persuaded us into a
morally evaluative attitude to the story.

What expectations do we have, then, about how the story will
proceed? It seems fairly obvious that there will be some threat to
Emma's state of happiness; indeed, there already is one, in the
fact that she is feeling grief for the first time. Moreover, two specified dangers are *at present* unperceived; so the development seems
likely to involve the exploration of those dangers, which lie in her
selfishness and vanity, which in turn lie in her situation. Moreover, since the dangers are unperceived, the action may well
involve her perceiving them: her undergoing a moral initiation, a
self-illumination. Certainly it would seem that if Emma is to be
happy again in this novel, it will not be in the same way that she is
happy at the beginning. But in addition to these expectations
about events, we are also being led toward expectations about how
to evaluate those events. We have sensed a moral vocabulary in
the story, but it is not entirely clear: we need to learn its terms.
The novelist appears to presume a certain agreement on our
part with that moral vocabulary, but obviously we must, in fact,
be taught it. It will clearly be a delicate one. It would seem that
Emma is being praised for having a happy disposition, but not for
having her own way; being praised for her strong friendship with
Miss Taylor, but not for the degree of grief she feels at losing her.
There is a moral language to learn and the novel must teach us
that. There are perhaps other presumptions we can make, about
the field of the action (it seems to be set very much in a world of

households and marriages) but it will take more reading before we see the confines of the particular world. At least, though, we have a strong sense of guidance and control that the novel will go on further to develop.

At what sort of date was it written? We might note again some marked features: the confidence of the moral assumptions and the nature of the social ones; the degree of externality about the telling, and the way in this case it is suffused by an ironic moral scepticism; the way in which every event is stylised into a moral drama involving a notion of life as a matter of responsibility. (For author, title, date of publication, see end of chapter.)

OPENING NO. 3

She waited, Kate Croy, for her father to come in, but he kept her unconscionably, and there were moments at which she showed herself, in the glass over the mantel, a face positively pale with the irritation that had brought her to the point of going away without sight of him. It was at this point, however, that she remained; changing her place, moving from the shabby sofa to the armchair upholstered in a glazed cloth that gave at once—she had tried it—the sense of the slippery and of the sticky. She had looked at the sallow prints on the walls and at the lonely magazine, a year old, that combined, with a small lamp in coloured glass and a knitted white centre-piece wanting in freshness, to enhance the effect of the purplish cloth on the principal table; she had above all, from time to time, taken a brief stand on the small balcony to which the pair of long windows gave access. The vulgar little street, in this view, offered scant relief from the vulgar little room; its main office was to suggest to her that the narrow black house-fronts, adjusted to a standard that would have been low even for backs, constituted quite the publicity implied by such privacies. One felt them in the room exactly as one felt the room—the hundred like it, or worse—in the street. Each time she turned in again, each time, in her impatience, she gave him up, it was to sound to a deeper depth, while she tasted the faint, flat emanation of things, the failure of fortune and of honour. If she continued to wait it was really, in a manner, that she might not add the shame of fear, of individual, personal collapse, to all the other shames. To feel the street, to feel the room, to feel the table-cloth and the centre-piece and the lamp, gave her a small, salutary sense, at least, of neither shirking nor lying. This whole vision was the worst thing yet—as including, in particular, the interview for which she had prepared herself; and for what had she come but for the worst? She tried to be sad, so as not to be angry; but it made her angry that she couldn't be sad. And yet where was misery, misery too beaten for blame and chalk-marked by fate like a 'lot' at a common auction, if not in these merciless signs of mere mean, stale feelings?

This is the most complicated of all the openings we have looked at, and it is possible to give only a few brief suggestions about its striking features. Here, too, the story is told in the third person, but a much greater degree of inter-relationship or interaction exists between the narrator and the character from the start. All events and sensations are focused on her, the scene enacted through her; her mind is the passage's apparent centre of consciousness. In this case there is little past and little future; and all the nuances that the novelist wants to introduce about either are brought into the present, into her mind at this point of time. The narrative present is the enforced scene for everything, and it is held very close to the character indeed. This high degree of 'internalisation' is established with the very first words; the convolution of 'She waited, Kate Croy' may seem affected, but it sets the story closer to the character's awareness than the more direct phrase would. Nonetheless, the novelist does feel the need to *state* the character's name, as much, it would seem, to preserve his narrative independence as anything else; for the process of internalisation is not quite total. It is as if the way of telling is enacting a complicated inner debate about through what eye the story is being perceived. A phrase like 'a glazed cloth that gave at once—*she had felt it*—the sense of the slippery and of the sticky' has this curious double effect; the object is being drawn into the range of Kate's sensations as well as of her observations; yet the novelist describes the cloth before stating the act of touching it. The same sort of ambiguity persists in, for instance, the later use of the word *feel*. It can mean sense perception (touching an object) and internal sensation (having an emotion about an object): both notes are there in 'To feel the street, to feel the room . . .' etc. So once again we might ask what end the author has in preserving his lightly stated independence.

One clear consequence is that it prevents our identifying ourselves completely with Kate Croy. The words all belong outside as well as inside her; they dramatise her but in a noted relation to the narrator. And the narrator not only preserves certain stylistic graces belonging more to patterns of written discourse than to that rendered immediate human thought in which he is clearly interested (so the formality of: 'She tried to be sad, so as not to be angry; but it made her angry that she couldn't be sad'); he also has very much his own *style*, a distinctive manner of discourse which determines what is seen and felt as much as does the flickering attentiveness of Kate Croy. It is a delicate style enacting a psychological attentiveness; it is also a very oblique one, taking the occasion to generalise and to broaden; it contains many abstract words ('the publicity implied by such privacies') that do not normally come readily to the mind; it also seeks clearly to dramatise grammatically the special relationship that exists between narrator and author, producing a species of unusual sentence construction. Hardly ever does a sentence become totally the property of Kate Croy, so to speak; though none becomes the property of the narrator either. So we see the room as Kate moves about it, feels about it, and we see its objects in terms of her movements of looking, touching, walking, and her emotions. But we also have a sense of seeing it independently, as an environment being explored by the author too. Equally we have the sense that the room is a dramatic stage for the mind of the character, with things serving almost human roles; we also have the sense that Kate's drama is not our drama, but is placed at a certain distance.

If the passage complicatedly enacts the relationship between the character and author, it also complicatedly enacts the relationship between the character and what surrounds her. Things have their own independent emanations; they affect Kate's sensibility as well as being a part of it; that is why the room can become a drama. How does it? In the first sentence Kate is described as showing herself her face, pale with irritation, in the mirror. This seems an odd proceeding; why are we not simply told that she is irritated? In fact, this is surely part of a principle that marks the whole opening: a refusal to give a clearly defined identity to the self, an intention to blur the edges of being, to relate inner to outer life. To a large extent, this is what the drama is about; the intensified emotions of the passage have something to do with the meaning of the room and its relation to Kate. It is not simply a realistic environment but a source for recalling emotions and creating them; and in doing that it involves the self struggling with itself. Kate is about to go; but she does not, the room keeps her. She keeps standing outside herself to see herself, to know where she stands in relation to the room. It is beneath her, meaner than her, yet the meanness somehow threatens her; produces a sense of guilt and a sense of threat. She exists in a strangely divided world, then; she makes what is outside herself, because it is through her irritated walkings and touchings that the room takes shape and objects have a meaning attached to them; but she is also made by

what is outside herself, because things have their emanations.
They are 'merciless signs' of people's feelings; they also have the
contingency, the flat reality, of things as things. The scene is
very much concerned then with the way in which immediate impressions affect Kate's more enduring psychology and attitudes,
attitudes basically toward meanness and vulgarity. And every impression is a kind of crisis for the self, a problem in determining
our freedom from or exposure to things.

What *events* happen in the scene? Almost none in the direct
sense; Kate is waiting to see her father and reacts to his room,
with guilt, a sense of his misery and also his staleness. So, apart
from supposing that the coming interview will be important, we
are not likely to be able to predict the sort of events that will
follow. What we have come to expect, though, is that events as
such are less important than what people make of them; they
will be conceived of in a sequence of emotions and responses, or in a
pattern of striking impressions. What is more, the process of
dramatising all that comes into vision or experience seems to work
by a principle of reiteration; phrases recur, objects are constantly
rearranged, the world of words and things is constantly being
remade, out of the same things in new relations. So, just as in the
last passage the writer seemed concerned to establish not so much
the events as such as the moral terms through which we might
view them, here the writer seems concerned to introduce us to a
way of seeing: of relating impressions, things, emotions, and *words*.
This gives a symbolistic resonance to the story; we have to keep
focusing on the sentence, on the sentence in the paragraph, on
the way it might live beyond the paragraph. Finally, we might
also expect that this linguistic and technical attentiveness on the
part of the author could have some moral resonance. For Kate is,
it would seem, a snob; her relations with her environment are
uneasy; we could then perhaps predict that some other balances of
persons and things might develop. But if so they would not develop
in the way of the last passage we looked at; rather out of following
not so much a moral vocabulary as a separation of writer and
character enacted through the very structure of sentences and
paragraphs themselves.

What date? What, this time, we might note is the degree of
internalisation and symbolisation, and what goes with this: a
kind of questioning of the firm lines of identity. We might also
note the attentiveness to psychological rendering and sensation,
the obsession with the way life operates between persons and things,
the shimmering impressionism, the way in which an image becomes a part of a mind. We might note, that is, the way in which

the novel's universe is made by processes of perceiving and feeling it, rather than being given to us ready-made, so to speak. And we might, finally, note the degree of technical precision and writerly sophistication forced upon the author by these presumptions. (Author, title, date of publication: see end of chapter.)

OPENING NO 4

If you really want to hear about it, the first thing you'll probably want to know is where I was born, and what my lousy childhood was like, and how my parents were occupied and all before they had me, and all that David Copperfield kind of crap, but I don't feel like going into it. In the first place, that stuff bores me, and in the second place, my parents would have about two haemorrhages apiece if I told anything pretty personal about them. They're quite touchy about anything like that, especially my father. They're *nice* and all—I'm not saying that— but they're also touchy as hell. Besides, I'm not going to tell you my whole goddam autobiography or anything. I'll just tell you about this madman stuff that happened to me around last Christmas before I got pretty run-down and had to come out here and take it easy. I mean that's all I told D.B. about, and he's my *brother* and all. He's in Hollywood. That isn't too far from this crumby place, and he comes over and visits me practically every week-end. He's going to drive me home when I go home next month maybe. He's just got a Jaguar. One of those little English jobs that can do around two hundred miles an hour. It cost him damn near four thousand bucks. He's got a lot of dough now. He didn't *use* to. He used to be just a regular writer, when he was home. He wrote this terrific book of short stories, *The Secret Goldfish*, in case you never heard of him. The best one in it was 'The Secret Goldfish.' It was about this little kid that wouldn't let anybody look at his goldfish because he'd bought it with his own money. It killed me. Now he's out in Hollywood, D.B., being a prostitute. If there's one thing I hate, it's the movies. Don't even mention them to me.

Where I want to start telling is the day I left Pencey Prep. Pencey Prep is this school that's in Agerstown, Pennsylvania. You probably heard of it. You've probably seen the ads, any-way. . . .

If the last opening was complicated, this is at first sight extremely simple: so simple as to appear to need little comment. A first person narrative, it is presented in such a way as to dramatise the character's own consciousness, to preserve his own language and his own way of telling, so completely that it seems less an order

than a sequence of immediate responses. It deliberately discards
and mocks familiar literary conventions and orders: the conventional opening of the first person novel of adventures ('that
David Copperfield kind of crap'), the convention that everything
can be revealed about one's background, even information 'em-
barrassing' to other characters, the convention that a character is
entitled to inflict his story on his readers ('If you really want to
hear about it . . .'). The writer yields language up to his character
so completely that the language is a total enactment of the character; he, entirely, is going to make this world, out of his own
vernacular, his own preferences and dislikes, his own limitations
and strengths. But if it is a personal language, it is also a fairly
familiar one in many respects; it not only suggests the narrator's
youth and background but *broadly* draws on the chatty speech of
the American young, which gives it a public as well as a personal
authenticity. In fact it deliberately engages with the reader's
sense of recognition, and draws him in as someone the storyteller
is chatting to ('You probably heard of it'). To a point it is banal
and repetitive; yet these very characteristics become stylised, so
that, for instance, the stresses taken from speech ('my *brother* and
all') and transferred into print acquire a vigorous new existence on
the page.

Most of the passage seems to be concerned largely with putting
a frame round the story to be told and providing a certain moral
vocabulary for judging it. We do know, for instance, that the
events the character wants to tell are over, recently, and that these
events—'this madman stuff that happened to me around last
Christmas'—seem to have to do with the present situation; he
got run down and is out in California to 'take it easy'. The story
seems to be complete, then; in the form of a line of adventures left
somewhere behind him, though presumably not completely detached from his present state. As for the moral preferences, these
come out of a confident pattern of likes and dislikes ('If there's one
thing I hate, it's the movies. Don't even mention them to me') and
a simple moral vocabulary: 'lousy' and 'crap', 'nice' and 'terrific'.
But although it is simple it is based on a strongly generated emotion
that ends up as by no means a simple view of the world; the
affections—for his father, his brother, and the 'little kid' in the
story—seem generous, the critical preferences fairly severe, the
attempt at self-honesty scrupulous—this, mainly touched in by
minor qualifications ('You probably heard of it. You've probably
seen the ads, anyway'.) The effect, finally, is of moral comedy that
is capable of generating quite a sharp critical centre, a centre that
derives from a kind of innocent human view that does not take

itself too seriously and yet thereby has the right not to take any other pretensions very seriously either. Once again, it is rather from the tone than from the prefigurings of the story that we take our sense of what is to come; what, I think, we expect is a larger application of this critical 'innocence' to a story that begins on the day the narrator leaves his prep school and ends with an explanation of why he is in California, on the other coast of the States, in a 'crumby place'. As for when the story was written, its internal detail gives this away; it is obviously contemporary, but is it in any sense dated? (Author, title, date of publication: see end of chapter.)

FROM BEGINNINGS TO MIDDLES AND ENDS

The novelist, we have said, must devise in each novel a relationship with the reader by which he creates all the terms—the standards of probability, the kinds of sympathy and repulsion, and so on—that are needed for evaluating his book. What we have been looking at is only the beginning of this process as it occurs in four very different novels. But from this point on, there are many different kinds of structure, many different principles of growth, many different threads we can follow. In some novels we will be most concerned with the narrative sequence as such; that will provide the main thread of attention. In other novels our attention is likely to fall on some other principle of cohesiveness that, while it may work through a sequence of events, invites us to fix our attention elsewhere. The transcending of the merely narrative, the establishing of orders more complex, is— as we have seen—one of the things that has obsessed many writers, particularly modern writers. But in any case the threads that take us through a novel, that lead us onward as principles of continuance, are rarely stories alone. There are certain things or themes in novels that seem to dominate, to be persistent, that suggest a pattern of relevance which informs each particular stage of the developing literary act. They are different for every novelist and we need to be sensitive readers to catch them. In one novel they may take the form of a complex interaction of symbols; in another a groping toward the universalisation of the plot-sequence itself; in another a moving toward a moral awareness or a psychological discovery. We start making hypotheses, grouping themes or following emphases, from the first words; we keep testing them and perhaps discarding them until we reach the last. And in each novel we are guided and helped by the novelist as persuader, though we must take it that the novelist is himself learning as he goes along. For him, the growth will be a matter of a kind of organic development which is natural and instinctive as well as severely deliberate; the making of a novel is not a mechanical logic. But it *is* a logic, for which both writer and reader are searching.

N.B. The authors, titles and dates of the four novels whose opening paragraphs we looked at are as follows:

1. Tobias SMOLLETT, **The Adventures of Roderick Random** (1748)
2. Jane AUSTEN, **Emma** (1816)
3. Henry JAMES, **The Wings of the Dove** (1902)
4. J. D. SALINGER, **The Catcher in the Rye** (1951)

Reading a Novel

The formal growth, the persuasive order, of a novel keeps developing until the novel reaches its last word. Until then nothing is finally determined, and all our assumptions, guesses and expectations remain provisional. But then, as we close the book and set it down, we do possess it complete. And we are likely to want to go back through it mentally and trace the threads we have been following, the logics we have found significant, and see if they really do work for the novel as a whole. Now we no longer see the book with the innocence, the open-ended expectation, that the first reading has given us. What criticism in fact *normally* deals with is not that new, developing experience but this finished view of the novel as completed whole, as an entire organism. It takes the book less as a continuous enactment than a whole object, moving forwards and backwards through it. My comments in the last chapter were partly designed to guard against this way of seeing things. It is not, for instance, how writers would usually see them; they are much more aware of the imaginative growth that has taken place as they wrote. Critics, who say that what should interest us are the words on the page, sometimes discount this sort of growth. The fact remains that novels are very long works of art and many of their main effects lie in extended sequences rather than in concentrated, distilled moments (as we saw in the second chapter). And, as Henry James pointed out, parts of them tend to be a good deal more incidental or passingly illustrative than others. The discovery of the central threads is therefore a considerable imaginative effort for the reader—an effort of comprehension that demands holding a sense of the entire book in mind as he attempts to place each part in some relation to the force, significance and logic of the other parts.

We have seen that, in that effort, we need to follow out the working of a novel at various levels. We must appreciate the sequence of life that it enacts, both in the way it gives the feel of particular moments and sensations, of the vivid existence of persons and places, emotions and scenes, and in the way it draws that

life into a sequence and a shape. And we must also follow the more
technical links that hold the novel together and order its development, bearing in mind that these features—of point of view and
shift of consciousness, or of imagery and symbolism, or of linguistic repetition—are not fixed systems but can be given a constant and perpetual variation. 'What interests me in the last stage
was the freedom and boldness with which my imagination picked
up, used and tossed aside all the images, symbols which I had
prepared. I am sure this is the right way of using them—not in set
pieces, as I had tried at first, coherently, but simply as images, never
making them work out; only suggest.' This is Virginia Woolf,
noting in her diary how she had completed her novel **The Waves**;
this is the creative process as imaginative growth. 'Don't let anyone persuade you—there are plenty of ignorant and famous
duffers to try to do it—that strenuous selection and comparison
are not the very essence of art,' wrote Henry James to Hugh
Walpole; this is the creative process as stringent control. Both
aspects of the creative process are involved in the growth of a
novel. And in most novels this growth will focus on an illuminating
sequence of *event*, a causative sequence commonly—though not
always—followed through time. This is the sort of thing we normally mean by 'plot' or 'story', it is what we usually speak of when
asked to say what a novel is 'about'. One of the purposes of this
book is to suggest the complicated existence in a novel this 'plot'
has: how it is deeply embedded in an elaborate context of language
and structure. It seems best to conclude the argument by illustrating it in relation to one novel: to offer a reading of it and some
suggestions about the way our own individual readings may proceed. The book I have picked is a contemporary novel: one that,
like many contemporary novels, probably makes its first impact on
us through the recognisableness of its world, the probability of
its life, the present-day nature of its vision. With such a book,
questions of form and structure often seem relatively incidental:
in fact, they are indispensable for talking about it seriously as a
novel. The book is J. D. SALINGER'S **The Catcher in the
Rye**, at whose opening we have already looked.*

A READING OF *The Catcher in the Rye*

At first sight, *The Catcher in the Rye* seems to be a fairly loose
comic novel of adventures, some of them amusing and some not,
which happen to a boy of sixteen when he slips away from his
prep-school in Pennsylvania and goes off to New York on his own.
Over a period of forty-eight hours, from the time he is expelled

* See page 53.

from the school to the time he rejoins his family, Holden Caulfield, who narrates his own story, is in a kind of limbo, a state of extreme freedom. He has escaped both from his responsibilities and from those who are responsible for him, and it would seem that, in the big city, almost anything could happen to him. A great deal does; once he is in the city, the novel's action moves rapidly through a great many settings and involves many different kinds of character, people met casually from the crowd and then lost to sight again. In short, the novel is picaresque, proceeding not through old-established relationships in a stable community but by passing encounters in a constantly changing one. These adventures can be in significant sequence, which can be of a very loose kind, illustrating how very various and unexpected life is, or of a very tight kind. And I think that normally, as we reflect on a novel, we would start looking for lines of development that link the sequence together or explain *how* it develops, why these events should follow in this order. So we can ask all sorts of questions: about the world that is explored, and about the character. Does that world have any features that make it consistent? By the end of the novel, have we acquired a sense of the workings of one whole sector of society? Or is it perhaps consistent in a different way: do, for instance, most of the episodes seem in some way to illustrate how immoral or corrupt society, or this society, is? And what of the character's way of experiencing his movement through the novel? Does he or she develop, undergo a psychological or emotional change, or learn something from his experiences?

As we do this kind of sensing out of the internal world of the story, this reading back of lines and sequences having to do with the action and its effects upon the character, we are also likely to notice certain ideas, themes, images, motifs that are a persistent part of the discourse of the book. In this book, they are perhaps most obviously there in the repeated presence of a few basic motifs—like the recurrent question about what happens to the ducks in Central Park when the ice freezes over; like the way in which Holden keeps holding onto certain fixed moments of experience, such as the death of his brother Allie. In addition, there are repetitions of certain types of relationship, usually involved with the relationship of innocence and responsibility. Particularly, there is one emphasis which is focused in the title and the passage in the book which most closely refers to it: the idea of an innocent, protective responsibility which Holden feels he must provide for others younger than himself. The passage that picks up the title is the one (Penguin ed. pp. 179–80) where Holden, talking to his sister Phoebe, misremembers the song by

Robert Burns as 'If a body catch (not *meet*) a body coming through the rye':

> 'I thought it was "If a body catch a body",' I said. 'Anyway, I keep picturing all these little kids playing some game in this big field of rye and all. Thousands of little kids, and nobody's around—nobody big, I mean—except me. And I'm standing on the edge of some crazy cliff. What I have to do, I have to catch everybody if they start to go over the cliff—I mean if they're running and they don't look where they're going I have to come out from somewhere and *catch* them. That's all I'd do all day. I'd just be the catcher in the rye and all. I know it's crazy, but that's the only thing I'd really like to be. I know it's crazy.'

The passage stands out from its surroundings because the title draws our attention to it. But it may suggest a basic aspect of Holden's character and therefore of his quandary or development in the novel. Some critics take it as the essential meaning of the story: the book is basically about Holden's quixotic gestures of love, and that is the prime value in the novel. But since it is only one conversation in the novel, and part of its total development, how much we emphasise it will clearly depend on how we find ourselves seeing the book as a whole.

If what the critics have said is a guide, we can see it very variously. Is it a picaresque novel of adventures, perhaps mainly calculated to produce a comic effect? Is it a novel about the squalor of the world and how it cannot really be lived in, a novel presenting Holden as a 'rebellious saint' trying to overcome squalor with love and protect the innocent against life? Or is it a novel about a boy who sees through the sham of his society, recognises it as commercial and exploitative: in short, a classic work of protest, as other critics have suggested? Or is it perhaps a novel less reacting against the given world than a novel of quest, involving a psychological development in which Holden seeks to see how his beliefs and attitudes square with those of an adult world that he is on the verge of entering? All these amount to very different suggestions about how the novel coheres: about the primary basis of its development and structure. And to come to a view of it, we will need to look closely at the whole book and try to come to some conclusions about what Salinger is seeking to develop as he writes. There is not space enough to do this in the kind of detail we should, in our own minds. And even if we have done it properly we could, of course, still disagree; indeed the book itself may thrive on such an ambiguity.

How, then, does the novel develop? Let us look first at the world

in which the action is conducted, and how we are led through it.
Clearly, we are led by a narrator who is not the novelist but is an
agent implicated in the action: who is, in fact, at its very centre.
The world is formed entirely around him and what happens to
him. He leads us through the two main settings of the story:
Pencey Prep, the exclusive boys' school in Pennsylvania where
he is a boarder, and New York City, or rather those parts of it
that are likely to be known to a college boy who is a resident. The
social world of the book is a middle-class one, and Salinger/Holden
creates it with a kind of lovingness, a realistic fascination with
places and *mores*, tones of voice and styles of behaviour, that give the
book a dense specificity. Holden is a very exact recorder of his
situation and what is more, of his environment, which he fills out
even as he reacts to it. He is always observing, watching, registering; the world is a crucial lesson in all its detail. And because he
reacts to what he understands, we see more than the surface of
this world; we see its inconsistencies, its oddities of behaviour, its
primary obsessions. The obsessions are with wealth and getting
on, with money and success, with ordering and systematising experience so that it fits those forms of success, with refusing to be
interested in failure. So many of the events and settings illustrate
all this, in precise ways; Holden moves from one scene to another
in the narrative present, then illustrates from the narrative past,
in order to build up the web, a web from which the human centre
is often missing. The events through which he passes are vignettes
of a fairly consistent culture, in which—at least by Holden's view—
most people behave in the same kinds of way.

So the society has a general tendency, as we see it through
Holden and through the novelist. But it is not a society created as a
social realist would create it; Salinger isn't attempting to show us
the dark underside of American society or the complex social
tensions of urban life. He illustrates through manners and inter-
ludes, and as the novel builds up and we relate those vignettes, we
recognise a squalid consistency in the entire order while not, I
think, finding only a basically social *origin* for that consistency. In
other words, it does involve a consistency in the particular society
of America in the late 1940s in which Holden lives; but it also involves a consistency in the world of adult life as such. Adulthood
is seen very much as a state of social acceptance—or at least is
seen, as in Mr. Spencer and Mr. Antolini, as a way of thinking
about life in terms of being mature and thinking about the future
and having a realistic view of one's place in the world. But that is
because adults tend to think like that, by a kind of adult necessity.
And of course Holden is trying to be an adult, to be mature, in

certain respects at least. He wants to appear sexually and socially sophisticated, and a lot of the comedy derives from his assumption of very sophisticated attitudes. But at the same time he stands somewhat outside this society. This is not because he protests in a general way about its basic relationships as such; it is not in that sense a novel of protest. It is rather because he stands at a time of life when he must neither accept nor reject it completely; where he is innocent enough to gaze in bewildered wonder at its inconsistencies; but where of course he is ironically implicated, because boys of sixteen must grow up into men.

This society is of course created by the author, who invents all its details, but it is created in relation to Holden and he is made capable of providing a judgment on it. The judgments need not be the author's; that, too, is something we must sense out. As far as Holden is concerned, it is not an invention but the given world he has to live in. So how is it evaluated? To a large extent, of course, it is evaluated through Holden's judgments, which at first often seem comically quirky but which gradually take on a consistency and depth. By choosing to evaluate it through Holden, Salinger of course is able to explore not only the society but Holden too. And in doing that he is able to make Holden's perspective, which at the beginning seems simply one of amusingly created responses, into a moral integrity. And that too is a principle of the novel's development; the events and episodes being calculated toward doing that as well as toward exploring the social world. That is to say, most of the events in the novel, however episodic they may seem at first, are calculated either to extend his knowledge of the world as it is or to reinforce or extend his particular values and preferences. This means that Holden's values don't just come out of the world as it is, the world we explore, but have certain more personal sources. Holden sees, as we have said, from an adolescent perspective; but it isn't the perspective of all adolescents, as the school scenes at Pencey show. Rather they come from Holden's way of grouping certain significant moments in his life and putting a special value on these. And these moments usually have to do either with nostalgia about childhood, or children, or about his own family: especially his sister Phoebe and his dead brother Allie. This gives him a localised moral world from which to see life. So the ethic Holden expresses is more or less present in him from the first. He normally expresses it in terms of strong immediate responses and preferences, stated through an evocative, value-laden, adolescent slang ('It made me puke'; 'She gave me a pain in the ass'). Holden is perfectly open to experience; he does, however, have strong convictions about it. And to see all these

effects working—the creation of a broad world, the creation of values
and attitudes toward it, and the creation of a smaller world of
the family and children out of which these attitudes come—we
need to start grouping certain of the scenes of the book and getting
them into perspective.

There is not space to do this in detail, but a few broad hints here
can be given; rather they are tentative suggestions. In the early
part of the book, the events of the day at Pencey, on the Saturday
of the football game, are given in loose sequence. Holden does
this and that; people come in and out; from time to time Holden
remembers something in the past and introduces it in the telling.
The sequence builds up to Holden's 'impulse' to leave that night
and rest up in New York for a few days. But there is in fact a
certain degree of consistency about what we are told. For instance, we see the school in two different lights: the light of its
function in the world, to minister to the needs of society, to attempt to mould boys for their social roles; the light of its more
'real' culture of dormitories, dating, bull-sessions in which the
boys compare sexual experiences. Holden is in fact separated from
both cultures, which in fact link up with one another. He is
not separated completely, though. He clearly needs to withdraw
from the school's world of damaged innocence, but at the same
time he needs to involve his affections in it, and 'miss' it. His
emotions take him backwards toward nostalgia but forward to
new events.

When he gets to New York, the same pattern extends and also
gets complicated. On the one hand it is a confusing anonymous and
vast city, a city for growing up in; a city of adulthood where things
are not what they seem and the signs of turmoil are finally those
dirty words about sex that are written on the walls and cannot be
erased. But it is also the city of Holden's childhood, and of other
children. Holden's movements and emotions again seem casual;
but he does have certain set patterns to follow deriving from both
of these versions of the city. He knows college-set New York,
sophisticated and mildly experienced: you meet girls under the
clock at the Biltmore, you go to the theatre and the skating rink
at Radio City, you go to Eddie's in the Village and listen to jazz.
You ask for liquor and if the waiter thinks you are under age you
drink coke. But behind that map of Manhattan lies another—the
schoolchild's New York, an unsophisticated world of the lake in
Central Park, the Museum of Natural History, the zoo, the carousel.
Holden explores both worlds at once and tries to bring them into
relation. So the episodes of this section are very mixed but again
have certain patterns to them. Some involve salutary shocks about

the world ahead (the episode with the whore and the elevator man (pp. 107–9); others are both instructive and salutary (the conversation with Luce (pp. 152–4) or Mr. Antolini (pp. 188–200), with its ambiguous conclusion in Antolini's apparent homosexual advance); and some seem to suggest a role for Holden in relation to childhood—he can be a catcher in the rye, the adult who is the protector of childish innocence. Over these episodes, Holden obviously develops and his attitudes change. He is hunting for his own adulthood, but doesn't want to lose his childhood. He sees his childhood dropping away from him (as in the scene on p. 128 when, after recalling the joys of going to the museum, he decides not to go in). He realises the impossibility of rubbing out all the dirty words from the world. He also realises that many of the characters who might help him to an adult world finally disappoint him. He ends up in the middle of a complex of contradictions. He thinks he will leave town and 'go out west and all'. But he doesn't, because Phoebe persuades him not to; and he ends the sequence apparently as the catcher in the rye, watching from the sides as Phoebe turns and turns on the carousel of her childhood and feeling 'so damn happy all of a sudden'.

The episodes fall into clusters, then, as we sense a number of threads running through the story: manifested in themes, emphases, particular images, and indeed a kind of subdued symbolism. The symbolism becomes most apparent at the end, because it is not imposed on the novel but comes out from its threads. In the final scene with Phoebe on the roundabout, there does seem a meaning that is created not only out of Holden's emotions but out of the way words, phrases, images draw together —so that we see more about Holden than he sees about himself:

> She ran and bought her ticket and got back on the goddam carousel just in time. Then she walked all the way around it till she got her own horse back. Then she got on it. She waved to me and I waved back.
>
> Boy, it began to rain like a bastard. In *buckets*, I swear to God. All the parents and mothers and everybody went over and stood right under the roof of the carousel, so they wouldn't get soaked to the skin or anything, but I stuck on the bench for quite a while. I got pretty soaking wet, especially my neck and my pants. My hunting hat really gave me a lot of protection, in a way, but I got soaked anyway. I didn't care, though. I felt so damn happy all of a sudden, the way old Phoebe kept going round and round. I was damn near bawling, I felt so damn

happy, if you want to know the truth. I don't know why. It was just that she looked so damn *nice*, the way she kept going round and round, in her blue coat and all. God, I wish you could've been there. (p. 219)

The scene is, in a sense, more than Holden says it is, because it not only tells his happiness but draws together various themes and depends on various contrasts—with the commercial Christmas-time we have just been seeing, for example. It recreates the pattern of the 'catcher in the rye' story: Holden as the older, protective watcher observing the happiness of childhood and its lack of concern about where it is going. Holden wears his hunting cap, a protective device he has kept donning through the story, and which has been associated with childhood: Phoebe has just been wearing it, and it has almost become for us a mildly symbolic badge of innocence. It is the novelist who creates this sense of significance, finally; particularly in the interesting verbal ambiguity of the last line, which suggests that religious feeling is what, in an oblique and unstated way, Holden has been looking for. The absence of God, the absence of veneration for things, seems here to be re-deemed; we recall other moments like this one, such as the scene (p. 40) where Holden refuses to throw snowballs at the car and the fire hydrant because they 'looked so nice and white'. If the image serves Holden as a secure moment of happiness, it serves the reader even more. But there are also ironies in it that are surely beyond Holden's seeing. It starts to rain, and the hunting cap gives him 'a lot of protection, in a way' but doesn't stop him getting soaked. Holden has already been feeling ill, and the next thing we learn— Holden deliberately doesn't give the reasons or the details—is that this is followed by illness. 'I practically got T.B.,' Holden has earlier told us, from his post-narrative position, on p. 9. Holden's real power to protect childhood, moreover, is already in question; and, as in the image of the catcher on the cliff, with Holden him-self threatened with toppling over backwards too, the scene suggests that his position is neither lasting nor safe. He does not belong on the innocent roundabout of the young; he is out and exposed to the weather. His idealised image is real enough here, but also qualified—and really by the novelist, who would seem to be suggesting in the situation more than Holden actually under-stands or knows.

This brings us back to the question of the point of view of the book. The main action takes place some time before the time of writing; but between those two points in time something has happened to Holden, which is not stated directly by him. Holden

has indeed gone 'out west and all', but not in the way he intended
—he is in hospital on the west coast, apparently with something
like T.B. but also under psychiatric treatment. The story he tells
is set off in the past, as 'madman stuff' (p. 5); and he says himself
that he doesn't really know the meaning of the story ('. . . D.B.
asked me what I thought about this stuff I just finished telling you
about. If you want to know the truth, I don't *know* what I think
about it' (p. 220)). All this brings alive in the story those signs of
oncoming illness we have had touched into the telling; Holden's
feeling 'spooky' (p. 204) and his getting wet in the rain; the warn-
ings of Mr. Antolini about 'This fall I think you're riding for'.
This involves additional meanings—meanings beyond Holden's
way of looking at these events at this time and place—and these
have to be worked into the story by the novelist: the novelist who
in some fuller sense *does* know what the story means. Salinger has
created a world of very immediate experiences and actions; created
a narrator who is very open to experience and does to a considerable extent interpret it for us; but there are certain touches of
distance that separate novelist and his narrator Holden.

The question of whether Holden is a reliable narrator, a sane
or honest one, is one possible area of separation, but perhaps not
the most important. Holden's engaging admission that the story
is 'crazy', 'madman stuff', doesn't so much throw doubt on his
accuracy or viewpoint as encourage us to respect his independence.
But it does provide a way in which he is seeing the story in a
different way from us. The real touches of distance come from tone
and technique. At one level, they come from the comedy, which
makes Holden sympathetically farcical. But even that is under-
standable in terms of his viewpoint. More important is the way
Salinger creates a contradiction in Holden; between his essential
openness to experience and his essential innocence. All that is
important to Holden comes out of life, and so his attitudes can be
presented as moments of immediate emotional response that flow
out of the run of the living. But it is innocence that makes Holden
open to experience; and it is also experience that is the obverse of
innocence. One has to grow up, face 'reality', be mature. The
childish eye cannot *remain* childish. So Holden's adventures
bring him to the edge of the crucial cliff that brings the innocent
out of childhood and which is—in this novel, surely—a version of
the fall of man. 'I think that one of these days', he (Mr. Antolini)
said, 'you're going to have to find out where you want to go. And
then you've got to start going there' (p. 195). Holden sees himself
that simply by continuing through the line of experience one
reaches a point where the vision is questioned. Hence perhaps his

getting run down; hence perhaps the gap between novelist and narrator; hence the discovery that Holden is thinking of going back to school, and his experiences must start opening out again. 'A lot of people, especially this one psychoanalyst guy they have here, keep asking me if I'm going to apply myself when I get back to school in September. It's such a stupid question, in my opinion. I mean, how do you know what you're going to do till you *do* it? The answer, you don't. I *think* I am, but how do I know? I swear it's a stupid question.' (p. 220)

The story, then, focuses on a crucial phase in Holden's life, the point at which one crosses the line from innocence to experience. The crossing involves a fall and a decline; it also involves a kind of moral schizophrenia. The innocent eye involves a love of the world, an appreciation of it, an attempt to reconcile the love and the squalor in it. But the squalor itself threatens to engulf the innocent eye. Holden comes to learn that 'you can't ever find a place that's nice and peaceful, because there isn't any' (p. 210). The theme of the novel is indeed in some sense religious: how do we come to accept a world in some respects evil and corrupt, yet is our only world. The presence of the novelist in the themes and episodes raises these questions, and raises them beyond and outside Holden. He, in fact, must go on to grow up; but the innocence of vision he presents may help us to perceive the world in a different way. So we, in seeing not only Holden but the way the novelist has created Holden and his world, see the book as a much more enduring meaning than Holden does. We know, more than he does, what to think about it; we know it as a fictional work, a created whole.

CONCLUSION

In discussing *The Catcher in the Rye* I have not so much tried to give a final reading of the novel—that, I think, should be left to the reader—but to suggest a way of reading. And in particular I have tried to suggest how our questions will tend to move from following out the sequence and development of events within the story, we will start to make orders and find themes which will draw attention to the technical and narratorial aspects of the story. To a considerable extent, *The Catcher in the Rye* is a book that follows life through with an empirical curiosity, and many of the things in it are surely designed to interest in that life for its own sake. At the same time, it is also concerned with making central and crucial a particular point in human experience—the point at which the child becomes adult and at which an innocent and hopeful love, a desire to protect life, becomes a profound human problem. Holden's special world does not stay intact, but it has been

imagined and created up to the limit of its possibilities, and out
of it a value and a meaning emerges. It is a value and meaning that
comes from Salinger's control and management; and we will not
really understand it unless we respond, whether consciously or
unconsciously, to that control and management. It consists of a
story that moves us through a social world and a moral world internal to that story, and it is up to us to look how the values by
which we judge the story come out of what is given of that internal world. This world grows, changes, develops and the perspectives are always shifting and enlarging. But at the same time
the novelist has always to keep alive his ways of guiding the
reader—by such devices as telling us events belonging to the seeming end of the story before their beginning. How does this change
a story? How does it affect our ways of perceiving it? In what ways
does it become a part of the total meaning? How do the 'human
plot' and the 'verbal plot' converge?

It is the intense power novels have to generate a sense of life,
in its development and its flow, that gives the form its importance.
If it were not for that, the novel would not be one of the most
central, perhaps still the most central, of the literary forms. The
first thing that a novel demands of us is that we yield ourselves to
it, to relish it and enjoy it. We have to grant as much as we can to
the imaginative reality created by the novelist if a good novel is to
do what good novels do: illuminate human experience out of the
fullest awareness of it that the writer can find. The novel is one of
the most sophisticated forms of dialogue that culture can have with
itself. But as with all dialogues, they are best understood if we
comprehend the terms in which they are created. Criticism at its
best is a way of illuminating the dialogue without killing its force
or reality. Ideally it should seek to see the sophistication, the complexity, the human and the technical depth of what is done without
suggesting that it is mechanically done. If we look at a writer's way
of telling his story and solving the needs and problems appropriate to it, we must remember that his mind, too, has lived through
his story. His ways are means of persuading, and not abstract
technical devices; they are ways of making his story live, grow, and
mean. We, as we order, will start to parcel out sectors of the novel;
to distinguish characters from plots within the action, to speak of
points of view and narrative voices in relation to the action. But
that is not the novel; it is our way of getting into it, and talking
about it. And these distinctions and separations that we make are
only meaningful if they are finally related to our comprehension
and appreciation of the whole. They are an enabling language for
us to talk in and see better with; but they are not a final summary

of the novel. They simply provide a means—which can well change as novels change or as critics do—for talking about that complex interfusion of realism and fictiveness which, in different degrees and with different emphases, all novels are. But in making these distinctions—which are inevitable, and which correspond with our sense that orders and shapes are being created—we must always try to retain a sense of the whole. The best advice on the matter, though, is a famous warning that Henry James issues in *The Art of Fiction*:

> People often talk about these things [plot, character, etc.] as if they had a kind of internecine distinctness, instead of melting into each other at every breath, and being intimately connected parts of one general effort of expression. I cannot imagine composition existing in a series of blocks, nor conceive, in any novel worth discussing at all, of a passage of description that is not in its intention narrative, a passage of dialogue that is not in its intention description, a touch of truth of any sort that does not partake of the nature of incident, or an incident that derives its interest from any other source than the general and only source of the success of a work of art—that of being illustrative. A novel is a living thing, all one and continuous, like any other organism, and in proportion as it lives it will be found, I think, that in each of the parts there is something of the other parts.

Notes on Further Reading

This is a short list of novels and critical works for anyone interested in exploring further the topics raised in this book. In addition, the novels and works of criticism mentioned in my text are, of course, recommended.

A. NOVELS

Some Major Novels of the Past:

CERVANTES	*Don Quixote*
DANIEL DEFOE	*Robinson Crusoe*
SAMUEL RICHARDSON	*Pamela*
HENRY FIELDING	*Tom Jones*
LAURENCE STERNE	*Tristram Shandy*
JANE AUSTEN	*Pride and Prejudice*
STENDHAL	*The Scarlet and the Black*
BALZAC	*Old Goriot*
EMILY BRONTË	*Wuthering Heights*
CHARLES DICKENS	*Great Expectations*
GEORGE ELIOT	*Middlemarch*
HERMAN MELVILLE	*Moby Dick*
IVAN TURGENEV	*On the Eve*
FYODOR DOSTOYEVSKY	*Crime and Punishment*
HENRY JAMES	*The Portrait of a Lady*
LEO TOLSTOY	*War and Peace*
THOMAS HARDY	*Jude the Obscure*

Some Major Novels of the Twentieth Century:

JOSEPH CONRAD	*Lord Jim*
D. H. LAWRENCE	*Sons and Lovers*
MARCEL PROUST	*Remembrance of Things Past*
JAMES JOYCE	*A Portrait of the Artist as a Young Man*
E. M. FORSTER	*A Passage to India*
THOMAS MANN	*The Confessions of Felix Krull*
VIRGINIA WOOLF	*To the Lighthouse*
EVELYN WAUGH	*Decline and Fall*
GRAHAM GREENE	*Brighton Rock*
ERNEST HEMINGWAY	*The Sun also Rises*
WILLIAM FAULKNER	*Light in August*
F. SCOTT FITZGERALD	*The Great Gatsby*
ANGUS WISON	*Hemlock and After*
SAUL BELLOW	*The Victim*
ALBERT CAMUS	*The Outsider*
RALPH ELLISON	*Invisible Man*
VLADIMIR NABOKOV	*Lolita*
IRIS MURDOCH	*Under the Net*
GUNTHER GRASS	*The Tin Drum*
J. D. SALINGER	*The Catcher in the Rye*

B. CRITICISM

On the History of the English Novel:

Walter Allen, *The English Novel* (London, 1954; now in Pelican paperback). A general survey of the English novel from its origins to the present.

Arnold Kettle *An Introduction to the English Novel* (two volumes) (London, 1951; now in Grey Arrow paperback). A study of selected major English novels with a 'practical criticism' approach.

F. R. Leavis, *The Great Tradition* (London, 1948). On Jane Austen, George Eliot, Henry James and Joseph Conrad; a brilliant critical study of one basic vein in the novel.

On the Technique of the Novel:

E. M. Forster, *Aspect of the Novel* (London, 1927). An excellent study which is however the statement of an individual aesthetic as well as a general analysis of the novel-form.

Henry James, *The Art of the Novel*, edited by R. P. Blackmur (London, 1934; now in Scribner paperback). Henry James's prefaces to the 1907 edition of his novels; a brilliant collection of statements by the most self-analytical of modern novelists.

Percy Lubbock, *The Craft of Fiction* (London, 1921, now in Viking paperback). An excellent study of the techniques of the novel.

Philip Stevick, editor, *The Theory of the Novel* (Free Press, New York, 1967 (paperback)). An excellent and full anthology of critical statements about the novel.

Miriam Allott, editor, *Novelists on the Novel* (London, 1959; in paperback). An excellent anthology of statements by novelists about various aspects of their form.

David Lodge, *The Language of Fiction* (London, 1966). An excellent study of the way the novel is presented through language.

Ralph Ellison, 'The Art of Fiction', in *Shadow and Act* (London, 1964).

Angus Wilson, *The Wild Garden* (London, 1963). One important writer's statement about the writing of fiction.

On the Modern Novel:

Leon Edel, *The Psychological Novel: 1900–50* (London, 1961). A good study of the development of the modernist novel.

Jonathan Raban, *The Technique of Modern Fiction* (London, 1968). A good study, with a 'practical criticism' emphasis, of the techniques of immediately contemporary fiction which in many ways complements my own.

Index